Abdi Aden grew up in Mogadishu, Somalia, until, at the age of fifteen, civil war broke out. Separated from his family, Abdi abandoned his home in search of a safe haven. Following a harrowing journey across Somalia to Kenya then back to Mogadishu, he escaped to Europe and, finally, Australia. Abdi attended university, completed postgraduate studies in adolescent mental health and was a youth worker for many years. In 2007 he was awarded a Victorian Refugee Recognition Record for outstanding work in the community. Abdi was eventually reunited with his mother and later found his sister, now living in the UK. He is married to the daughter of British immigrants and lives with his wife and three sons in Melbourne.

Robert Hillman is the author of more than eighty published works, ranging from biography and autobiography to textbooks and literary fiction. His most recent publications include the biographies, *The Rugmaker of Mazar-e-Sharif,* with Najaf Mazari; *My Life as a Traitor,* with Zarah Ghahramani (shortlisted for the 2008 Prime Minister's Literary Awards); *The Boy In the Green Suit* (winner of the 2005 Australian National Biography Award) and *Gurrumul: His Life and Music.* His journalism has appeared in newspapers all over the world. His fifth novel, *Joyful,* was published by Text Publishing in 2014. Another new novel, this one for a teenage audience, *Malini* (Allen & Unwin), was also published in 2014.

SHINING
THE STORY OF A LUCKY MAN

Abdi Aden and Robert Hillman

HarperCollins*Publishers*

HarperCollins*Publishers*

First published in Australia in 2015
by HarperCollins*Publishers* Australia Pty Limited
ABN 36 009 913 517
harpercollins.com.au

HarperCollins*Publishers*
Level 13, 201 Elizabeth Street, Sydney NSW 2000, Australia
Unit D1, 63 Apollo Drive, Rosedale, Auckland 0632, New Zealand
A 53, Sector 57, Noida, UP, India
1 London Bridge Street, London, SE1 9GF, United Kingdom
2 Bloor Street East, 20th floor, Toronto, Ontario M4W 1A8, Canada
195 Broadway, New York NY 10007, USA

National Library of Australia Cataloguing-in-Publication data:

Aden, Abdi, author
 Shining: the story of a lucky man / Abdi Aden with Robert Hillman
 ISBN: 978 0 7322 9984 2 (paperback)
 ISBN: 978 1 4607 0372 4 (ebook)
 Aden, Abdi
 Orphans – Somalia – Biography
 Unaccompanied refugee children – Somalia – Biography
 Unaccompanied refugee children – Australia – Biography
 Self-reliance
 Self-realization
 Somalia – History – 1991–
 Other Creators/Contributors: Hillman, Robert, 1948– author
967.73053092

Cover design by Darren Holt, HarperCollins Design Studio
Front cover image by Roberto Schmidt/Getty Images; all other images by
shutterstock.com
Back cover image by Andrew Bott
Typeset in Adobe Caslon by Kirby Jones
Printed and bound in Australia by Griffin Press
The papers used by HarperCollins in the manufacture of this book are a natural,
recyclable product made from wood grown in sustainable plantation forests. The fibre
source and manufacturing processes meet recognised international environmental
standards, and carry certification.

Contents

Abdi's Journey

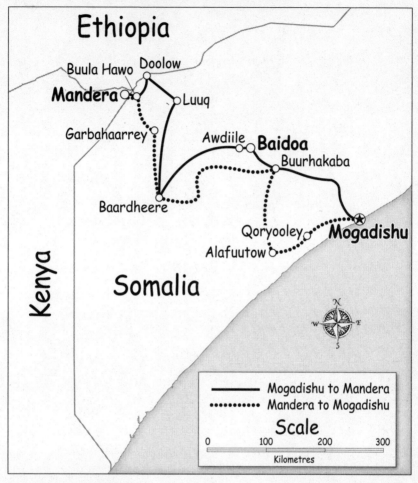

Ethiopia

Buula Hawo   Doolow

Mandera   Luuq

Garbahaarrey

Awdiile   **Baidoa**
Buurhakaba

Baardheere

Qoryooley   **Mogadishu**
Alafuutow

Kenya

Somalia

— Mogadishu to Mandera
····· Mandera to Mogadishu

Scale

0   100   200   300

Kilometres

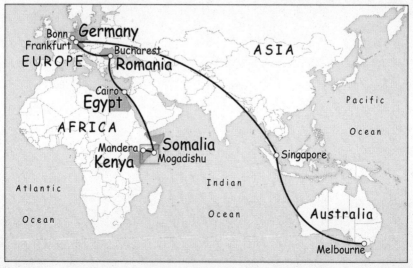

Bonn   **Germany**
Frankfurt
Bucharest   **Romania**
EUROPE

Cairo
Egypt
AFRICA

ASIA

Pacific

Ocean

Mandera   **Somalia**
Kenya   Mogadishu

Singapore

Atlantic

Ocean

Indian

Ocean

Australia

Melbourne

CHAPTER 1

An African Life

In a classroom, the world begins. Even in a school such as mine, a very poor school in a very poor country.

'Listen to me, children,' says Macallin Yousef, our teacher. 'Who knows of a country that has more animals than people?'

Macallin Yousef's question has come out of the blue. There is no reply. The students in the classroom with me, maybe fifty of them, boys and girls ten and eleven years old, are thinking of an answer that will please Macallin Yousef rather than one that can be found in a textbook. This is Mogadishu, the capital of Somalia on the Horn of Africa, and here all geography is local. Macallin Yousef knows something of the neighbouring countries of Ethiopia and Kenya, something of Yemen, Oman and Saudi Arabia across the Gulf of Aden. The rest of the world? Not so much.

Now, a country that has more animals than people is a prosperous country. In Somalia, since forever, the ratio of beasts to humans has been used to show a community's wealth. A thousand beasts, fifty people – good. A thousand people, fifty beasts – a problem. So the answer that Macallin Yousef is seeking is probably Saudi Arabia – many more beasts than people, very wealthy, and a great favourite of our teacher.

But:

'Yes, Abdi?'

I have raised my hand, willing to attempt an answer.

'Macallin,' I say, standing beside my desk in my white shirt and khaki shorts, the uniform of the school (with a long skirt in place of the shorts for girls), 'Australia is such a country.'

Giggles break out all over the classroom. Australia? What is it? *Where* is it? Ridiculous!

Macallin Yousef says: 'Australia?'

'Macallin, yes,' I say.

Macallin smiles with all of his white teeth. He has barely heard of Australia. Who in the Horn of Africa has, other than me?

'It is mostly empty,' I volunteer.

'Mostly empty?' says Macallin Yousef. 'No people?'

'Yes, people, of course,' I say, 'but more animals than people.'

'More animals than people,' says Macallin Yousef. 'Indeed. And Abdi, you are sure of that?'

The other pupils, sensing that I am on safer ground than our teacher, begin to warm to the exciting idea that I'm losing my mind to be telling Macallin Yousef that I am right, even if he says I am wrong. Unheard of.

I say: 'Sir, I am sure.'

And I *am* sure. I read it in a book my mother, Aalima, gave me. My mother is an educated woman and she would expect me to stand up for the facts. I have no intention of changing my answer to Saudi Arabia.

Macallin Yousef holds back. He's thinking I might be right. But if he accepts my answer, he's saying it's okay for every other student to come up with information that might take the class to all sorts of ridiculous places.

In the end, he gives in. It's the best thing to do, and a big relief for me. 'Yes,' he says. 'Australia. Of course. More animals than people. Australia.'

I sit down again at my desk, dizzy with pride. A question has been asked, an answer given. It pleases me that I've been able to match the two. I'll tell you the truth: knowledge delights me. I'm bursting to get home and tell my mum. A question has been asked, an answer given.

Knowledge.

★

There are moments in our lives – maybe almost forgotten – that much later begin to shine so brightly that they throw a light over everything we've ever done. A day is coming when I will have the good fortune to speak for hours about Australia and Australians; a day when I will become an Australian citizen, buy a house and start a family in one of my new country's great cities, win some praise for the work I do in migrant communities. But on the day of Macallin Yousef's question, a life in Australia is as far from anything I can imagine as living on the moon or the bottom of the sea.

The life I *can* imagine has Mogadishu at its beginning, middle and end. Most of the events that will soon turn my city into the most dangerous place on earth, full of intrigue and violence, are yet to happen. Mogadishu still has some of the charm of its famous past when it was ruled by the Muzaffar dynasty and was known as the pearl of the Indian Ocean. Dhows laden with cargo from the Arabian Peninsula arrived in fleets; caravans of camels loaded high with fabrics, spices and pewter made their slow way to the city from Cairo, from Ethiopia, from Sudan. Mogadishu was filled with the noise of commerce, the happy sounds of people making a good living. The city was said to be the most beautiful on the African coast, the white walls of its villas glittering under blue skies.

★

What remains of Mogadishu's beauty in my time is found in the city centre and a couple of classy suburbs with views of the ocean. The rest of the city is either the well-known mudbrick houses and blocks you see in every East African city, or concrete structures painted white, or shanty towns on the outskirts made from corrugated iron, plastic sheeting, cardboard and hardboard.

The first inhabitants of what would become my city kept close to the shallow harbour, and for centuries Mogadishu was all about the ocean. Even today, Mogadishu is a not much more than a strip of coast with a desert behind it. The harbour trade these days is not what it was in the past. A breakwater reaches out into the ocean, providing shelter for vessels that don't sit too deeply in the water. The monster ships of the twentieth century can't dock here. The only true natural harbour of Somalia is found much further north at Berbera on the Gulf of Aden.

★

With the hell to come not yet guessed at, I experience Mogadishu as a type of paradise. My family is not well-off, but nor is it among the poorest of Mogadishu. If I can't have anything I want it doesn't matter much because most of what I want is free: football, the beach, the love of my mother, books, learning. And of course, my father's love, too, far from Mogadishu though he is. Dad took a position as chief cook to the Military Legation at the Somali Embassy in the rue Dumont d'Urville, Paris. I have seen the address on the back of envelopes in which he sends his letters.

★

School runs for six days a week, starting at seven in the cool of the morning and finishing at one in the afternoon, just when the heat is building up like murder, with the golden sun in the centre of the sky and everything on the ground hot to the touch.

The main street of my suburb of Medina runs east all the way from my house to the school, the police station, the law courts and the Majestic Cinema, seven blocks along. This whole section of the city, taking in four suburbs, is laid out in a grid pattern. The dwellings are all close together. Rooms are added in any way you choose, not like in Australia, where councils have to approve everything down to the nails you use. Our home is not far from the corner, one storey, well built. If you walk to the corner, you come to the back wall of the most important building in the area – the United States Embassy. Big wall. Very big.

The walk to school takes me past shops and stalls setting up for the morning; steel roller doors rising with a crash, merchants calling greetings to each other in Somali or Arabic, or in an African version of Italian that sounds like a song. Within a few years, you will see soldiers with rifles slung from their shoulders mixing with the crowds of shoppers on Wadijir Jaale Siyaad Street, and crews of young men rolling past with machine guns mounted on the back of Toyota utilities.

But in 1985, everything is fairly friendly, at least on the surface. The earliest stallholders to set up are the *baajiya* sellers – the fast-food merchants of Mogadishu (*baajiya* is a type of spicy bean paste that is eaten with a coating of chilli). The merchants know us; we know the merchants.

'*Warya*, Ali! *Warya*, Nuurow! Pick up your feet or God will take them back!'

I must tell you here that I am often called 'Nuurow' in my suburb of Medina. It is what in Australia is known as a nickname. It means 'the Shining One'.

'*Warya*, Awa Mohammad!' I call back. 'Good fortune to you this day!'

'Listen to your teacher!'

'We always listen to our teacher, Awa Mohammad!'

The gelato seller, Ay Fartun, a woman of maybe forty, also calls a greeting, but not with any hope of a sale on a school day. In truth, there's never much hope of a sale to me or my sister, Jamila, who trails behind me. When I go to Australia – years away yet – I will hear the expression 'once in a blue moon', which means, I think, 'almost never'. Well, treats come along in the Aden family once in a blue moon. Ay Fartun's gelato is what the future, Australian me will come to know as an icy pole – frozen red cordial. If you wish, you can drink the cordial in its liquid form, or wait half an hour while Ay Fartun freezes the cordial with a stick inside it in a refrigerator that is used by a hundred people.

My suburb of Medina is so different to the big shopping malls of the suburb I will call home in Australia, where I can buy a jumbo pack of icy poles from Woolies without thinking twice. But the street life of an East African suburb like Medina is rich in its own way, and will become the source of my inspiration when I find work in community development, bringing Mogadishu to Melbourne. It is a clever community, Medina, always making do with what's at hand. In the market, you can buy Bic lighters that have had a hole drilled in them, been refilled with liquid gas and closed with a rivet – one lighter can be recycled in this way three or four times for the equivalent of five cents. The many colourful spices on sale are kept in cut-down cans that once held vegetable oil. Plastic bottles that started out filled with Pepsi or Coke are refilled with a mystery drink that is the same colour as Pepsi or Coke, but tastes very different. Making do even extends to the cars and trucks that roar along Wadijir Jaale Siyaad Street. Engines are held together with wire; spark plugs are filed down to suit cars they were never intended to fit; carburettors are fiddled with in various ways to overcome the need for a part that can't be purchased any longer; cracks in sumps are welded shut. The noisy motor vehicles of Mogadishu mostly belong in a car museum or a wrecker's yard. But the clever drivers of Mogadishu keep them on the road. In Medina, and all over Mogadishu, everyday life depends on invention.

There are wealthy citizens of Mogadishu, but only a few, and the Somali middle class is just eight per cent of the population. For most Somalis, there is no security of employment, no unemployment benefits, no reliable pensions of any sort. Opportunities for improvement barely exist. My existence is not hand-to-mouth, but it is on the edge. It's the same for my friends, and for most of the kids in my class. Real hardship is only one disaster away.

And yet there is such a thrill in being alive in Medina, a joy that I won't find anywhere else in the world. Every story in Medina is like a small stream that joins up with every other story, and the flow of all these small streams makes a river. The river is the community. The merchants calling greetings to me and my friends know that my father is in Paris, know exactly how long he's been away, and what keeps him there; they know of the letters and tapes he sends

AN AFRICAN LIFE

9

back to the family, and in some cases, what he says in those letters. The whole community of Medina holds me in its arms, sometimes as closely as if I were a blood relative, sometimes simply as an interesting boy in the ripples of gossip that run through the houses of the suburb. Everyone is interesting, some more than others, of course, but no story is dismissed. Medina is my teacher. The values of the Medina community make up for all that my teaching lacks in other ways – in sophistication, if that is the word I'm looking for. You know, the role of the parent is different here. Every adult has the right to lay down the law to every child, or to reward every child, as if that child were his or her own. If I am guilty of some naughtiness or other as I wander about Medina, the nearest adult will chase me and box my ears. Or if I need help, that same nearest adult will come to my aid, support me and console me. In Medina, and in Somalia as a whole, if you're a parent to any child, you're a parent to every child.

★

My school has a name: President Mohamed Siad Barre Government Primary School, or Siad Primary for short. The kids of my school are never likely to forget the name of the president of the republic because we sing his praises each morning at assembly, in the way that Australian kids in times past (so I have been told) rejoiced in the reign of Queen Elizabeth II. And the kids make quiet fun of the reign of Barre just as Australian kids once made jokes about the Queen. (An Australian friend told me that he used to sing 'God save our gracious Queen, long live our Ovaltine'.) Fifteen hundred kids aged from six to twelve attend Siad Primary, with about fifty to a class. The Somali government wants schooling for primary-aged children to be compulsory, but that hasn't happened yet. Maybe it has in Mogadishu, but out in the rural areas schools don't exist. Even in Mogadishu, school attendance is not a serious matter. It comes down to the hopes and dreams of the parents. My mother's ambition for Jamila and me is plain and practical: get a qualification, get a better one, get a job. My father's ambition for Jamila and me is more … poetic. Down the centuries, his ancestors looked an ox in the eye with the type of admiration that people in other lands saved for looking at gold nuggets. Rahanweyn songs and legends are all about the beauty of oxen, camels, sheep, goats. But at the age of six, after the death of his father, my father, Isak, was taken from his village to live in Mogadishu with an uncle, and the entire livestock heritage was lost to him. What he wants for Jamila and me is an education that will permit us to make a happy life in the Somalia of the twentieth century – primary school, high school, university. He sees us as giants of the decades to come, taking jobs in government, making big plans, getting things built.

I will be forced to leave my African life behind within a few years, and for my survival, I will rely on the lessons both of my mother's simple, get-things-done way of looking at life, and my father's more poetical way of seeing things. Going from A to B by putting one foot in front of another – that's from my mother, Aalima. But imagining that I could do it – imagining the 'B' of where I am headed – that's from my father, Isak.

CHAPTER 2

Paradise

The buildings of Siad Primary are not beautiful, but at least they are functional, laid out in the fashion of bungalows, with overhanging verandahs to save us from the fierce midday heat. No lawns, no green sports grounds, just a dusty *garbi* tree (apple acacia), a *qurac* (umbrella thorn), a *dheddin* (myrrh tree). Even if a little down-at-heel, the school is a big advance on what was provided for Somali kids before the socialist era, when parents had to band together and find a few rooms at scattered locations where teachers on a pauper's wages taught classes of a hundred. My third-world education at least gives me the basics: maths, geography, Arabic, Somali, science (including agriculture), social studies, physical education, arts and crafts. The teachers are never absent and student morale is high. There's a sense that education is valued; a belief that our generation of Somali kids will lead the way towards universal literacy and numeracy. Many of my fellow students also attend religious classes on Friday, their one free day of the week. In my family, religion has its place but it doesn't regulate every thought and action. When it's convenient, my mother, Jamila and I observe prayers and uphold the sacraments of Islam, and that's considered enough. The 1979 Islamic Revolution in Iran hasn't exported its fever to Somalia, and another two decades will pass before the jihadist Harakat al-Shabaab al-Mujahideen (Mujahideen Movement of Striving Youth) finds a big place for itself in Mogadishu.

My teachers, my macallins, are honoured as men and women of great learning. Although teachers at primary and secondary level are not paid much, their public status is high. In the case of most teachers, their knowledge does not really merit their reputation, but what they know far exceeds anything their students have learnt independently (except in my case and that of two or three other kids – my hunger for facts is unusual, and is considered just a little bit crazy). Somalia is, at this time, in a struggle of transition from almost universal illiteracy to a hoped-for literacy rate of forty per cent by the year 2000. This is where my mother and my father's profound belief in the benefits of education comes from; they detect a Somali momentum, a feeling that our country is not to become yet another failed state that staggers from disaster to disaster, its young men and women forced to leave their homeland and struggle along in neighbouring countries such as Kenya, Ethiopia, Saudi Arabia. Change is coming, yes, but the tragedy is that the change that is desired – growth and development – is about to be overtaken by a more brutal change that will be measured by the number of Kalashnikov assault rifles in the hands of young men, and by the laying of land mines.

★

School's over in the early afternoon and, out of range of a teacher's supervision and free at last, fifteen hundred students whoop and shriek like kids everywhere in the world. Now, for me, as I picture the Siad Primary kids hurrying home for lunch in their droves, the whole scene is tinged with grief. What we don't know amounts to more than what we do; what the Siad Primary kids don't know is that some hundreds of us will no longer be alive in a few years' time, and that the imagination and creativity behind this experiment in education will soon fall to pieces.

What we kids *do* know is that the main meal of the day is awaiting us as soon as we reach home. For Jamila and me, the meal on this day will be *bayini* chicken, seasoned with *xawaash* (a potent spice mix); flavoured rice; *muuso* (flat bread) and, afterwards, maybe *doolsho* (cakes). The cuisine of Somalia is a banquet that comes from almost everywhere *except* Somalia: Arabic recipes from Yemen across the gulf; more traditionally African fare from Ethiopia and Kenya; and a great number of Indian dishes introduced by traders from the subcontinent five hundred years ago. More recently, the Italian colonists made pasta, especially beef lasagne, as widely known in Mogadishu as the native *baajiya*. In other Medina households, the meal will be chicken stew, *muufos* or *sambusas* stuffed with peas and mashed potato or tuna.

★

Over lunch, served in the Somali manner on a cloth spread on the floor, *Hooyo* – Mum – asks the question that she is bound to ask, the question that I have been anticipating all morning: 'What did you learn today?'

'Macallin Yousef said, "What is a country that has more animals than people?" And I told him.'

'Told him what?'

'Australia!'

'What are you talking about?'

'That was the answer. I put up my hand and said "Australia".'

'You should have said Saudi.'

'I said Australia.'

It is always difficult to wring a compliment from Aalima. Even when she is pleased, she's just as likely to pretend indifference.

'Okay,' she says. 'Australia. Good. But don't make Macallin Yousef angry.'

'I didn't.'

'Okay. Now eat.'

Lunch is followed by siesta. It would be insane to do anything other than stay indoors when the temperature outside is at its fiercest. Keeping out of the heat in the middle of the day had been a big thing in Africa long before Europeans came to the continent, but it was the Italians who made a nap the foundation of refreshment later in the day. I might nap, or I might not. I might read instead. Our household includes a number of books apart from reference volumes such as the atlas. I enjoy yarns from Somali history telling of colourful deeds on the Horn of Africa reaching back to King Parahu and Queen Ati and the fabled Land of Punt. Or, in the more recent past, the Dervish State of the fierce Mohammed Abdullah Hassan, who drove the British out of the inland and back to the coast in the eighteenth century. Our modest library also takes in romances, nothing too volatile, but the fact that love stories are represented at all is unusual. Islam endorses the reading of sacred texts and maybe the classic poetry of past ages, but fiction as a whole is thought to be trivial at best, and romantic fiction in particular is considered a total waste of space. I enjoy it. And if I'm reading all through siesta, I'm drawing – faces, figures, animals.

★

Later, when the heat is waning, the kids of Medina emerge from their houses and head for the beach, the bottle-green water of the Indian Ocean, the lapping waves, the fawn sands.

My friends and I make a carnival of the experience – shrieks, jeers, challenges, laughter, ducking, a few tears. This is the beginning of the revels; next comes football on the beach, two teams rapidly chosen, the goals fashioned from sticks picked up on the way and placed exactly 7.32 metres apart. Will it sound as if I'm bragging if I say that I am the organiser, the go-to guy and problem solver, the one who sees to it that everyone who wants to play gets a game? It's essentially the role I will play later in life, off the football pitch. Trust me, I'm not bragging. Many things I can't do, or do poorly, so maybe I can be permitted a few lines of self-congratulation for a few of the things I do well.

'Ali! Ali, here!'

'Me, Ali!'

'Abdi, get forward!'

'Hey, Hassan, I'm by myself. Are you blind?'

'Abdi, I said get forward!'

'Hassan, pass to Abdi! Fast!'

'Goal!'

'Offside!'

'Who says offside?'

'Abdi was offside!'

'Bullshit!'

A few punches, threats of further violence, then I concede I was offside and the game goes on. Later, I take on the role of referee and allow some other kid to play. It's a game, yes, but it's serious, and it's serious, yes, but it's a game. The evening comes in with a rush and the sunset turns the sky gold above the sand dunes to the west. This is the heaven that settles over each day – the beach, football, an African sunset. I call time, the game ends with whoops of joy and a few cuss words from a boy who had a clear shot on goal two seconds too late. I hide the sticks that served as goals and fourteen boys, still panting from the exertion of the game, head for home.

★

The only cloud that sometimes blots out the East African sun is my father's absence. *Abe* – Dad – had departed for France one fine morning in 1980 when I was just a little kid. He didn't return until 1985, and then only for a visit. In Somali culture, more than in the West, the father is a lordly figure who disciplines, rewards and reproaches, and even if Dad's gaze is strict at times I mourn his absence, I truly do. Mum went to see him in Paris in 1982 and came back a little annoyed, I think. Maybe my dad was not as attentive as he should have been. Letters arrive now and again bearing French stamps, letters that include messages for me and for Jamila, sometimes a photograph of Dad and his pals smiling broadly for the camera (*la Tour Eiffel* in the background, of course) and, maybe, once a year, a cassette tape, all sorts of news about Paris. Then 'love to you, Abdi, my son, love to you, Jamila, my daughter, be good, Abe'.

★

My mother is compelled to bear almost the entire burden of raising her two kids. This is not thought unusual in Mogadishu. Men are free to turn their gaze north, south, east and west; women are expected to focus exclusively on the family. But Mum is an unconventional woman, and although she fulfils her role as mother, she could never be accused of going overboard. Her manner is tough and uncompromising, at times remote. As I said, she's educated, speaks fluent Italian and considers herself a feminist, in the broad way she looks at life.

As a girl, Mum was promised to an older man in her town of Awdiinle, near the city of Baidoa, north-west of Mogadishu, an arrangement she couldn't stomach. She ran off, choosing the hardship of the independent female over marital servitude. Somali culture has zero tolerance for initiatives of this sort, rooted as it is in pre-Islamic tribal beliefs reinforced by the strict protocols of obedience of the post-Islamic era in Somalia. Disapproval does not go as far as homicide, what you might call honour killings, although just being constantly frowned upon can take a daily toll almost as cruel. Whatever the cost, when Mum did marry – in Mogadishu, far from her home town – she married Isak, my dad, a man of her own choosing. As she explained to me when I was old enough to be curious, Isak's great attraction was that he was 'different'.

'"Different?"' I asked, hoping for some elaboration.

'Yes, different.'

'How?'

'Just different.'

One of the ways in which Isak was 'different' was in his willingness to marry a woman who was strong and independent. He's educated too and, like Mum, he can speak fluent Italian. Without rebelling but just by making different choices here and there, Dad took on tastes better suited to the life he was to lead in Paris than his hometown of Awdiinle, or even Mogadishu. Dad has a nomadic tribal background, but allegiance to the customs of his tribe and clan was not the first thing he wanted to speak about if you met him on the street in his Ray-Bans; more likely, the rock or reggae bands he enjoyed. He was politically clever but not full of slogans, all-in-all, the best example you'd ever see of Mogadishu cool, and he wasn't even trying.

In his liberty and independence, Dad was also a product of the erosion of tribal and clan identity in Somalia over the decades before his birth and its acceleration in the decades that followed. Somalia, for its entire history, had been dominated by the loyalties, pacts, conflicts and jealousies of its tribes and clans, some hundreds of them. Dad's tribe was Rahanweyn and his clan, the Heledi. The Rahanweyn were nomadic cattle herders, and with their history of judging almost everything in its relationship to the ownership of livestock, they were unprepared for the social and political upheavals in nineteenth- and twentieth-century Somalia.

The clan system had aspects that I doubt I could ever support, but it did give all Somalis a structure for their lives. The observance of obligations and courtesies that went back a thousand years and more had begun to wane under the colonial rule of the British, the Italians and the French from the middle of the nineteenth century. By the time of my dad's birth in 1950, the clan system, although still acknowledged, imposed only a few bits and pieces of the order it had once done. It could not explain the world that emerged after the European industrial revolution, in which great powers shuffled whole chunks of Somalia about on a map and gifted sections to Ethiopia, to Kenya.

★

Socialism came to Somalia in 1969, when Dad was nineteen. The military putsch overseen by Major General Mohamed Siad Barre and the declaration of a Somali Democratic Republic led to radical change in Somali society. A literacy program that reached beyond the cities to rural Somalia introduced boys and girls, men and women, to books and writing for the first time in their lives. Women were allowed to vote, and encouraged to assert themselves in ways they had never contemplated in the past. Growing into adulthood in this new, altered Somalia gave both Isak and Aalima options in life that their parents and grandparents would never have known. Dad could make those choices that caused Mum to describe him as 'different'. For her part, as a woman less restricted by tradition, she was free to think of her entitlements in life. She was free, in fact, to recognise 'difference' in Isak.

I am the product, in part, of this liberty of thought that had come the way of my parents. All over Africa, boys like me were heading into a post-colonial future that would be characterised by fierce conflict, the decay of tradition and the intervention of Western powers pursuing Cold War agendas. When I raise my hand in my Mogadishu classroom to answer my teacher's question, I cannot know that within a few years the forces at work under the surface of my African life will thrust me into a hurricane of violence. Some of the boys I see in the streets will become more familiar with the mechanism of an AK-47 than with the narrative and customs of their clans, and the average life expectancy of a Somali male of fighting age will halve between 1980 and 2000. But the thrill of answering my teacher's question in the classroom that day, the delight of connecting with a bigger, broader world, will remain with me throughout the ordeal that awaits me. I am Rahanweyn, I am Heledi, I am Somali, I am African; I am my mother's love for me, and her discipline; I am the longing that makes my heart ache when I think of my father in the rue Dumont d'Urville. And I am also myself; I am Abdi, cheerful, optimistic. All the forces ranged against me will have to contend with my determination to stay alive, keep breathing, love and be loved. And those forces opposing me, as formidable as they are – they will fail.

CHAPTER 3

Falling Apart

My East African paradise is a very local Eden. Away from Medina, from my home and school, Somalia is becoming a land of warring tribes. President Barre's regime, socially progressive at first, has lapsed into negligent disregard of the people it rules. There is no commitment to any national agenda within the government; every minister, every member of parliament, jealously guards the interests of his particular tribe and clan. Corruption has spread to such an extent that it's impossible to run a business, build a house, even buy a car without paying off a number of government stooges. The bitterness and resentment felt by the chieftains of every tribe and clan has become so entrenched by 1985, sixteen years after the putsch that gave Somalia to Siad Barre, that militias are arming themselves to the teeth with foreign aid money channelled down by ministers and army commanders. During the years of Barre's rule, the institutions that support a secure civil society with an elected parliament have had their authority eroded; the judiciary is owned by influential ministers; censorship makes it impossible to even talk about a free press. For years, Barre has made sure only members of his own tribe have positions of power. My dad lost his job as a head nurse at Mogadishu's biggest hospital because he was Rahanweyn. That's why he now works as a chef. In other parts of the world, the Somali government (which is really no more than a corrupt military dictatorship) has earned a reputation for running a type of slaughterhouse in Somalia. My country has one of the worst human rights record in Africa.

As early as 1987, warlords are plotting my murder, and the murder of thousands of other Somali kids like me.

★

For the time being, though, Somalia's dangerous drift towards civil war doesn't show up in my day-to-day life, nor in the lives of the people of Medina in any dramatic way. There's trouble here and there, sure, but there's always trouble. In Kismaayo down south, a man is found shot dead in a vacant lot with a sign around his neck in three languages naming him as a traitor. In Bosaso on the Gulf of Aden, a tyre factory explodes – something to do with extortion. In Baidoa, a truck is hijacked and the driver left on the roadside with a fractured skull. In Beledweyne, the old Dervish town on the Shebelle River, the remnants of the Western Somali Liberation Front (WSLF – a much more powerful force in the 1970s) is in the midst of a battle with the Ethiopians. There are mortar attacks, a small-scale massacre at a camp in the desert, bodies everywhere. That's what it says on the television news. But nobody knows if the left-behinds of the WSLF were really involved, or if the Ethiopians were anywhere near Beledweyne – there are no 'facts' in Somalian television news, just what it is convenient to say. But everyone believes there was bloodshed – that makes sense. Violence of this sort is background noise in Somalia; what's happening a hundred kilometres to the south can be left to take care of itself, almost wished away, until it's fifty kilometres closer.

★

It's 1987, and I'm in my final year at Siad Barre. As I walk down the main street each morning, I'm aware in a troubled way of a change in the mood of the merchants. My name is still called and I still reply, but there's a wariness abroad. The laziness of the day is gone; everyone is watching for what the next hour might bring and nobody expects anything good. More police are out and about. A meanness that was never part of Medina's street life has taken all the silkiness out of the ocean breeze that springs up in the late afternoon. Football has lost its zest.

★

The rumour is that my father is going to return to Mogadishu from Paris. I hear this from people in the street – not from my mother. How do they know? Well, how do they know anything? They heard it from someone who heard it from someone else. For me this is like news that a hundred angels are about to come down from Heaven and dress me in golden cloth. Each day I wait for further details, but I hear nothing; the people who first mentioned my father's return now deny that they said any such thing. The only way in which I can learn anything more definite is to visit my father's family in Janale, further south.

I've never been to Janale alone. And only maybe twice with my father – I'm not sure. Certainly not with my mother. She has nothing but contempt for my father's family, partly because they belong to a clan that she considers far inferior to hers, and partly because she believes the whole pack of them to be as lazy and unmotivated as Isak. And after I hitchhike to the town – it takes hours – I can see Mum's point, except that it's not laziness I notice in the faces of uncles and cousins but that languid disdain Dad has for people who don't know how to take it easy.

'Hey, Abdi, sit down, tell us what the world is doing, if you know!'

'Comrades, *saahib*, it's Abdi from the big city! Bring him some guava juice!'

I ask if anyone has heard that my father is coming back to Moga.

My uncle says: 'Isak, sure, he's coming back. A good time for you, Nuurow. Make you happy to see Isak, I think.'

A surge of happiness runs through me, and for a moment I look down to hide the tears of joy.

'When is he coming?' I ask.

'When is who coming?' says my uncle.

'Dad. When is he coming?'

'Oh, Isak. One day, for sure.'

'But how long?'

'Who knows? One month, one year. He's coming back, for sure.'

This is the sort of vagueness that drives my mum crazy when she sees it in Dad. It drives me crazy, too. I try to get something more definite out of my uncle, but it's hopeless. I hitch back to Medina knowing nothing more than I did before.

★

Finally, Mum confirms that Dad is indeed returning from Paris, and she even gives a date, a couple of weeks away. Dad's reason for returning is vague, but it may be to do with the political situation in Somalia. Perhaps the general who employs him in Paris has been ordered back to Moga.

I ask Mum again and again over the next ten days if it's still true that Dad is coming back. She stops answering me.

And, you know, the way Mum is makes me uneasy. It should be a joyous occasion – I haven't seen Dad for almost three years. I want Mum to be as happy as I am about Dad coming back, but as the day of his return approaches, she turns down the chance to go out to the airport to greet him, and she barely acknowledges his pending arrival. For Somali children, marital strife is a disaster that they quietly and stoically watch unfold. They are not encouraged to think of themselves as stakeholders in the outcome as Australian middle-class kids are. ('We'll tell the kids, okay? They deserve to know.' I can imagine those words being used in Australian homes.) I can't say anything, can't ask questions, but when Dad finally arrives, it wounds me to see him and Mum coolly ignoring each other. Dad walks in the front door, nods at Mum, and immediately joins a card game between friends and relatives.

I stay close to my father, waiting for a touch, a wink, a quick hug.

Dad is deep in a game of baccarat. He glances up at me. 'You don't want to play football, Abdi?'

'No, I'm okay.'

'Really?'

'Really.'

'Something wrong?'

'No.'

Dad smiles quietly and returns his concentration to the game. Of the four men at the table, my dad is the most relaxed. What am I saying? Of the four men at the table? Of all the men in Mogadishu, my dad is the most relaxed. He never looks any other way. He knows he's wicked cool, he knows he's handsome, he knows that women are attracted to him, but it's part of his cool that he never makes a big deal of it. It's just him, and it's part of what I so admire in him. Times will come in my life when I think of trying on my dad's cool, but I know I can't pull it off. It has to be natural. Jamila adores Dad as much as I do and, for her, too, his cool is part of the love. About my mum, you could never say the same thing. She's a beautiful woman, but relaxed? No. There's an anger burning in my mum so much of the time. And there's an anger burning today. It's woman anger, wife anger, the sort of anger that you see in women in all cultures all over the world when they know that the husband they married isn't working as hard at being a husband and a dad as the woman is at being a wife and a mum. It's disappointment that has taken on a tinge of bitterness. Mum took a risk when she married Dad – there were signs that he might not be as driven as she was. Mum thinks that Dad should be doing a hell of a lot more to smooth a path for me in life than he's done. He's away in Paris making hay while the French sun shines, overseeing a big shot's kitchen, maybe exercising his allure up and down the Champs-Elysées, returning smiles from smitten French girls, and Mum is slaving away in Mogadishu without the consolation of a husband's touch, a husband's caress. All of that would be okay with her, sort of, if Isak was making the most of the Paris opportunity to set things up for me, maybe bring me over to France, put me in a French school. Somali women have a different set of expectations in life than women in Western countries. They're in the back seat of the car, looking out the windows, not in the front seat holding the steering wheel. No, that's the husband in the front seat, one hand on the wheel, lounging back, big smile, dragging on a cigarette, winking at the ladies on the footpath. Not much in Somali culture is there to make things easier for women; it's nearly all there to give the man the feeling of being a lord. Sure, women make the best of it. They find ways to wield a bit of power, and in some Somali marriages the wife simply takes the power that the culture withholds. But not in our household. Dad is the lord; Mum is the resentful stay-behind. Because Mum would love to see more of the world. She's full of curiosity – she wasn't made to be a stay-behind. She wants to sashay along the avenues of Paris, buy herself a cashmere scarf on the Boulevard Saint-Germain, wander up and down the river on the Left Bank, where they have all those little kiosks that sell books and pictures. It's a big part of her resentment – not so big as Dad not taking better care of me – but a big part. In her heart, she's burning to show what a Somali woman can do in the world. She's a queen.

So what plans does Dad have – apart from kicking back and playing cards and smiling his big 'Hey, chill, what's the rush?' smile? That's what I'm wondering while I'm standing nearby, giddy on hero worship, watching him deal. He's here now, but will he stay? Because, apart from being super cool, Dad is also restless. It seems like a contradiction, but it's like that for men like him. No rush, no panic but, at the same time, restless. What I'm thinking is that I won't be able to bear it if he hops onto a jumbo jet and flies away again. Years later, when I'm blue down to my boots about my dad, who by then is dead and buried, my mum will say: 'Abdi, I never saw any boy who loved his father like you loved Isak. I have to say that. Never in my life.'

As it turns out, Dad is going to hang around for a time. He moves into the house, reestablishes himself as the lord of his domain. He's still in the employ of the general who took him to Paris, still goes each day to the general's villa way across town to make sure that his boss is properly fed about forty times a day. The reason that the general has come back to Mogadishu – and the reason Dad is here – is that the system of political alliances and secret deals that has made socialist Somalia viable is starting to fall apart. The general is an ally of Barre, and Barre needs his buddies around him at this time. It's a tribal thing. You sit the most powerful people in your clan down at a big feast of *iskudhexkaris* and chicken *baasto* and big piles of *lahto* and small dishes of *xalwo*, *bur*, also maybe a bottle of Coke or Fanta, and fill their bellies. You tell jokes about your political enemies, probably suggesting rude things about their organs of generation. Then the boss gets serious, and tells you who has to die for the good of the whole of Somalia, and everybody agrees. Later, a certain amount of money and a number of favours are quietly dispensed. This is the way politics is practised in my land of Somalia. It's not polite, and usually it's barely civilised. If you want a better idea of Somali politics than I've given you here, think of the great plays of Shakespeare, think of *Macbeth* – that's what Somali politics is like. Axes and daggers and blood and ghosts and betrayal: the old king is murdered; the new king sleeps with a knife under his pillow.

★

My dad isn't involved in the politics of the whole thing. That might be one reason why the general trusts him. Anyone who is deeply political has an appetite for power that dominates every other motive. He can be turned if his interests seem better served elsewhere. My dad is simply the general's friend, not his political ally. Friendship is a much better foundation for loyal service.

★

While Dad is living at home, he's in charge of the cooking. That's one thing Mum is glad about. It's something Jamila and I are glad about, too. Mum can cook, no worries – she knows her way around the kitchen – but Dad is a master. If you teach yourself all there is to know about Somali cuisine, you can get a job in a restaurant anywhere in the world, because Somali dishes come from all over the place, as I mentioned earlier. Dad knows how to cook Italian, Yemeni, Egyptian, Iranian, Indian, Iraqi, Palestinian cuisine. You watch him in the kitchen, you're getting an education. He looks like he's got all the time in the world. He looks almost lazy – he smiles, he jokes – but his hands are always busy, and when you smell the aromas, you want to clap with pleasure. There's another thing about my dad I haven't told you: he's a type of genius. I don't mean like Albert Einstein or some famous guy from the universities. I mean with his hands. Dad is a chef, but if he'd chosen something else, he would have been a genius at that, too. He might have chosen car engines and become a motor mechanic and, okay, he would have made you clap if you watched him fixing a Toyota. If he'd become a carpenter – same thing.

★

Mum is happy to leave the kitchen to Dad, sure, but that doesn't mean she's forgiven him for one tiny part of the disappointment he's caused her. The house stays chilly. Jamila gets angry with Mum, tells her to give Dad a break. My mum is too proud to defend herself, too proud to give her daughter a detailed explanation. She just lifts her chin and, like a queen, ignores Jamila. It's a hard thing, trying to stay comfortable in a house ruled by a king and a queen. They should have seen that before they married. Mum should have said: 'Isak, I'll be the ruler.' And Dad should have said: 'Lady, please yourself, because that's what I'm going to do – please myself.'

In this time of chilliness between my parents, Dad must have noticed that I could use a surprise. And he provides one. He says: 'Abdi, I want to show you something. Are you ready?'

We're at home. Mum is out somewhere. Dad's standing at his bedroom door – the bedroom he doesn't share with Mum.

'Something to show me?'

'You want to see?'

'Sure.'

I follow him into the bedroom. A suitcase is lying on the green throw that covers the metal-frame bed, a cheap black suitcase with brass latches. Dad clicks open one latch, then the other and lifts the lid. I'm staring down at a great heap of American dollars. How much in total I don't know, but a big sum, very big.

'Seen anything like this before?' Dad asks softly. He knows I haven't seen anything remotely like a suitcase stuffed with American dollars before.

'No, never.'

'This is from Paris. American money, American dollars.'

'I know, Abe.'

'Touch it.'

'You think?'

'Sure. Touch it.'

I pick up a wad of dollars, hold them on the flat of my hand, then carefully replace them with all their friends. The money is fine, of course – who doesn't want to take a look at a suitcase full of American dollars? – but what I'm responding to is *being shown* the money, being trusted to know of its existence.

A quiet, steady little flame of pride burns in my chest. I'm getting towards thirteen, and it's as if my dad is saying, 'Abdi, you wouldn't have got a peek at this a year ago, two years ago, not at any time until now, because you're not a kid anymore, you're becoming a man.' It's an endorsement, the sort of thing I crave from my dad, proof that I have a special place in his heart. This time, when Dad's back from Paris, is the beginning of my fever for accomplishment. Because that's what it is, this burning need to win praise from Dad so that, even today, myself now a father of three kids, I find myself whispering to him whenever I've taken some important step, passed a landmark. I say: 'Dad, what do you think? Three kids! Lovely wife! What do you think?' Or 'Dad, new car, two-year warranty, automatic locking, air con, independent suspension, special light in the glove box when you open it. Wow!' And I like to imagine the big smile on my dad's face as he lifts his sunglasses and gives a nod, nothing too extravagant. 'Not bad, Abdi. Not bad at all.' What I'm so aware of now, looking back, is my insecurity in that house with a mother who walks about with her chin held high, a queenly bearing, radiating disdain for my carefree dad, and a father who's there today, sure, but could at any moment put a hand on my head and say: 'Kid, you know I love you, don't you? I do. But I'm flying back to Paris in an hour and won't see you for another five years.' Achievement is important for everyone, but for me it's like those thermal drafts that birds and humans in gliders use to take them higher and higher into the air. I am lifted up by the sort of achievement that brings me face to face with Isak, high above the earth, and love fills my heart. And I am happy to confess that Isak was, in all honesty, a problematic sort of guy to have as a hero. 'Look at me, Dad, in big demand in this multicultural country, telling my story to kids in school, to Rotary meetings, to audiences of high school teachers, always lots of applause.' Off I soar, and Dad, who is dead, takes a vivid shape in my imagination, lifts his sunglasses, flips his eyebrows, and then offers me that big, white smile. 'You've done good, kid. Proud of you.'

★

The reason my dad has thousands of US dollars in a suitcase hidden in a secret nook, when it is not being displayed, is that the banks in Somalia are getting closer and closer to collapse in 1988. No Somali is going to trust his money to a Somali bank when the government can no longer guarantee the security of deposits. The government doesn't actually *say* it can't guarantee deposits; on the contrary, the government says that all deposits in Somali banks are one hundred per cent secure. But the spokesman who tells us how secure our banks are makes this sort of announcement so frequently that it is obviously a lie. For a year or more, all over Mogadishu people have been fashioning little hidey-holes for US dollars. If my suburb of Medina burnt down, you would have to add millions to the estimate of the damage to cover incinerated bank notes.

Mum also has a stash concealed in the house. I know where Dad's money is kept, and Mum's too. She's more devious than Dad, and normally wouldn't share the hiding place with Jamila and me, but our birth certificates are stored with her money so she has to tell us. She's also hidden our passports there – she's taken the trouble to get them for us, in case there is a sudden need to get the hell out of Somalia. Sometimes she says: 'I have nothing. I am the poorest woman in Somalia.' And I think, *Yeah, sure, Mum, sure.* Poor people do not boast about how poor they are. Mum's stash is probably not as big as Dad's, and that's why she prevails on him to fund a trip to Italy, where she intends to have a medical procedure, something to do with 'female complications' – she doesn't elaborate – that will be quite expensive.

Mum has always been distressed about having produced only two children. In Australia, two kids, a boy and a girl, is great. It's closing time for Australian wives after the birth of baby two. But in Somalia, a wife would be expected to provide four kids at a minimum – six is better, eight is getting towards the upper limit. You might even go to ten if you've only managed a couple of boys in the first eight. Your husband will say: 'What's the matter with you? I'm doing my job. How come you're not doing yours?'

I don't know for certain what sort of deal lies behind this all-expenses-paid trip to Italy, but I can guess. 'Husband, I have worked my fingers to the bone caring for your kids while you pleased your sweet self in Paris. Okay, now I need an operation. I've heard of a surgeon in Rome. Time for you to shell out.' And Mum probably added: 'If all goes well, I'll give you more children.'

Jamila and I only hear about this trip to Italy the day before Mum hops on the jumbo jet. As I've mentioned, Somali parents don't consider themselves under any sort of obligation to share news of this sort with their kids. Your dad could be an astronaut planning a moon landing and all you'd hear is: 'Oh, by the way, I'm taking a rocket into outer space today. Should be back in a year.' Or your mum could say: 'Kids, I've joined a circus. I'm secretly an acrobat – meant to tell you. Anyway, I'll see you maybe five years from now.'

When I hear the news, all I can think is: *What the hell? To Italy? Who's supposed to look after me and Jamila?* My Aunty Amina has been helping Mum out around the place for the past year, cooking, cleaning, shopping, being on hand when my sister and I get home from school. So is Amina about to become my full-time mother?

'No,' says Mum. 'Your cousin Fadema will take care of you. Don't worry.'

Don't worry? Mum's heading off on a journey of five thousand kilometres. I have no idea when she'll be home again, and she says 'Don't worry'? Meanwhile, Dad has moved into the general's mansion and only sees us – his kids – on weekends, and not even every weekend. In the Australia I will come to know and love, a social worker would take out an order to get custody of my sister and me. 'Hmm, father away most of the time. Mother's on a lengthy holiday with no fixed date of return. These kids now belong to the state.'

★

My cousin Fadema is seven years older than me and married with three kids. Jamila and I like her and get along with her. But I have such a longing for signs of love and concern from my parents that I can't properly see the goodness and generosity of Fadema's offer to care for me and Jamila.

With all this disruption and anxiety, my grades are suffering. I was once the brightest kid in the school, but now I'm among the strugglers. The truth is, I'm demoralised. I've noticed in my life that people become demoralised when they feel they have lost the power to make things happen or to choose the path they will tread. It's not the other way around – people don't lose that power because they're demoralised; they become demoralised because they lose that power.

I don't know it at the time, but I am about to enter a stage in my life when the only power I will have left is the power that fills you in moments of extreme panic. Because that is a type of power, the power of panic. A man will lash my hands behind my back in preparation for resting the muzzle of his Kalashnikov against the back of my skull, ready to pull the trigger. He will become distracted for a moment, and in that moment I will get to my feet and run like a hare across the sands. That's the power of panic, but when that is your only power, you are in very bad trouble.

★

Out in the streets of Medina I am always being shouted at by the merchants, or by anyone who knows the story of my family. I am Nuurow, the Shining One, but the shine has faded.

'Abdi! Have you seen a ghost! Aiee!'

'Nuurow! My dear, I want to weep as soon as I look at you!'

Ay Fartun, the gelato lady, calls me to come to her. She is chatting with another lady, a neighbour, and with a man who is using her refrigerator to cool soft drink. She says: 'My brother, my sister, *akhii wa ukhtii*, this is Nuurow. Alas for him! His mother has flown away like a bird. The father, Isak – what can I tell you? Medina is not good enough for him. He lives with that old rogue of a general in his palace. The boy's heart is broken! Aiee, such a mother and father!'

After this announcement, Ay Fartun puts her chubby arm around me and squeezes me hard. 'Who know?' she says. 'God will have a plan for you. Today, a little suffering, tomorrow, you become a prince. Who can say?'

'Thank you, Ay Fartun.'

When Macallin Yousef at my old primary school hears of my situation he will be torn between disappointment in me and satisfaction with my downfall. A boy who comes from such a family as mine may well know strange facts about distant lands like Australia, but if the mother flies off to Italy and the father pleases himself on the far side of town, of what use is that knowledge?

I have become a pathetic figure.

★

For the past few years, Siad Barre's Darood clan has been fighting the Isaaqs (this clan has the same name as my father, but my father is not of that clan) from Hargeisa in the north of Somalia. The Isaaqs do not recognise Barre's authority. Everybody in Mogadishu knows this. It is part of the patchwork of information that makes up a mental map of Somalia – which tribes are fighting with each other, which tribes have made peace, the members of which tribe are about to start murdering the members of which other tribe that they have had a truce with for the past few years. I've made all this sound much more haphazard than it really is. There is always a reason for the breakdown of a truce, for the renewal of fighting between tribes – it is never about nothing. With the Isaaqs, the motive is, as I have said, that they do not recognise Barre's authority. They never have. Perhaps for a year or two after Barre came to power did the Isaaqs put up with him, but probably only because they didn't have enough weapons to come out into the open and shoot a few of Barre's Daroods. So they remained patient, quietly making arrangements to acquire Kalashnikovs and grenade launchers. How do they make such arrangements? The Isaaqs speak to the Chinese, or to the Russians, or to the Iranians, the Saudis, the Palestinians, to Hezbollah, or even, in a super-secretive way, to the Israelis. They make an offer. A big shot amongst the Isaaqs says to the Chinese, 'Hey, you want to dock your warships at Berbera? Give us some rocket-propelled grenades, we'll take over the whole of the north and you can dock your warships.' If the Chinese say, 'We have other plans,' the Isaaq big shot talks to Hezbollah. He says, 'Hey, give us some of those Kalashnikovs you've got and we'll take over the north. The Saudis hate you – this is a chance for you to drive them crazy.' Now Barre has ordered the Isaaqs' annihilation and flattened their cities. Hundreds of thousands are dead. Hundreds of thousands more have fled to Ethiopia. Barre's killing the Hawiye too. Trouble is, Mogadishu is Hawiye territory. A huge card game is being played in Somalia, ten people or more sitting around a big table with each player representing a tribe or a clan within a tribe. The cards have been dealt, the killing begun.

Now it has started, the killing can go on forever. People I talk to in Australia don't usually understand what is happening out there in the third world. Sure, they know about poverty and disease, they know about the various wars in Africa, in the Middle East. What escapes them is that these wars are an industry, the best industry in the world for an unemployed young man who yearns to escape the boredom of his life, the hopelessness. Someone says, 'I have a job for you,' and puts a Kalashnikov in his hands. The weapon is not just a gun, it is power. He has only to display the weapon and a doorway opens leading to adventure, authority. When he is unemployed and bored, nobody takes any notice of anything he says. When he becomes a soldier, everyone listens. He is surrounded by his comrades, young men who support him, slap him on the back, congratulate him on becoming a fighting man. If he needs a philosophy to explain his job of killing people by the hundreds, of burning down villages and throwing children into the flames, there is always someone close by to say, 'My friend, we don't kill for the sake of it, we kill to make a better world, a purer world, one free of the pollution of unbelievers, one honoured by God.' Or maybe this: 'My friend, those guys in Mogadishu, they're the enemies of our clan. Who the hell do they think they are? We're not going to let them push us around. And so it's our unhappy duty to shoot those guys, blow them up. We don't like killing but they've forced our hand.' The justification is easy to come by. Here's your Kalashnikov. You've got a job for life.

CHAPTER 4

War

1990. I hear the shelling, a number of terrific explosions, but I don't immediately know what I'm hearing. And then I do. I don't make myself believe that I'm listening to thunder, or some sort of industrial accident. No, this is what everybody in Mogadishu has been waiting for, the event that transforms tension into war. Such a strange thing! People have been going about their business, knowing that some catastrophe is looming but unable to prevent it. I never meet anyone who says, 'We can't just stand by and do nothing. We must stage a rally, we must make signs, we must let those in authority know that we are against violence.' People continue to smile, continue to joke, continue to act as if this catastrophe they are anticipating might not happen for another week, or another month. But even as they smile and joke, they are sick with fear. In Mogadishu, war means that people who have no politics, no stake in the outcome of any fighting, will die in the streets. Nobody knows who is destined to be found dead with a bullet wound in the chest or head, but we know that it will be someone we know, a hundred people we know.

We are in our house, in the kitchen, almost ready to leave for school. Jamila says, 'Brother, tell me what has happened.' And I say, 'Why ask me? How should I know?' My heart is banging inside my chest like some creature that is struggling to break out. Jamila can see the terror in my eyes. She says again: 'Brother, tell me the truth.'

I don't say another word. My schoolbag is packed. I am ready to go down to the main street and catch a lift to school with a man who knows my father. He drives a utility, and it is the habit of many of the kids in Medina to jump into the back of his vehicle when he slows down then jump out again at the school. He charges nothing. It is a custom of our city to get about in this way. Fadema is just as terrified as Jamila or I, but she disguises her feelings. She says: 'Abdi, my dear, Jamila, both of you, take care today.'

Out on Wadijir Jaale Siyaad Street people are milling about, hoping to pick up gossip, rumours. All wear anxious expressions. Ay Fartun, the gelato lady, is clapping her hands together slowly in the way she does when something bad has happened, something that worries her. She calls to me, and I shuffle over.

'Nuurow, in your clever brain is there an answer? What has happened?'

'Ay Fartun, I do not know.'

'Aiee! Is it all a mystery? I am told that soldiers from Barre have gone crazy in the city. Killing people. What hope for us?'

The utility is coming and I make my escape. If I were to stay, Ay Fartun would hold my arm and shoot a hundred questions at me. No sooner have Jamila and I scrambled into the back of the utility with a dozen other kids than my friend Ali says to me: 'Why were you talking to Ay Fartun? Do you know something?'

'I know nothing. I heard the explosions, that's all.'

'I think you know something,' says Ali. He was in the classroom on the day of triumph when I answered Macallin Yousef's question. Ever since, Ali believes that my genius must also take in secret information about everything under the sun.

'If I knew, why would I not tell you? Do you think I am an oracle?'

'Do I think you are what?'

'Don't worry about it. I know nothing.'

The vehicle hurtles through the streets in the Mogadishu fashion, for I must tell you that in our city all driving is a matter of inspiration. You see an opening, you take it. Even if you don't see an opening, you try to make one. And if the reader will pardon me, I will take this opportunity to leap ahead for a moment. In the city in which I now live – that is, Melbourne – I have accustomed myself to obeying all the road rules, hundreds of them, that apply here. But every so often I am compelled to take a taxi, and it has happened once or twice that I have found myself in the cab of a brother from Somalia. From the back seat, with my wife and a child or two to safeguard, I sit in terror as the driver roars along Nicholson Street, leaving maybe a centimetre between his panels and those of the cars around him. I want to cry out: 'Brother, I did not survive a war to die with my family in this law-abiding land! For God's sake, slow down!' And if I did cry out? The driver would smile and call back to me: 'My friend, listen to me when I tell you to relax. You are in the hands of a genius.'

Now, back in Mogadishu, in the hurtling utility, all of us are swaying in our efforts to keep our balance, which we do, expertly. We round a corner and without warning the driver brakes to a halt. None of us in the back fall over – we know the knack of keeping our feet, no matter what. A small crowd has gathered here outside the mansion of a general who recently changed his allegiance from Barre to another soldier-politician by the name of Aidid, of the Hawiye tribe. The iron gates of the general's mansion have been twisted and buckled and the earth all around is torn and pitted and red with blood. All of us in the back of the utility have learnt at the one time where the explosion of an hour ago took place. Who the victims were, we don't know – perhaps soldiers standing on guard at the gates – but what we do know is that a war has begun. If Barre is firing rockets at the Hawiye, then Aidid's Hawiye will fire rockets at Barre. I stare down at pools of blood that are turning black in the sun and sickness floods through me. I have never before seen blood spilt in this way. The twilight of anxiety over what might come to pass is swept away and I stand in the harsh dawn light of a new reality. War is now only a few streets from my neighbourhood, and I'm sure it will come closer still. Siad Barre and his army are being hunted in Mogadishu. The city will become a battlefield.

I put my arm around my sister's shoulders and hold her close.

Jamila says, 'Brother, what is this? What is happening here?'

I say, 'A bad thing.'

'Will we die?'

'No, but it is a bad thing. We will tell Abe and Hooyo.'

I feel a shudder of dread pass through Jamila's body. She says, 'What will they do? Hooyo is in that place. What will they do?'

By 'in that place' Jamila means Italy.

'They will do something,' I say, but in my heart I doubt it.

The utility picks a path through the crowd and we continue on our way to school. In such a situation as this, with war coming over the horizon, all that any of us can do is behave as if life will go on as usual. In the back of the truck I can feel the fear of all those around me but nobody says: 'What is the point of going to school? Soon the Hawiye soldiers will come and kill us.' When you are powerless, the only ally you have is hope. But you don't believe in that hope.

After school, in the afternoon, I call my mother in Italy from the house of a neighbour. The neighbour doesn't mind so long as I call *collectico*.

Mum asks me why I am calling. She sounds relaxed – not worried in the least.

'Hooyo, we have to get out of here.'

'Get out of where? What are you talking about?'

'Out of the city. Out of the country.'

'Are you mad? No. You must go to school. You are safe.'

'Safe? Hooyo, things have changed. It is much more dangerous now. Bombs are going off. I'm scared, Hooyo. Jamila is scared.'

'Where is your father?'

'I don't know. At the mansion, I suppose. Come back, Hooyo! Do something! We will be killed.'

'You're hysterical. Calm down. I can't come back yet.'

'Then when?'

'I don't know. You're worried about nothing. Go to school. Fadema is there. Talk to Isak.'

I don't want to put any pressure on my mother or make her feel obliged to come back to Mogadishu. I shouldn't have said that. This will sound strange to people in the West, but in Somalia the relationship between parents and children is, well, shall I say 'more casual' than it is in Australia, for instance? Yes, more casual. My mother feels that she has made adequate arrangements for our care by asking Fadema to take over her role, and she can't be accused of negligence. I know that Mum is enjoying herself in Italy, that she is travelling far and wide, not only within Italy but elsewhere in Europe, and that she feels she deserves this holiday from motherhood. And she knows, too, that Dad is here. When she says 'calm down', what she really means is, 'Tell your father to act like a father'.

I walk and hitchhike across town to the mansion of Dad's patron, the general. What I hope to achieve, I don't know. Dad will say, 'Nuurow, the Shining One, to what do I owe the honour of this visit? Tell me everything.' And I will say: 'I'm scared, Dad. Barre's soldiers are attacking the Hawiye. It's war.' Dad will smile and rub the top of my head. Then he'll say: 'It's nothing. Chill, kiddo. Hey, do you want a piece of watermelon? Of course you want a piece of watermelon! Let me cut you a big piece, okay?'

I find Dad in the kitchen, directing the more junior workers.

'Nuurow, hey what's up, kid? Do you want some *baajiya*, what do you say? Hey, maybe some *quraac*, maybe some *khamiir*? You sit down. I'll make something good.'

I say: 'Dad, people are fighting. Close to Medina, very close. They blew up the gates where that guy lives who went over to the Hawiye. I saw blood on the ground.'

'Yeah? Blood on the ground? Where was that?'

'I told you. Where the general lives who went over to the Hawiye.'

'Blood on the ground? Hoo! I don't like the sound of that. That's those G4 guys. Crazy guys.'

'G4' is the name of the death squad that Barre has formed to carry out the dirty work. The soldiers of his regular army are happy to kill the people Barre hates, I'm sure, but the G4 squads murder in secret, and Barre can deny any involvement.

'I'm scared stiff, Dad. There's going to be a war.'

'You think? Maybe, yeah. Could happen.'

He goes about his work while I sit on a stool, feeling sick. Every so often he catches a glimpse of me and asks me, once more, if I would enjoy some *baajiya*. Finally he puts a plate on my lap – not *baajiya*, but a couple of tuna *sambusas* and some bread. I nibble at the bread, try to enjoy the *sambusas*, but I can't. Dad is whistling a Bob Marley song – 'I Shot the Sheriff', one of his favourites. The workers in the kitchen call out to him, 'Hey, boss, how much of this chicken we need? Boss, this *cadriyad*, what do you think?' After half an hour or so, I put the plate on a bench and quietly leave the kitchen to return home. I'm not resentful. I don't hold it against Dad that he finds it difficult to worry about war and pools of blood.

I find a ride part of the way home but when the driver lets me out I walk the rest. I need time to think. I'm trying to imagine what Dad would tell me to do if he could get his head around what's happening here. I'm attempting to become my own parent. It hurts my brain to think in this way. I hate it. I want Dad to say: 'Abdi, I'm going to get a car and pick you and Jamila up and drive you to Kenya. We're going to live in Kenya where there's no fighting. That's what we'll do.' In the way these things happen, this most recent disappointment reminds me of the whole grotesque episode of Jamila's betrothal a little while ago. Some guy from Dad's tribe asked for Jamila's 'hand in marriage', as they say in Australia. Jamila was twelve and, sure, these marriage agreements involving young girls and creepy older guys are still part of Somali culture, but it's hillbilly stuff. Jamila comes from a sophisticated family with a feminist mother and a father who's lived in Paris and seen the Eiffel Tower. No way Dad should be accepting proposals from horny guys in their thirties or forties. But Dad said: 'Sure!' My impression at the time was that he gave it about fifteen seconds' thought. The whole deal fell over, but I was amazed that Dad even considered it. And now he's taken this happy-go-lucky attitude to blood and death and open warfare. Like I say, I don't hold it against Dad, any of this stuff, but it's getting harder and harder to keep him up on that pedestal.

It's late in the afternoon but the sun's still hot. This is that time of the day when I would usually be out at the beach playing soccer then cooling off with a swim. It's normally my habit to walk with my head held high – the same for all Somalis, men and women, except that women make sure they never look a man, a stranger, in the eye as they pass, as that would be considered very immodest. But I used to look every stranger in the eye and offer a big smile. It didn't matter if I knew the guy was from another tribe, didn't matter if he was rich or poor, I looked him in the eye, sure, because that was me, Nuurow, the Shining One, the kid with the big smile. Not today, not for a while now. I walk with my gaze on the ground unless I hear a sudden sound, like a car going a bit too fast, or a really loud shout, or someone with a shop banging the roller door down hard. I'm in a state that I later saw referred to in a magazine article I read in Australia as 'hyper-alert'. It's a condition found pretty often in people who've experienced some sort of violent trauma – say, guys returning from Afghanistan or refugees from regions of the world where bullets go whizzing around your head at any old time of the day or night. Hyper-alert, hyper-vigilant: Abdi, the Shining One, scared out of his mind, thinking that the next sound he hears might come from drug-crazed G4 madmen blazing away with a rapid-fire cannon from the back of a Toyota ute.

I reach Medina and stop on the footpath to watch the merchants closing their shops. It's sunset. The heat is fading. The leaves of the few trees that grow along the street hang limp after bearing the sun's rays for the whole day. In the morning they will look fresh again. The red dust of the street rises in small, wispy clouds as people walk. The whitewashed buildings along the street – some as high as three storeys – take on a pinkish colour as the sunset intensifies. A breeze will come in from the ocean soon, a soft breeze that brings a smile to your face. Across from me, a merchant is having trouble getting his roller door down. It's stuck halfway. He calls out: 'Why today?

I'm in a hurry! Will you force me to strike you with a hammer?' He hauls on the door again, without any success. He calls to me: 'Lend me your strength!' I shuffle over to offer what help I can, and the door loosens and descends. The merchant – one I don't know; he sells electric light switches and cable – throws his arms around me. 'God grant this boy long life!' He presents me with a cigarette, but I wave my hand and smile. 'For your father, then,' he says, and again I wave my hand. 'He doesn't smoke,' I say – not the truth – and I head off down the street. For a minute or two, I smile, then a strange, uneasy feeling creeps over me. I stop and look back up the street the way I have come. I think: *I'm going to lose all this.* It is a feeling of foreboding, very strong. It is almost as if I can see into the future when all the whitewashed buildings will be pock-marked with bullet holes and scorched by flame, and piles of rubble blasted away from the walls spill out onto the street. The trees will be torn by explosions, limbs hanging down. The steel rods that are normally concealed beneath the cement of the walls and roofs will stand up like antennae, turning orange with rust. The merchants will all have fled. Tears spring into my eyes, and I weep all the rest of the way home.

★

The teachers are abandoning the schools. War is coming to Mogadishu, and will be around for a long time – everyone knows it. Those who have some safer place to go to are taking the chance to get out before the fighting sets in. Many of the teachers owe their jobs to their tribal allegiance. They are Darood, the same tribe as Barre. Most of the people who have government employment belong to the president's tribe. That's the way of things in Somalia now.

But nobody expects the president to win this war. Five years earlier, he was badly injured in a car crash and had to go to Saudi Arabia for medical treatment. His deputy took over until he returned, but Barre is still suffering from his injuries, and he looks older than ever. Somalis are very superstitious people. They think that Barre must have been injured and weakened for a reason. They think that God has said goodbye to him. His luck is finished. He will never win the war.

★

Nothing that happens over the following months lessens my sense of imminent disaster. The foundational tribalism of Somali culture has survived below the surface during the years of peace. It remained a potent force, yes, but people were more relaxed about it. You're not of my tribe, not of my clan, okay, it's possible that you are still a good man. But now that war is coming, people hold tighter than ever to their traditional allegiances. You are not of my tribe, not of my clan, it might be best to shoot you before you cause any trouble. Soldiers are everywhere, now, riding in the back of Toyota utes and on the top of four-wheel-drives with their AKs ready to fire. I used to spend my whole time walking to school or to the shops waving to people who passed in cars. I don't do much waving now. To wave could be taken as a gesture of aggression. Does that sound mad? It is mad. People with guns want to use them, more than anything else. They want to shoot someone. Soldiers want to say to their commanders: 'Some kid in the street was trying to be smart. I put a round into him.' There are no more friendly gestures.

At our house with my cousin Fadema and her kids and her husband, we live as if we are under siege. We don't smile. I still go to middle school, as I have been for the past three years, almost, but if I didn't return one day, my sister, my cousin, her kids, her husband – none of them would be shocked. That's because boys are being kidnapped off the streets of Mogadishu every day. Barre has run out of soldiers in his war against the Isaaqs so he's replacing them with kidnapped boys. Now, when I'm on the street and a government truck approaches, I limp, because surely they don't want a boy with a limp. But, as I say, if I didn't return home from school one day, no one would be surprised. They would mourn me, of course, but no one would say: 'But how did this happen? It's impossible. He was just a boy walking to school.' No, they would think: 'It was the soldiers. Poor Abdi. So young, so clever, so friendly, and now he's gone. Ah, God! How sad.'

Now the city is divided in half by a barrier – razor wire, concrete blocks – erected by Barre's soldiers a few months ago. You can't cross it. My father is on one side; I'm on the other. We are now completely cut off from each other. The barrier gives those of us who live in Mogadishu a taste of Barre's paranoia. He must think that by putting up a barrier he has made himself safer. How? It is one of those things that desperate men do without ever thinking hard about the logic of it. If someone tries to cross the barrier, he will be shot. It could be someone like me, who simply wants to see his father. But the soldiers tell their commanders: 'We shot ten people tonight trying to cross the barrier. All bad guys.' And the commanders tell Barre. And Barre says: 'We are winning the war.' One thing you have to get used to in war is craziness. People lose their wits and believe things that in normal times they would laugh at.

This is what they are saying now in the streets of Mogadishu: that Barre has sent a new general to south Somalia to take charge there. Is this a good thing? There is some sort of craziness going on in the south, and the new general, Manur Hassan, who is always called Mad-dheer ('the Tall One') is expected to sort it all out. What sort of craziness? It is said that soldiers are looting houses, factories, killing people, that they are out of control. These are Barre's soldiers, but they seem to have lost all discipline and turned into a gang of murderers. They do whatever they wish. So the people in the south are fed up, and sick of Barre, and maybe don't care if someone else seizes control of Somalia. Or maybe the people in the south, like many in Mogadishu, have no idea of what's happening. Maybe all they think is what I think: that the country is falling to pieces, and that any man with an AK is the law.

Fadema and her husband make the decision to move away from Mogadishu. They send Jamila to live with a family we know in another part of the city, for safety, because now girls are being kidnapped off the streets.

When I am told Jamila is going, I just nod. 'Okay,' I say, but I am terrified. I will be alone. Fadema says she will leave money for me to support myself, but not much.

My entire family has fractured into pieces. It feels as if there's no reason for me to even stay alive. I have never thought of Abdi as a person by himself. I only think of Abdi, the son of Isak, the son of Aalima, the big brother of Jamila. There is no 'Abdi' who stands by himself.

I say goodbye to Jamila briefly, no tears, as a male Somali does. On the surface, I'm pretty cool, but there's a big, big pain in my heart.

★

September 1990. Every day now on my way to school – sometimes in the back of a Toyota, sometimes on foot – I hear rumours. Often I want to say: 'But where did you hear this rumour? Do you know this for certain, or are you just repeating what someone else said?' The more extravagant rumours I disregard. A man in the market is telling three other men that Barre has taken a billion dollars and flown off in a big Boeing to Qatar. Then he says: 'Brothers, the man who told me this swears it is the sacred truth, on the heads of his sons.' He has another story to tell: that the Hawiye in the north are coming to Mogadishu with half a million men in uniform and a thousand tanks. He says: 'The Saudis gave them the tanks. After they destroy Mogadishu, they will make a Sunni state.' Here is another rumour: the Palestinians are behind everything, and they will make their own state of New Palestine in Somalia, and build atomic bombs and destroy the Zionists of Israel. I don't believe any stories told by men who say, 'Brothers, I swear this is true.'

But I believe a new story that I hear from the women who sell green bananas in the market. They say that Mad-dheer has been shot dead by his own soldiers. The women see me listening and they become quiet. One of the women I know says: 'It's okay. It's Abdi.' Then the woman telling the story takes up her tale again. 'The soldiers have abandoned God. They have made whores of the women in the south. Mad-dheer tried to stop them. Barre sent an assassin. First the fool wanted Mad-dheer to restore the law. Then he sends an assassin. Aiee!' The woman telling the story shakes her head and claps her hands together softly, in sorrow.

But, can you believe it, sometimes I still play football with my friends, set up the goal posts, organise two teams, though there are not so many players now.

One afternoon I call out to Ali, my neighbour, ask him if he wants to come and play.

'See you there, Nuurow,' he says from the doorway. His mum has given him a job to do first.

But Ali doesn't come and the game goes on without him. I'm about to take a shot on goal when we hear that sound again, like thunder but much more frightening. We're playing not far from my street, and that's where the sound is coming from. We run to see, and there where Ali's house had stood half an hour earlier are blackened walls and a heap of rubble. Ali was inside, which means he's dead.

★

Four houses down the street from our house lives Eedo Khatijo – Aunty Khatijo, as she is called by all who know her. She is a beacon in our neighbourhood, not simply because of her bright clothes and the scarf she wears around her head, but because she is the woman you go to when you are troubled, the woman you seek out when you need light. I have been to her many times over the past few months.

This time, though, she comes to me; that is, she calls me when she sees me coming home from school. 'Abdi, it worries me to look at your face. It worries me to see you walking like a child who has a stone in his shoe.'

'Eedo Khatijo, I apologise for offending your sight.'

'Apologise for nothing, Abdi Aden. But listen to me, now. We are leaving this place. The soldiers are madmen. Barre is the king of the madmen. If we stay, we die. We are leaving this place.'

I look at Eedo Khatijo's face, so full of determination, and tears gush from my eyes. 'Eedo Khatijo, what hope for me if you leave our city? My father is on the other side of the barrier. My mother is nowhere. Ali killed. What hope for me?'

Eedo Khatijo puts her hands to my face and pats my cheeks, not all that softly. 'Is Fadema still caring for you?'

'Eedo Khatijo, she has left with her children and her husband. She is gone.'

'And your sister? The little Jamila? Our princess?'

'Eedo Khatijo, Jamila has left us to stay with another family in this bad time.'

'Aiee! Do you think I will leave you here alone? Am I a monster? Aiee! Listen to me with all of your ears. You will come with me, with all of us. Abdi, many of us will make this journey. Many. All of us together. Are you asking me where we will go?'

I hadn't asked, in fact. The relief of being in Eedo Khatijo's care is so great that I don't mind where she takes me.

'To Baidoa, in the west. Rahanweyn territory. Not so many of these bad soldiers up there.'

When I look back on this day and remember the relief I felt when Eedo Khatijo reached out for me, I realise that I was still a child. It is difficult for me to grasp, you know, that I had a childhood. I have written all about my childhood, yes, that's true, but sometimes, in my heart, after seeing so many things I wish I could forget, my childhood disappears and all that I can bring to mind of my life in Somalia is blood on the ground and the crazed expressions on the faces of soldiers, some of them children themselves, as they shout at me: 'Don't run or I will kill you now!' I ran, of course. Even today, if I heard a voice shouting at me in the streets of my peaceful suburb in such words as this – 'Stay where you are! Don't run!' – I think I would just take off without a second's reflection. Now and again in my present life, a terrible panic gets into my blood and I begin to think that what I saw in Somalia is going to overwhelm me and I will become a crazy person. It is as if I can hear a voice whispering: 'Do you think you can escape Somalia just like that? Do you think we will stop hunting you? Never, fool. We will come with our guns – we are coming now.'

I have made my will, and left everything to my wife, Angela. It is important for me to have such things organised. And Angela has become used to me hurrying to her in a sweat, my hands trembling, my voice unsteady. I say: 'If things go bad for me, get rid of me. The will – do you have the will in a safe place?'

Angela says at these times: 'The will is safe. We are all safe. This is Australia, my love. We are all safe.' After a few minutes of frenzy, I calm down. I walk about the house and look at the lovely home we have made. I sit for a time on the sofa and watch my kids playing a video game, or bent over their homework at the long wooden table; at Angela making fruit salad at the kitchen bench. I look at the pictures on the walls that beautify the house. I hear the sprinkler outside watering the green lawn, the droplets of water striking the window above the kitchen sink and running down in streams. It takes me a little while to accept that this is my life and not a fantasy. Then I smile. The kids glance at me, thinking: *Dad's having one of his panic attacks. He's nuts but he'll be okay.* And that's what I say to myself as I sit there on the sofa: 'Abdi, Nuurow, what's the matter with you? Relax, moron. You're okay.'

★

We set off early that evening, sixty of us from the neighbourhood, amongst them many I have come to know over the years at school – Abdile, Eeden, Yousif, Usmaan, Suleymaan, Sheeq, Ibraahin, Nuurtey, Aliyow, Timire, Fadima, Warsame, Anyuure, Haaway,

Isha, Abuukar, Eedo, Luuley, Daadiray, Feylehey. Some carry a small bundle. I'm in such a hurry I've brought nothing. No one smiles. I am not the only one travelling without my parents. Others have become separated from their families by the fighting or by the barrier. No one smiles. This is not an adventure. This is a desperate act. We may all be dead within a week. Moving about is considered very suspicious by the soldiers. It is quite possible that they will stop us and shoot us all.

CHAPTER 5

The Grand Tour

When Eedo Khatijo says 'we are going to Baidoa' she means we are heading in that direction, not that the town of Baidoa is our destination. By going north-west, we will be closer to the border with Kenya, which is almost five hundred kilometres away, although I don't realise it's that far. If things go badly, we may have to cross into Kenya. At this time, I don't have a very good understanding of the word 'refugee'. The closest I can come to a definition – picked up from adults who might have used the word – is 'nuisance'. Refugees are people who make nuisances of themselves by appearing in a neighbourhood and asking for food, for shelter. Certainly none of us call ourselves 'refugees'. But that is what we are, in truth; we are refugees inside our own country. The framework of the society that we once belonged to has been torn up and cast aside. We are afraid, all of us, but not as afraid as we should be. Most of us believe that our danger is a short-term thing. The bad guys – that is, the crazed soldiers – will come back under the control of more reliable people. Three or four weeks of roaming around in the countryside, then maybe we hear better news from Mogadishu. The most optimistic of us might imagine it will be a few months before things truly calm down. And the more pessimistic? Ten years. Twenty. Never.

Our group has joined a larger one, and now there are three hundred or so travelling. We will be relying on trucks to pick us up, sometimes cars. We know it will not be possible for us to stay together. But will the trucks stop? They will. This is one of the strange things about countries like mine. No matter how many people go crazy and start thirsting for blood, there are always other people who recall the lessons of our faith and show generosity to those who are struggling. It is one of the lessons of Islam that I honour.

We will cross the big river Shebelle on our journey west, one of only two rivers in my country on which the skinny fishing boats made of reeds can navigate. The Shebelle and the other big river of Somalia, the Jubba, flow down into Somalia from the mountains of Ethiopia, and I have heard tales told by those who have been to Ethiopia and seen the source of the big rivers that the streams in the mountains glitter in the sun and flow so fast that a man will be swept away if he tries to stand up against the current. The Shebelle comes out above Kismaayo on the Indian Ocean, past Merca, Baraawe and Jamaame down the coast from Mogadishu. Baidoa is in Bay Province, where the land in some places, as I remember, is not much better than the scrub of the Ogaden further north. In the Ogaden, as all Somalis know, to survive you have to have the strength of a billy goat and the ability to live on thorns and grass and lick the dew from leaves, for there is no water except from wells. But other parts of Bay between the two rivers Jubba and Shebelle are much greener than Ogaden, and the people who live there stay in the one place year round and plant crops of maize. I must hope that we spend most of our wandering journey in this region of the two rivers, for elsewhere there is only water in the creeks and wadis during the wet season, and for a month after.

Outside Mogadishu Eedo Khatijo stands in the middle of the road and raises a hand to stop a big truck heading west. The truck is carrying a load of timber to a cluster of villages close to the town of Wanlaweyn, about a hundred kilometres along the highway. Eedo Khatijo says to the driver: 'Sir, will you carry some of my friends with you in your fine machine? I ask you in the name of your honoured parents and in the name of our God.'

The truck driver climbs down from his cabin. He wears a big smile. 'My honoured parents, you say?'

'If they are still living, they will weep with joy to hear news of the help you give to weary people such as my friends.'

The truck driver chuckles to himself. Eedo Khatijo has a fancy way of speaking and he is enjoying it. Another woman might say: 'Let us ride with you or I will curse you to all the gods of the world.' But Eedo Khatijo knows better than that.

'They are still living, Aunty,' says the truck driver. 'I will take twenty of you. More than that, the axles will bend.'

Eedo Khatijo quickly picks out twenty of our number, children and adults, and shouts at them to climb up on top of the timber. 'We will meet again, that is my hope!' she calls out as the truck roars away. Then she waits with those of us remaining for another truck. When one comes, this one without a load, she waves it down. 'Will you take my friends west?' she calls to the driver. 'Even at this moment, God is looking down. Your honoured mother and your honoured father will weep for joy when they hear of your good deed.'

The truck driver steps down from his cabin and lights a cigarette. He looks at Eedo Khatijo. He looks at the crowd of us, each with a bundle. He says: 'One hundred dollars, yankee.'

'Aiee!' says Eedo Khatijo. 'If I had dollars I would pay you with a thousand! But we are poor, sir, very poor. Sir, will you take my friends out of the goodness of your heart? That is my hope.'

After a lot more pleading by Eedo Khatijo, the truck driver agrees to carry some of us without payment. Now only twenty-five of us remain. Eedo Khatijo herself has gone on the second truck to care for the children and to protect the women from abuse if soldiers stop the truck. It is up to me to stop a third truck. I have none of Eedo Khatijo's flair and one truck after another passes without paying me any attention. It is well into the night before I am able to stop even a car.

The driver says to me: 'Are you mad, boy? I almost ran you over!'

'Sir, I bless your honoured mother and your honoured father. I –'

'You bless what?'

'Your honoured mother, sir, and your honoured father. They will weep tears of joy when –'

'My mother and my father? What have my mother and father to do with you?'

'Sir, I was only saying that –'

'My father is dead. My mother is in Canada. Do you want a ride? Just come out and say it, in the name of God!'

Now, this is blasphemy. I have never heard anyone say such a thing. I say: 'No, no ride, sir. I am sorry for interrupting your journey.'

By this time the driver is lighting a cigarette. 'I'll take six of you,' he says.

'Six?'

'Are you an echo? Six. Get in.'

I pick out six children and adults to ride with the driver, but I am ignored and six different people pile in. As the car drives away, the six people I'd first chosen shout at me, telling me to be strong.

The truth is, I hate this responsibility. I want Eedo Khatijo to come back and take charge. So do all the people still waiting.

Now a truck pulls up with two men high up in the cabin. 'Get in,' the driver says. Without a word from me, though I am supposed to be in charge, the last of us climb up onto the back of the truck and sit down amongst bags of white onions. This is the beginning of our wandering from place to place, but all I am thinking about is the day I will return to our house and find my mother there in the kitchen reading a book, and my father cooking *muuso* in sesame oil, and *cambe*, which is mango, waiting for us to eat after the rice. Jamila will be there, of course, and no harm will have come to her. She will be saying to my mother: 'Hooyo, braid my hair.' My mother will put down her book and find a comb and begin to braid my sister's hair. The only sounds in the kitchen will be the crackling of the *muuso* and the song my father is whistling, probably, 'I Shot the Sheriff'. All of us are happy. All of us have become a family again. That is my dream.

★

It seems at times that the whole of Mogadishu is travelling on the roads and highways. I see trucks ahead full of people going nowhere in particular, just away from the city and the crazy soldiers. When we stop at a shop on the side of the road, I meet up with people I travelled with a week before. All of us are going around in circles. I say to a boy I met at this same shop five days earlier: 'Did you get to Baidoa?'

'No, not to Baidoa. But we saw Buurhakaba.'

'Are the soldiers there?'

'We saw no soldiers in Buurhakaba, but we saw plenty on the highway.'

'Did they search you?'

'Sure. They always search you. They searched us and took anything they wanted to take.'

'But no one was hurt? The soldiers didn't hurt anyone?'

'Sure they hurt us. Sure. They hit me in the face. Can you see?'

He had a swelling on his cheek.

'I'm sorry for you,' I said.

'Don't be sorry for me. Be sorry for Jamal. He's dead.'

'Aiee! Don't say such a thing!'

'Sure, he's dead. The soldiers were searching him, looking for dollars. He said he had no dollars. But they found five dollars in his shoe. Then they shot him. I don't know whose soldiers they were.'

★

The trucks let us off whenever it suits the driver. Maybe we go for fifty kilometres, maybe for ten, sometimes for more than fifty. If the driver fears that soldiers are waiting up ahead and stopping all the trucks, he might tell us all to climb down. You can't predict what mood the soldiers are in. Not even the soldiers know what they will do. They might stop a truck just to check IDs, then change their minds and shoot the driver and the passengers. It all depends on their mood. Maybe they have had nothing for breakfast and they are in a bad mood and decide to kill some people. The journey feels crazy. We drive on and on for weeks, for a month, more than one month, almost two. We change trucks sometimes twice a day, sometimes five times a day, and some of the people travelling with me stay behind and a few new ones climb on board. It is almost like a video game, where dangers are lurking everywhere, and some of the dangers take the form of soldiers who are crazy mad on drugs, and the soldiers jump out and destroy a few people but the rest of us keep going, waiting for the next danger. If we keep going, eventually the soldiers will kill everyone. They have killed so many that they don't care about it anymore. It doesn't make them sick. They are used to it. They don't know what's happening any more than we do.

What do I see at different times from the back of different trucks heading in a roundabout way to Baidoa? I see the landscape of Bay Province in its various forms: the greenery of the big area between the Shebelle River and the Jubba River; the crops of those who are still able to grow things – sorghum, maize, a crop with a yellow flower whose name I never learnt. So sad, those crops, for they are threatened not by drought in this well-watered region but by soldiers who are likely to burn them. I see the many small shops that appear in clusters along the highway, some displaying signboards that say in faded lettering Coca-Cola, Kent, Gauloises, Lucky Strike, Pepsi, San Remo pasta. Or if they don't promote well-known brands, they say, in Arabic, in English, sometimes in Italian, Best in the World Quik Foods, Stop and Try My Egg Noodles. Sometimes the signboards just say the name of the proprietor. These shops and their signboards are mostly portable. They might all move to another location if they feel threatened by the soldiers. Each time they move, a little town grows up around them; a town of tents, of rags, of cardboard, of plastic sheeting. I see people sleeping half in and half out of their ramshackle dwellings, and children playing with sticks or with empty Coke bottles. In such places, the only hope people have is that they will somehow remain alive. They do not think of a better future – that would be too luxurious a way of thinking, a fantasy. Unlike me, they do not have a house to return to. Husbands pray that their children will not be shot, and that their wives will not be captured by the soldiers and abused.

Maybe I am living in a fantasy myself, believing that I will one day get back to Medina and sit in the kitchen with my mother and father. But if it is a fantasy, it is one I am not yet ready to give up. Such a strange thing, but it is possible to hold tight to a fantasy and at the same time know deep inside that what you believe will never happen. You can say to yourself – as I do – 'I will believe this for a few more weeks, that's okay, just two more weeks, I can't give it up just yet.'

From the back of the truck, I also see the dusty parts of Bay Province, places where no crops are planted. Small acacia trees stand above dry grass. Maybe once or twice each day, I see a man with a few cattle trying to find a little bit of feed for his beasts. And, every so often, two or three men driving camels. In ancient times, long lines of camels came across this land on their way to Mogadishu from Addis Ababa in Ethiopia or, if not to Mogadishu, to Cairo, or Yemen, carrying spices and salt. I have read that these camel caravans would follow the Jubba River down to Baardheere and Jilib, then turn northwards and follow the Shebelle River until they had to leave the well-watered routes behind and travel through the dust of Hiiraan and the Mudug and Nugaal, coming at last to the country now called Djibouti, where boats would carry their wares across the Gulf of Aden to Yemen. That was a different world. Not so many guns. Not so much craziness.

We see the small towns and the villages, too, all of them tense, not knowing what is happening in the busier parts of Somalia, except that it is nothing good. A few of the villages have had soldiers go through – Barre's soldiers and others. The soldiers are thieves, but they don't call themselves thieves; they think they are just doing the commander's bidding. Maybe the commander says: 'Shoot a few of them. Show them who's boss.' The worst that they do, even worse than murder, is violate the girls and the women. For most of these women, most of these girls, a whole lifetime will not be long enough to recover. For the younger ones, what was done to them will stay in their eyes, even when they try to hide it. Other people, those who were not there at the time, those who did not see the soldiers running through a village, grabbing girls, these others will say to themselves and to their neighbours: 'Maybe they made the soldiers do it. Maybe they were not modest.' When people talk like this, you can't say anything to change their minds. You can't say: 'But what if it was your daughter? Would you say the same thing?' There would be a fight. You would be accused of insulting the man's daughter. He would think of killing you. So when we hear the news in villages, those that the soldiers have come to, I never say a word. But in my heart is a hard pain of sadness. I think of Jamila and close my eyes and pray for her safety, wherever she might be.

I meet up with Eedo Khatijo every so often. We cannot always travel together. Some of her own children who she brought with her have died of starvation and disease. Her spirits are always good, but that is just for other people, those she is helping, especially for the children. Underneath she is heartbroken and fearful. I think she has seen worse things than I have seen. She says: 'Aiee! When will the sun come back?' This can sound crazy, because the sun is always over our heads, except at night. But I know what she means. She says: 'Nuurow, would we have started this journey if we had known? What do you think?'

I say: 'Eedo Khatijo, we had no choice.'

This is what she hopes I will say. And she says this, too: 'Nuurow, is it just us? Is it just this hot land that is so fearful? Are there countries where people are happy all day, all day, what do you say? You have famous geography, you must know.'

I always say: 'America is happy. England is happy. Australia is happy.'

'If you find a road to America and England and Australia, take us all with you, Nuurow.'

We have to beg most days. None of us has any money, except some who are hiding a few Somali shillings for when things are at their worst. We wait at places where trucks stop, outside shops, sometimes at wells where water is pumped up from the ground, sometimes in villages and towns when it's safe. Most people are kind to us. We are given biscuits and a type of porridge made from meal and water. But all of us are hungry for the whole day and the whole night. Even when we have eaten the biscuits and porridge, we are hungry. People are starving, some are dying. Everybody is sick, in one way or another. It is only the children who cry when they are sick. The mothers never cry. Boys of my age don't complain, no matter what the cause. Girls of my age never cry. Only the children, who know no better. Often when the children are crying, I think, *It's because they don't understand. They remember a time when they were comfortable. They don't understand war.*

There are days when we run. We will be at a stop, hoping for water and food. We hear a scream: 'Soldiers!' At the very second we hear that cry, we run. We don't all take the same direction. If we are in the open, we run into the fields, north and south, and hide in the grass and acacias, or in wadis, dry channels cut into the earth by the rain. In a village, we run into the back streets or hide in huts and houses, in drains, in water tanks. We are like sand foxes. When danger comes suddenly to a den of foxes they scatter, each fox taking a different direction and each fox fitting itself into a hole that you would not think could conceal a sparrow. We are all living lives of starvation and fear, and yet we do anything and everything to preserve our lives, as if we were princes with a palace to return to. The instinct for survival is the same in foxes and Somalis. We have almost stopped believing in anything but remaining alive, and yet we do not know why we want to live. But we do. Most of us. Some don't care anymore.

We see more and more soldiers as we head further west, when we had expected to see fewer. At one stop, a man tells me that President Barre and his entourage are taking the same route as us. God knows why, unless he is reduced to the same sort of plan as me and my friends and Eedo Khatijo – that of endless running. The man says: 'Some of the soldiers are protecting Barre, some are chasing him. Some, I think, don't know what they are doing, chasing or protecting.' So we have a president who is driving crazily about the countryside with soldiers who shoot people like us because we are running about the countryside ourselves. When I was told about the president's madness, it seemed to me, just for a few cold, cold minutes, that we were all trapped in hell. Hell to Muslims is a place of pain and desolation, the same as it is to Christians. In these bitter few minutes, I think to myself that hell could not be any worse than what we have here in Somalia, where a madman rules and soldiers take drugs to make themselves happy to shoot people, and children cry hour after hour. But you know, thinking that thought is too painful. I do not want to become a sad person who wears an expression of despair all day long. I think: *Abdi, listen to me, this is important. You will be happy again one day. If you don't believe that, go and sit on the side of the road and wait for the soldiers to kick you with their boots.*

CHAPTER 6

Predators

The soldiers are predators on two legs, but we also have to worry about the predators on four legs – the hyenas, the lions, the wild dogs. What these animals make of the war I don't know, but they probably can't believe their luck. Why spend the day hunting creatures in the fierce heat when humans, dead ones, others almost dead, can be found just by sniffing about? The female lions, I am told, are the hunters of their tribe; the male lions, larger still than the females, sit at home in the shade of a big rock and wait for their wives to bring them something fresh to eat. The lions will only eat what is fresh – a rotting body disgusts them. But people die every day from disease and starvation, or sometimes simply because they want to die, so there is no shortage of fresh meat. The hyenas are different. They will eat anything. If a body is rotted, they don't pause for a second. I have heard of a pack of hyenas running off in four different directions, each with a piece of dead body to devour in some hidden place. And more frightening still are the stories of hyenas stealing into camps where people are sleeping, finding a small child and dragging that child off into the darkness. A hyena has a set of powerful jaws that can clamp around the chest and throat of a child, and also great strength in its shoulders, so that it can lift that child off the ground and, if necessary, run into the darkness. Everybody in the makeshift camps off the roadsides fears the hyenas even more than the soldiers. We also hear wild dogs howling in the night, but don't see them. They are too stealthy to show themselves.

At night I listen in a state of dread to the harsh, coughing sound of the hyenas in the scrub, and the deep, grunting roar of the lions. On such nights, sleep is impossible. So strange, to think of my enemies, those with two legs, those with four, simply as creatures of the one sort. For the truth is, the hyenas and lions are only looking for dinner, and have their reasons for wanting to eat me, while the soldiers don't want to eat me, just kill me. I have to say, the wild animals will be easier to forgive, but it will be years later, in my comfortable home in Australia, before I get around to forgiving them. Here, in the darkness of the Somali night, all I can think is: *May God send a lightning bolt to destroy the lions, destroy the hyenas, destroy the crazy soldiers.*

★

Snakes, too, are our enemies. I fear them. We all fear them. The snake we see most often is the horned desert viper, brownish-pink, about a metre long with a horn above each eye. People who suffer the bite of the viper usually run around in circles until they fall over and begin bleeding from the nose and ears and mouth. Those horns on the viper's head are creepy, but even worse is the way it moves, so fast, very fast, curling and uncurling. It is like a machine that has been wound up tight, then the spring is released and it explodes into its zigzag motion.

On this day, I have joined a line of people crossing the arid plain, and we are trudging in the African way, single file, more than a hundred of us. Up ahead I hear the cry: 'Snake! Brothers, run!' We sprint away in every direction, wailing at the tops of our voices, so mad, for a snake can kill at most one person whereas a soldier with a gun can kill many more. We do not even have any idea of where the snake is, and yet we all run as if we are putting a distance between ourselves and the viper. Of course, we have always been afraid of vipers, of hyenas, of lions – at least, those of us who go walking across the plains. Fear of the soldiers is new in my life. When the line re-forms (the snake has hidden itself somewhere, probably as frightened of one hundred Somalis shrieking their lungs out as we are of it), I am still trembling. I think: *One day it is snakes trying to kill us, another day it's politics. What next? An earthquake?*

★

I have one advantage on this long flight to safety – a safety that is really a mirage, floating above the plain a long way ahead, never growing any closer – and that is my four dialects. I can speak the dialect of a kid from Mogadishu; that of my mother's tribe; that of my father's; and that of the president's tribe. Except for certain people of the north, who identify their tribal allegiance by colouring their teeth yellow (a primitive custom, thought to mark you as a hillbilly), Somalis do not alter their appearance according to their tribe. Men and women are nearly all tall and slim, one of the most handsome people of the whole African continent. Hawiye, Isaaq, Darood, Hiraab, Sade – I could say I belong to any one of these tribes rather than Rahanweyn, and nobody would know that I was not telling the truth. Well, not without asking me many questions, such as: 'Who is the great patriarch of the Hiraab?' or 'Where do the Hawiye live?' or 'On what day do the Sade celebrate the Victory of the Harvest?' But even such questioning can be negotiated like this: 'The great patriarch of the Hiraab? A good question. Some say there is no patriarch other than the Prophet Muhammad. It depends on how pious you are. Me, I am very pious. I would always say the Prophet, and disaster to him who does not honour our faith.'

It can happen that the soldiers who question me know that I am telling lies, but they respect my ingenuity. Still, with soldiers you can never tell. Maybe they have been smoking hashish or taking amphetamines. You can't always count on them to show an interest in your talent as a liar. But when it comes to using dialects, I am on safe ground. The soldiers say: 'Little cub of traitors, admit that you are Madhiban or we will hang you from a tree.' I say, in the Darood dialect of my mother's people, a dialect that I know these soldiers will recognise: 'Oh, sir, I am surely Darood, there can be no doubt!' The soldiers always seek to make a quick decision. Within thirty seconds of detaining you, they might shoot you or let you go. They are not about to begin a court case, and argue over the outcome like lawyers.

★

After weeks and weeks of travelling in this crazy, haphazard way, a day comes in late 1990, when I fall into the hands of soldiers who are ready to kill. I am not alone – nine of us are captured – but I am the youngest. Some of the others with me, I don't know by name. But I know Ibra, and I know Warsame. The soldiers are from the president's forces, all Darood. Although I can speak their dialect, they are too deeply involved in their theft of farm equipment and food from Baidoa to care about tribal allegiances. The theft of rice you could understand, but farm equipment? The truth is that the soldiers are willing to loot anything they can find that can be carried away, or driven away, and the front-end loader they have seized is a great prize. We had walked straight into them while we were skirting Baidoa, not through lack of wariness, but just through not knowing what lay around the next corner.

The soldiers, like all the soldiers at this time, are dressed in tattered camouflage uniforms that must have been worn day and night for months. They aim their guns at us from their two Land Cruisers – two soldiers in each vehicle, and another one driving the loader – and scream at us to lie facedown on the ground. I can see by their expressions that they have lost all human sympathy. They scream at us, sure, but their eyes are dead; they are both hysterical and emotionless at the same time. I lie with my face in the dust.

Now the soldiers get out of the vehicles, still pointing their guns at us. Then an argument of some sort breaks out amongst the soldiers. I can't make sense of it. My heart is pounding against the ground; I can feel a shudder running through my body. Now the soldiers tell us to stand. Their movements are rapid. They slap us, cuff us, jab us with the barrels of their weapons. One soldier says: 'You think you can go all day and do no work? Do you? Why are you not in your own towns? Why are you not working? Now, you work.' This soldier has an eye that is partly closed by a scar that runs all the way around to his ear. Beads of perspiration stand on his forehead. This is not the way Somalis sweat. We are used to the sun, to the heat. We can stand in the open at midday for an hour without much more than light moisture appearing on our faces. If he is sweating like this, he has been using drugs. Any sort of madness is possible.

On the ground are several big twenty-kilogram bags of rice stacked in a heap, and other bags stuffed with clothing. There is also a pile of spare parts that must have come from the same place as the front-end loader. I have seen others gangs of soldiers carrying off stolen booty in this way. They will take anything.

We are told to pick up the bags of rice, of clothing, the spare parts. I lift a bag of rice, trying to find the most comfortable way to carry it. The soldiers keep hitting us, slapping us, as if we were animals with whom they had lost patience. When the nine of us have lifted a load, the soldiers add more to our burdens until everything they have stolen is on our backs. I am carrying two bags of rice. The soldier in charge shrieks: 'March! Get moving! You stop, I shoot you!'

Along the bare earth of the road we stagger, thinking what everyone thinks in this desperate situation: *If I do what they say, maybe they won't kill me.* I carry my bags of rice on my back, with my arms stretched around to support them. Forty kilograms soon feels like twice its weight. Others, carrying a greater weight, moan with the effort. The soldier in charge, the one who shouts the loudest, every so often runs amongst us and gives someone a whack with his fist – such a stupid thing to do because we cannot go faster. There is no rest. My muscles ache so much I'm sure I will soon fall over and be shot. I think: *I will walk five more steps – then I can go no further.* After those five steps, I say to myself: *Five more – then I can go no further.* And again, and again. Ibra, in front of me, is beginning to lurch from side to side. He is carrying bags of rice like me, but his load is slipping lower down his back and I can see that he will soon let it drop. I hiss at him: 'Don't fall. They will kill you!' With great effort, he gets a better grip on his bags of rice and hoists them further up his back.

The sun on my head and shoulders is so hot that it feels as if my skin is being burnt from my body. I stop counting my steps and instead begin telling myself a story, one word per step. I say – not out loud – *The sun will set, the night will come, you will be cool. The sun will set, the night will come, you will be cool* … The region we are trudging through is open and barren, except for a few thorn bushes and those dry clumps of grass that turn green overnight when it rains. We don't pass anyone on the road. Anyone ahead of us or coming towards us would run off into the thorn bushes well before we reached them. A couple of times, I glimpse people who have escaped into the grass. They stand in the distance, far enough from the soldiers to avoid being shot. It is known that the soldiers are not very accurate with their guns beyond a range of thirty or forty metres, and the people I see are two hundred metres away.

For maybe three hours we march in this way. Now, just as my marching story promised, the sun is beginning to sink lower, our shadows on the ground are lengthening. Even when the soldiers stop to relieve their bladders or to drink from bottles of Evian, they do not allow us to put down our loads. The soldier with the scar is the cruellest of the four. When he drinks from his bottle of Evian, he makes a great show of feeling refreshed just to torment us. He says: 'So good, so good! What do you say boys, isn't this good?' And he laughs, as if he is the funniest man on earth.

Our destination is two new four-wheel-drives parked off the road. The cars would have undoubtedly been stolen and they are already packed with other stolen goods. We unload our burdens, one after another, and the soldiers are delighted with the great treasure trove they have built up. I call them soldiers, but it would be truer to say they are pirates. In years to come, my country of Somalia will be known as a haven for pirates of the sea, but these soldiers are pirates of the land.

Once I have relieved myself of the weight of the bags of rice, I am unable to straighten up. My muscles and bones have formed themselves into a saddle, and they won't resume their normal shape. But even in my bent shape, I can see that the soldiers are impatient to get going. They order us to lie on the ground as they had hours before, but this time they pull our arms behind us and lash our hands together with plastic rope. Now we are forced down on our backs, staring up at the sky. Whatever is about to happen will not be anything we would welcome, that's for sure. If our hands are tied, we can't carry anything, meaning that the soldiers have finished with us. I can hear someone weeping, his cries becoming high-pitched as a child's. But another guy, I don't know his name, is full of anger and is cursing the soldiers and calling them criminals and telling than they are a disgrace to their clan.

The soldiers pay no attention. They are chattering away like a flock of birds – 'Hurry, hurry, tie them tighter, be quick, why are you so slow? On their backs, on their backs, idiot!' And now, a new argument. One of the soldiers says that he doesn't want to kill us face-upward – he wants us to lie facedown.

'What difference does it make?' shrieks the soldier with the scar. 'Up, down – just do it!'

The soldier who is reluctant to kill us face-upward is stubborn. 'I don't want them to give me the evil eye. Don't you know that? If you kill them while they can see your face, a bad thing will happen to you.'

'Tell them to shut their eyes, fool!'

'No, I want them to turn over.'

The scarface soldier screams at us to roll over. And we do. We are lying in a row, almost shoulder-to-shoulder, our faces in the dirt. I have accepted that I am about to die, but who has ever practised dying? Who knows how to do it? I lie as still as I can, not knowing what comes next – pain, nothingness, I don't know. I can hear the soldiers climbing into the cars so that they can shoot at us through the open windows. I hear the clicking sound as the soldiers make adjustments to their automatic rifles, their AKs. Scarface shrieks: 'Okay, okay!'

Bursts of gunfire follow, a rapid rattling noise. Ibra next to me makes a slow, moaning sound. On my other side, a man whose name I don't know jerks quickly, as if he's convulsing – his body is pressed against mine. The firing stops, but only for a couple of seconds. Now the soldiers are sweeping their fire down the row, then up again. My eyes are shut tight but my face is sprayed with dirt as the bullets strike the ground in front of me. Another pause of two seconds, then the firing begins once more. The man on my right side is no longer moving, but Ibra, on my left side, is still moaning softly. One of the soldiers cries out: 'Son of a bitch!' And then: 'My rifle's jammed, man.' Ibra has fallen silent. The scarface soldier with the high-pitched voice screams out: 'Let's go! Let's go!' I hear the roar of the car engines, the crunch of the gears. The soldier who called out before is still complaining about his jammed rifle. I can't let myself believe that the soldiers are going. I can't risk opening even one eye. As far as I can tell, I am alive. But I am wet all down my left side, all down my right side, and the only thing that could make me wet is blood.

Sometime earlier, I heard a man speaking to some other men about a big scar on his chest close to his shoulder. He was saying that it is possible to feel as if you have escaped injury when you are being fired at, only to find, when you stop running, that blood is pouring from a big hole in your flesh. That is what happened to him. He didn't know he was wounded until he stopped running and hid himself. Then he looked down and saw that he was kneeling in a pool of blood. He reached a hospital and was saved. So the wet blood I am aware of must be coming from me. This causes a sickening panic to grip me, and it is only with a great effort of will that I keep my mouth shut. I want to scream my lungs out. My blood is running from my body. I have a vision of water dripping from a bottle, and the bottle emptying until it is only two-thirds full, then half, then less than half ...

Have five minutes passed since the cars drove away? Are five minutes time enough for safety? I say to myself: 'No. Ten minutes more. Fifteen. Don't move for another fifteen minutes.' I can't hear anything but the cries of harmless birds – linnets and starlings, to give them their English names. But what if the ravens come while I am waiting? The ravens that devour the flesh of corpses? Or worse, the hawk-eagles that will not eat anything that is dead, but will attack the wounded, like me? All I can hope is that Somalia is already such a banquet table for birds that eat human flesh that I will be spared.

I am trying to judge fifteen minutes, but it is hopeless. When I begin counting, my flesh shrieks back at me: 'Counting? Are you mad? Get up and run!' I open one eye, but slowly, a millimetre at a time. My blurred vision can make out the earth into which my face is pushed. I open my eye further. I can make out cartridge shells on the ground, many of them, many, many, shining in the setting sun. A starling lands amongst the shells and pecks at them, as if they were food of some sort, caterpillars, maybe. I watch the bird, one of those starlings with orange breasts and black feathers along its back, in its foolishness strutting amongst the shells. Starlings are cautious birds. If it has landed here, a metre from my face, it must believe that we are all dead, all harmless.

I lift my head in order to see further, and the bird rises into the air in alarm. I can see no one. Close to where the cars were parked, a Mars Bar wrapper lies on the ground, left by one of the soldiers, probably. With great caution I rise to my knees, my hands still lashed behind me. On both sides, the bodies of the other eight of my companions lie motionless, torn apart by the bullets – some have broken skulls.

Without waiting to check my own body for wounds, I struggle to my feet and run in the opposite direction to the soldiers. I run fast, leaning forward, hands behind me at first, until the rope loosens and falls off. Whenever I imagine the soldiers chasing me – they are not, of course – I speed up. My bare feet hardly touch the ground. I want to put kilometres between myself and the soldiers. I stumble and crash to the ground, but I am up and running again in a split second. It is only when I have covered as much ground as my strength can manage that I veer off the track into the scrub and sit down to regain my breath. I have a terrible stitch in my side from running. I wait for the stitch to ease, then immediately get back on the track and start running again, and I keep running, kilometre after kilometre.

I rest for a second time in a place where the scrub and trees on the sides of the track are thick enough for me to escape into if any soldiers appear. It is only now that I search my body for wounds. It will seem strange to my readers that I should have waited this long to see if any of the soldiers' bullets have harmed me. But this is what I thought: that I was certainly wounded and would likely bleed to death, but that I had to keep running whatever the cost. Do you see what this illogical thinking suggests? That I was more afraid of the soldiers than actual death. Perhaps this means that we are more afraid of what can cause our death than of death itself. As it happened, I was not wounded. The blood on my legs and my flanks came from those on either side of me at the time of the massacre.

How strange can things become? The soldiers raked the nine of us with automatic gunfire from weapons that can destroy you with a single shot, killing the men and boys to my left and to my right. And yet not a single bullet broke my skin. This is one of those occasions that everybody above a certain age has, I think, experienced, one of those times when you say to yourself: *Somebody is watching over me. My time has not come.*

CHAPTER 7

At the End of the Earth

The road I have been running on is not the road on which we were captured. Somewhere, this road branches off the one on which I was travelling hours earlier. The dark has come down in the African way, suddenly, as if some great hand has placed a lid over the world and blotted out the light. I am lonely, I am exhausted. But for the fact that I desperately want to remain alive, I would be happy to die. It is as if I am on a road that will go on and on for all the remaining years of my life. This is Somalia Road. In the darkness on each side, murder and despair. Why should this disaster have befallen my country? Why could we not find the desire to build, instead of the compulsion to destroy? I say 'we' but, really, I mean the big guys, the ones who put the guns into the hands of the soldiers. People like me, whatever tribe we belong to, small people, unarmed people, we detest fighting, and we are the majority. One man with a gun can stand in front of five hundred unarmed people and force them to do his will. That is all it is. Men with guns, a few thousand, forcing millions to do their will. One of the most horrible of my fears is that I will one day join the men with the guns. Who can say? Put an AK in my hands and I might be as bad as the worst. Perhaps I would kill one person, not wishing to do so, but after that I might be happy to kill more. The scarface soldier who tormented us hours earlier – maybe he was once no different than me. Maybe he hated murder. Now, it means nothing to him.

I can run no further. I walk instead. I see images of my mother and of Jamila in my mind. Before long I am sobbing; my cheeks are wet. I say: 'Are you weeping, little baby? Be a man!'

Up ahead, an orange glow shows off the track, in the black of the night. I stop and study the glow warily. I am in the middle of nowhere. Who would be out here with a fire burning? I approach with great caution, stopping every three steps to listen for the sound of soldiers boasting and shouting in the way they do. Not a sound other than the crackling of the fire. Or is that a voice singing? A very soft sound, very gentle. I can make out a few phrases of Arabic. I come closer to the fire, to the voice. I can just glimpse the silhouette of a man against the glow of the fire. Now a dog barks, just once. I stop where I stand. The silhouette turns and becomes an old man. He calls: 'Come in from the night.'

I step into the circle of the fire's glow. An aged dog trots up to me and sniffs my legs. He looks like a wolf. He can surely smell the blood. The dog seems puzzled for a few seconds, then decides that I am harmless and allows me to approach.

'You have been swimming in blood,' the old man says. 'Let me see.'

He bends over, with difficulty, and touches my legs here and there. 'No, it is good, it is good,' he murmurs. 'No wounds – it is good.'

'Not my blood, sir,' I tell him. 'The blood of my friends.'

'Everywhere in Somalia,' says the old man, 'people bathed in the blood of friends. A sorrow.' Then he says: 'Will you eat? You are surely in need of food.'

The old man prepares me some porridge and offers me a plastic bottle of Evian water. (The third world survives on Evian because it has to, because so much of the unbottled water is polluted. But in Australia, where the water from taps is pure? And people still drink from bottles? A big puzzle.) He doesn't ask me how the blood came to soak my clothing. Maybe he doesn't want to hear, or maybe he wants to spare me the ordeal of telling the story. We both sit in silence by the fire, the old man nodding his head as if lost in his thoughts, and me, thinking nothing, still stiff with fear. After some time, the old man says: 'And now?'

'And now?' I say.

'For you.'

'Now, for me, I must find my friends, those I was travelling with.'

'To where?'

'To where I don't know.'

Then the old man says: 'Your friends are west, two hours.'

'You have seen them?'

'I have. Two hours west.'

'I will go now?'

The old man says: 'No. Sleep, child. Your friends will not be any further away by the morning. Sleep.'

I lie down in the sand by the fire's edge, knowing that it will be impossible to fall asleep. The dog is stretched out between the old man and me. The dog makes faint whimpering sounds in its sleep, as if it, too, has seen dreadful things that plague its rest. I am preparing to lie here with wide open eyes the whole night, but I fall in and out of a light sleep, a sleep without nightmares, and wake finally with the fire reduced to a few smoking embers, the crimson light of sunrise colouring the peaks of the distant hills. I can smell the pleasant wood smoke of the fire.

The old man is sitting cross-legged with his dog's head resting in his lap. He smiles when he sees my eyes open. He says: 'God has sent you some sleep to restore your soul. Praise God, who sends sleep in his mercy.' He has already prepared porridge for me, which I accept with thanks. 'And drink,' he says, offering me the water bottle. And he adds: 'Not like the Americans and the Germans and the English and the Australians. Not like the Dutch and the Danish, all the UN men and women. They drink as if they were camels coming out of the desert after a month without seeing a waterhole. Drink like our people. A few sips.'

I smile. 'I know, sir.'

★

Exactly two hours west, as the old man promised, I find my friends, those who I and the eight others, now dead, were travelling with. There are a hundred of them crouched around cooking fires. The mothers are stroking the heads of their children, feeding them a thin variety of the much more substantial porridge I had for breakfast. The mothers and relatives of the eight others who were captured with me rush over and demand to know what has happened, all of them talking at once. The mothers reach for me with their hands and stroke my flesh, as if by being kind to me they will make me give them good news. They say: 'Ibra, where is Ibra?' And they say: 'Tell me Warsame is alive and I will bless you with my own portion of our bread.' And: 'Abdi, you are a good boy, you honour your parents with your charity. My son is alive, tell that to me, that my son is alive.' But others have seen the blood that has dried on my clothing, and they are hysterical with grief: 'Aiee, aiee! What news do you have? What terrible news do you have of my husband?'

I wave my hands and ask for some quiet. When all the women are quiet, or almost quiet, I tell them the story of the past twenty hours. At the end, I say: 'All are dead. They died in an instant when the soldiers raised their guns. All dead. I alone survived. It was God's will, I can say no more.'

Some of the women fall to their knees and pick up handfuls of dirt and throw it in the air so that it falls on their heads. Some rush about with their hands raised to heaven wailing in grief. I stand with my head bowed, ashamed to be alive when all my friends are dead. Two of the women and a number of the men are angry with me. They cry out: 'What, only this one left alive? How can this happen? Did he betray our sons? How can this happen?'

'The bullets missed me,' I tell them. 'The soldiers tried to kill me but the bullets missed me. I can tell you no more.'

My story does not satisfy them. But others come to my defence. 'What would you think of this boy? The soldiers kill everyone. Will you persecute him for his good fortune? Better to praise God that we have a witness to tell us this story.'

You cannot blame people for what they say when they are full of grief. It makes them crazy. It wounds me, of course it does, to hear myself accused of betrayal. It wounds me to be a survivor. But I say this to myself, for comfort: *God has a plan for you that is too strange to understand. He has left you alive. Let the life I live after this reprieve honour those who died beside me.*

★

Again, we are on the road, either walking in a long line across the open ground or travelling in the backs of trucks. We come one morning to Buula Hawo, a Somali town near the borders with

Kenya and Ethiopia. I am coated in dust from the journey. I know what I look like because everyone else in the truck is covered in dust, too – my face is a red mask with holes for eyes and mouth.

★

After three months of living as a refugee, I had thought I'd already come across the worst things my eyes would ever see. Then we jump down from the truck and walk across the border into Mandera, just across the border in Kenya, and on to the refugee camp outside the town. Within two days, Mandera changes my mind about that. Here, tens of thousands of people stagger about with nowhere to go – no destination. Some of the shelters are the sort that the United Nations provides – a hoop of wire at the front and back over which is stretched a white fabric, like the plastic fabric that our shower curtain was made from in Mogadishu. These tents are pinned into the earth with steel spikes. A few are big and provide a home for maybe fifty people; most are of a smaller size, with room for six people. But the UN tents are very few, and all are ripped and tattered. What most people live in here are low, makeshift shelters made by building a frame a metre high from sticks and wire and pieces of plastic piping then covering it with cloth, plastic sheeting, cardboard. Some people have found a bush to use as a frame. These low shelters – and there are thousands of them, in rows – are really piles of debris under which people hide from the sun. Thorn bushes are all that grow here in this arid place, and many of them are dead. Any rubbish that blows about becomes caught on the bushes and hangs there forever. And there is so much rubbish, so much, banked up against the walls of tents, against the fences made of sticks tied together with grass that once must have served as pens for animals, chickens, goats, not that there are any animals left. There are no toilets. If people can manage, they creep out beyond the edge of the camp and make use of the desert. If a big wind came, it would blow the whole camp of ten thousand huts off into the wilderness, but such winds only blow once a year.

Hundreds of people here are in the last stages of death by starvation. They're hoping to find something on the ground they might eat – a lizard, ants, a strip of vegetable peel. Mothers sit outside collapsing shelters with babies on their laps or at their breasts – babies who in some cases are already dead. Many people are burning up with malaria, stretched out on the bare earth or on strips of cardboard, sometimes pieces of cloth. There is little medicine. The UN comes to Mandera only sometimes. These people have virtually been abandoned by everyone in the world.

As I walk along the tracks between huts, looking for somewhere to lie down for an hour, small children, some naked, walk beside me and beg for food in a monotonous chant: 'Oh, sir, something for my sister, oh, sir, anything you can spare, oh, sir, God will bless you ...'

Who feeds these people? Who looks after them? As I say, the UN comes here only sometimes because it is usually too dangerous for their personnel – not dangerous within the camp but on the road that leads here. UN vehicles have been hijacked. I ask the man who is telling me the situation in the camp – he is not an official, just a resident of Mandera, sitting cross-legged outside his tent – what became of the UN people when their vehicles were hijacked. He looks at me without saying a word, as if the question does not require an answer. He is not an old man, but he looks old. He is not waiting here in hope. He is waiting to die.

I see empty plastic bottles that once held water, and here and there I see a resident with a medical dressing. What is being done for those burning with the fever of malaria, I don't know. By the looks of it, nothing. I have come to the end of the earth.

At night, the crying and weeping are continuous. At dawn, people hope against hope for a better day. They pray early, led by a stand-in muezzin. But at night the hunger is still there, nothing good has happened, and the crying begins. Faith is the last thing people relinquish. I am not a Muslim who prays five times a day; sometimes not even once. Certainly I do not rouse myself from a night fractured by the weeping of children to prostrate myself in worship. I believe in the God of our faith, and I believe He is merciful, but faith is not the engine of my existence. Nobody admonishes me for not heeding the call to prayer, and I do not despise those who are able to revere Allah and honour our Prophet from this gathering in front of the gates of hell. These people would share their last meal with me if they had any food, and I would do the same for them. They did nothing to bring about the calamity of Mandera. The mothers have struggled all their lives to raise their children; the fathers have toiled to put food on the table. How can they be blamed if struggle and toil no longer mean anything? I will come to know the efforts that charities make to raise money for food and clean water in such camps as Mandera. I will participate myself in these programs of relief some years from this day I am describing. In their generosity, people give millions each year, hoping that the money will indeed provide relief and not wind up in the deep pockets of some rapacious warlord. I always think back to Mandera. What ten loaves of bread would have meant to those famished people – one slice per person would have provided a ray of hope in the lives of two hundred people. A truckload of high protein biscuits would have fed the camp for a week. And yes, the next week would have been another matter, but a biscuit to bite, a small bowl of wheat and milk to sip from – that would have been a supreme joy for the people of Mandera. If they die the next week, then so be it. But to have tasted food before that fate overcomes them – that is something, at least.

It takes me only three days to see clearly that I will die in despair if I remain in Mandera. Even after three months of touring my suffering country of Somalia – an enforced tour, of course – three months of wishing for a full belly, my body is still strong. It takes almost six months of starvation rations before a healthy human being begins to succumb to illness in such a way that he will take a further six months on a good diet to fully recover. I have not reached that stage yet. I have avoided pellagra, rickets, respiratory collapse, anaemia, blindness or dementia, and such diseases as malaria and cholera, which are not brought on by malnutrition but that follow the starving more closely than the well-fed. My body is strong, my mind is strong and true despair has not made its way into my heart yet. I say 'true despair', but my readers may not know what I mean by that. I do not mean the despair that you might feel when you experience one unlucky event after another. That is easy to overcome, with a small change of fortune. No, I mean what I see in the eyes of the mothers of Mandera, and in the eyes of the fathers. Their children clutch at them, claw at them. But they stare straight ahead, seeing nothing. And their ears no longer hear the cries and pleading of their children. That is true despair, when you have already died and you are waiting for your burial to catch up with you.

I am going back to Mogadishu. I am going to cover the ground I have already crossed. I want to see if my mother and my father and Jamila have returned to our house. Does this sound like foolishness? Like a vain hope? So it is. But it is the only plan I can embrace.

And so I begin, in the company of three other boys who have made the same journey as me – Dahir, Idris and Jilow. On a day when the sun is already burning our skin at eight in the morning, with not a morsel of food between us, we walk out of the camp to the road, hoping for a truck, a car. We walk along the road in the sun, not hurrying. If we hear the sound of an engine, either heading east, the way we are going, or travelling west, we watch with eyes peeled. If it is the crazy soldiers, we have only a few seconds to run from the road into the acacia and sand. If it is a vehicle that might stop for us, we leap up and down where we stand and wave our arms and call out: 'Sir, blessings if you stop! Sir, a million blessings if you stop!' And the trucks stop, and the cars, unless they have no space. The people who drive out this way still have some kindness in their hearts. They have to have some kindness left or they would not come into this land of despair to start with.

Best of all would be if we can stop a UN vehicle or the vehicle of some charity people, for the UN people and the charity people will find something for us to eat and drink and will talk to us as if we are true human beings. But there is little hope of a UN ride, an Oxfam ride. The crazy soldiers have frightened them away. We have to be content with truck drivers who shout at us above the noise of the engine, and want to share their insane politics with us. Like this: 'Who is at fault! Saddam! He is a madman!' Or if it is not Saddam who is at fault, it is the king of the Saudis, or the president of the United States, or the Kenyans, or the Ethiopians, or sometimes all of them together. For some reason, truck drivers are always extremely talkative people. You pay your way by listening to insane conspiracy theories, or long tales of complaint about the driver's family members. It's okay. A small price to pay.

CHAPTER 8

Massacre

A day of great grief is about to come our way. May I apologise in advance for the story I am about to tell. It is in this book because it is the truth, and it happened to me, and the whole theme of this book is the truth and what happened to me. If God granted me one wish, it would be this: that human beings lost the ability to be cruel to one another; that one morning, everyone in the world woke up and could no longer remember how to torment others, and from that day forward, had to rely on kindness. But as of this day, God has not granted me that wish.

★

We are close to a small village west of Buurhakaba on our return journey to Mogadishu. Dahir, Idris, Jilow and I have joined up with other travellers taking the road to Mogadishu. None of the travellers has much of a motive for going to Mogadishu, except that it is there. Some have heard that Mandera is a place of death, and hope for something better in the capital, but most are on the road because there is no alternative.

Whenever we approach a town, it is our habit to send a few people ahead to check for soldiers. Today, it is my turn, together with three men from our group. We creep along stealthily, pausing to listen every few minutes. The landscape is fairly green here, on this side of Buurhakaba, and we know that, if needs be, we can run and hide in the scrub. I can smell in the air the smoke of a wood fire. Up ahead, the man who is leading calls back in a whisper: 'A fire is burning, I don't know why.' A fire suggests a camp, perhaps a place where we can find food, and so we advance quietly, feeling that we have come upon good fortune.

But good fortune is not what we find. As soon as we emerge from cover, soldiers step out from hiding and aim their guns at us. We have been ambushed. The fire deceived us, as the soldiers intended. I look quickly at the three others, asking silently, *Will we run?* The others, Jilow, Idris and Dahir, don't meet my glance. The soldiers are dressed in the camouflage uniforms of Barre's army, but very ragged. There is something else about them that chills me. They don't look simply crazed, like so many of the soldiers we have come across over the past few months, they look – this is the English word that I think is the right one – demonic, like men who have given themselves over completely to wickedness. Some are smiling, but without any humour.

One is holding a long, unsheathed knife. He stands before me, nodding his head. 'You are Rahanweyn,' he says to me.

On another day, in another place, I might have denied that I was Rahanweyn. But this day, for some reason, I reply with pride: 'Yes, Rahanweyn.' Perhaps I am fed up with denying my tribal allegiance. Perhaps I am crazy. But that's what I say: 'Yes, Rahanweyn.' I might have chosen a better occasion to show my pride. Do you know what I think? I think that when I stare into the eyes of this soldier, a lie would make me more like him, and I am repelled by the thought.

We are told to stand close together. One of the soldiers is guarding us, but in a very casual way. He knows that he could shoot us dead in five seconds if we tried to run, so he is untroubled. It soon becomes obvious that the soldiers, the pirates, have taken control of the village and are looting everything they can find in exactly the same way as the soldiers who murdered my friends a month earlier. These soldiers have stripped nearly all of the corrugated iron off the buildings in the village – hundreds of sheets of iron that are now stacked close to a grain bunker. The grain has not been destroyed, for reasons that will soon be demonstrated.

These grain bunkers are found wherever harvests are carried out in Somalia. They serve to preserve grain, mostly wheat, in certain seasons. An oblong trench a metre deep is dug into the earth and a trapdoor is fitted above the trench. The grain inside is kept dry and also safe from scavenging animals such as rats. But that is not what the bunker is being used for now. Instead, soldiers are herding people from the village into the bunker, packing them in, ignoring the screams of the mothers and their children. I close my eyes. I cannot watch. But the soldier guarding the three of us notices that I have my eyes shut and he jabs me with the tip of his rifle barrel. 'What is the matter with you, Rahanweyn?' he says. 'Are you falling asleep?'

When no more people can be crammed into the bunker, the soldiers lock the trapdoor. The day is hot and getting hotter. The temperature inside the iron bunker must be fierce, like an oven. The people inside will die horribly. The cries from inside the bunker amuse the soldiers. Why they wish to kill the villagers in this way, or in any way at all is something I can't understand. The soldiers have the iron; they have everything from the village of any value.

Why is it necessary to torture these people? I stand like a zombie, staring at nothing. The cries of the people within the bunker are like sparks from a fire that burn my flesh. And is this the death that the soldiers intend for me, for Dahir and Idris and Jilow? This, or something as bad?

The soldiers command us to load sheets of iron on our backs. We are to carry the iron to some destination we know nothing about. Four, five, six sheets of iron are loaded on my back. To carry them I have to remain bent over and reach around and grip the sharp sides of the sheets. This is a new version of my ordeal a month earlier, when I carried rice sacks. And these soldiers are a new version of the soldiers that herded us along on that day. It seems that I have survived one torment only to have the whole episode re-enacted. Better I had died when the bullets were fired at me. Better I now lay dead beside my friends – this is what I think. Somalia is one hell after another waiting to seize me. And if I survive today, a fresh hell is ahead.

And yet, just as on other days when despair builds up in me, I feel an instinctive need to fight it. Despair in your heart is itself a type of torture, and if it is left unchecked, it will surely kill you, or your soul, at least. And so I fight. Instead of picturing myself as a beast laden down with a load, I think of the atlas I left in my room at home months ago. I picture the page that displays the whole of the African continent and with each ten steps, I try to remember the name of a new country and its capital city. I start with my homeland of Somalia then go north, whispering as quietly as I can. I say: 'Egypt – its great city is Cairo, where you see the strange constructions of the ancient kings. And the great river that has the name of Nile, in its waters crocodiles are found. That is Egypt. And west of Egypt you will find Libya, where the Colonel Gaddafi rules. The great city of Libya is Tripoli, on the coast of the famous Mediterranean Sea. West again is Algeria, where the French kings once ruled and where the language of the French is still spoken. The great city of Algeria is Algiers. A very big country is Algeria. Between Algeria and Libya is the smaller land of Tunisia. Its great city is Tunis where, in far-off times, the strange people called Carthaginians had their towns and villages. They were a cruel people ...'

The sun heats the iron on my back and I feel my strength seeping out of my body. I say to myself: 'Abdi, if you survive this day, any work you do in the future will seem like a daydream, so think of that day to come, think of the wife you will find and the children who will come from God as a blessing. You are Rahanweyn, you are your father's son.'

After hours of this ordeal we come to a place that I have never seen before. I am permitted to lay down my burden of iron sheets, as are the others, my friends. It is only when I stand up straight again that I become aware of the horror of this place. I hear screaming coming from a shed of corrugated iron, the screams of people who are being tormented in some way. Smoke is in the air and a smell that is unmistakable – it is tar, the tar that is used to mend roads in Mogadishu. The soldiers within the shed are shrieking with laughter. Those outside glance at us, the new arrivals, and giggle to themselves at the expressions of dread on our faces. One jeers at us: 'Very hot! Aiee!' Many other captives are sitting on the ground, men, boys, girls, women, holding their heads in their hands. I cannot be certain, but my judgement is that they are all Rahanweyn. The soldiers are enjoying themselves by torturing their captives.

I have heard about this torture. An old man told me – he'd seen the soldiers cover a man in hot tar. He described how the poor wretched creature crawled whimpering on elbows and knees, nothing of life left to him, hoping for death.

The soldiers are amused. They giggle and shake their heads. I shake my own head, bewildered by such depraved cruelty.

This is the day of horrors that still comes back to me in my worst dreams. This is the day that I wish with all my heart that I could forget. Even now, in the comfort and safety of my home in Australia I am sometimes overcome by these horrors, as I have said earlier. Do you know what upsets me so much – not just me, I'm sure, but anyone who has witnessed the worst of what human beings are capable? It is this. I belong to the species that takes such delight in cruelty. I am a human being. I can never rid myself of this knowledge. I cannot say: 'Oh, those soldiers, such terrible creatures, thank God I am not of their make.' But I am. The soldiers grew up in communities like mine. Mothers bore them; fathers loved them; brothers and sisters played with them. And yet the time came when they thought: *How comical! Cover a man in boiling tar and see how he shrieks, see how he crawls on the ground! Oh, such a sight!* However kind we are, however much we sympathise with the suffering of others, we remain the brothers of monsters. I can say this: if a doctor somewhere in the world could operate on my brain and take away these memories that so plague me, so torment me, I would pay a fortune to be rid of them.

What the soldiers intend for me and my friends, I cannot say. Nothing good. We are forced into a yard surrounded on four sides by a stone wall. Our hands are not bound. The soldiers say 'Sit!'

and we sit. Then we are left alone while the soldiers return to the massacre.

Jilow whispers to me: 'Abdi, now what?'

'Now what? I don't know.'

Jilow says: 'Are we to wait here until they cover us in tar?'

I say: 'Maybe they want us to work for them.'

'Yes. And maybe they want to cook us.'

The stone wall is low, about the height of a man's waist. If we wished to, we could leap over it. Beyond the wall lie the outskirts of a town. I rise up on my knees so that I can see over the wall. Some way in the distance I can make out what seems to be a cemetery. How far? More than a kilometre. I say to Jilow: 'If we can run into the cemetery, they will not follow us.'

'Do you think? These devils? They would follow us past the gates of hell.'

'I do not think they will follow us.'

Why do I believe this? I have noticed that the more savage the soldiers become – these soldiers, and others – the more superstitious they are. It is as if they leave behind all that their faith has taught them, all the blessings and mercy of God, and grow more primitive. In Somalia, people still practise black magic, some of them, and talk of demons and witches and carry small dolls that they believe will keep them from harm. The mullahs say to these people: 'The dolls are a blasphemy. Cast them away.' How long has our country enjoyed the embrace of Allah? Maybe a thousand years? But for such people as these soldiers all the old gods still have power. A cemetery frightens them. They think they will be pursued by creatures with the heads of dogs if they venture into such a place. That belief is my only hope.

It is evening. Light is fading from the sky and the colours of sunset appear in the west, accompanying the hopeless cries of those being tortured. When the soldiers turn their back on us briefly, I give a signal and three of us vault over the stone wall and begin to run like madmen in the direction of the cemetery. The soldiers shriek when they see what we have done and fire at us with their Kalashnikovs. But we have an advantage of one hundred metres over the soldiers and they cannot shoot straight even over twenty metres, so we will surely reach the cemetery before they catch us. After all, for us escape is a matter of life and death; for the soldiers, our escape means less.

The cemetery is unwalled. We sprint through the grave markers, as deep into this area of sacred soil as we can manage. Then we flatten ourselves on the ground and listen. The soldiers are shouting to each other on the perimeter. One calls to the other: 'Get them, chase them!' And the other calls: '*You* chase them!' As I'd hoped, they will not enter the cemetery.

I am stretched out on a grave. I can read the sacred inscription in Arabic on the grave marker in the dim light, the *Salat al-Janazah*, or funeral prayer:

Subhaanak-Allaahumma, wa bihamdika, wa tabaarakasmuka, wa ta'aalaa jadduka, wa jalla thana uka wa laa ilaaha ghayruka.

'Glory be to You, Allah, and praise be to You and blessed is
Your name, and exalted is Your Majesty, and there is
none to be served besides You.'

I dare not move. I can hear the soldiers stalking the perimeter of the cemetery, shrieking to each other, and to us. One soldier calls:

'Come out! You will be safe!' On the other side of the cemetery, a second soldier calls: 'We find you, we kill you like goats!' The first soldier calls: 'Don't say that, fool! Do you think they will come out to be butchered like goats? Are you mad?' Then the soldier who had threatened us changes his tune: 'We will feed you!' he says. 'Very good food! Come out!' He may excel at torture, but he is no genius, that's for sure. I don't move a muscle. The soldiers will have to depart soon. It is now dark. I can no longer read the inscription on the grave that is my haven.

The threats and promises of the soldiers cease. I feel certain they have gone, but I'm not ready to stand up. What would be the point? In the dark, I can't see where to go. No, I will have to wait until the first light of dawn. I doubt the soldiers will come back that early. They can't think that far ahead. I can't even call out to the others, to my friends. Well, I could, but I'm not willing to risk it. We are all isolated from each other in this cemetery – or perhaps the others have crept out. I return to imagining my atlas open at the continent of Africa, and continue my journey to the west, to Morocco, with Rabat as its great city, and also Casablanca on the coast of the Atlantic Ocean. Now I picture the map of Europe – so many countries. Could I escape to Europe from Mogadishu? Oh, what joy that would be! Of course, I know very, very little about the countries of Europe but what I do know is that the people of Europe are rich. Each man and each woman – yes, even the women! – have automobiles of their own, modern automobiles, Mercedes-Benz, Audi, Volvo, Ford, Volkswagen. And in the houses of the Europeans are two television sets, radios, giant refrigerators filled with food. I picture the peninsula of Spain, Madrid at its heart; further north is France, where my father has lived and worked, the great city of Paris, famous for a thousand things – its beautiful river named the Seine, the Arc de Triomphe, the Champs-Elysées, where Dad has walked with his friends. Italy is close by, the famous land of Italy. Mum is in Italy even now, and just to picture her dressed in her stylish Italian clothes makes my eyes brim with tears. I whisper over and over into the earth of the grave that my face rests on: 'Mum, Mum, it's Abdi. I am still alive, keep me in your heart. Jamila, sister, think of me …'

★

Dawn comes at last. The starlings chatter as the light expands in the sky. I lift my head and get my bearings. As far as I can see, the soldiers have not returned. Taking great care, I stand upright. I make a sort of whispering call to my friends, three or four times. No response. They must have found their way out of the cemetery in the darkness. I creep between the grave markers, crouching down whenever I hear a sound from the village – gunfire, shrieking. On the far side of the cemetery, I gaze around to get my bearings. The sky in the east is growing brighter. I can make out the shapes of hills in the far distance. It is towards the south that I must travel. During the night I made a plan to search out the village of Qoryooley, where my father's cousin lives – Sharifa, the wife of Sheikh Abdullah, a famous religious teacher. If I can find the village, I will ask Sharifa for sanctuary. In Somalia it is a sacred duty to give comfort and assistance to any relative who comes to you. We know all of our relatives and the map of the broad, extended family we carry in our heads takes in every cousin, second cousin, third cousin. There is not the slightest risk that Sharifa will say to me: 'Abdi? I have never heard of an Abdi. Go on your way.'

I know the direction of Baidoa, and I know that Qoryooley is to be found to the south. At other stages of my journey, I had given thought to the possibility of calling in on Sharifa, but circumstances were never quite right. I am glad I left Sharifa's house as a haven of last resort.

I am in rags now. My legs are covered in cuts, scratches and bruises. In all of Somalia, there is probably no boy who looks more like a beggar than I do. And yet, just for a few minutes, I enjoy a feeling of great gladness. I am alive. My heart beats, my lungs take in the air of the morning, my feet carry me along this dirt road. Death has not yet been able to take me away to the silent land. So many times now the angel of death has come so close that I can hear the beat of his wings, and yet I am alive. This is the song of my soul rejoicing in life.

★

When at last I reach Qoryooley, people glance in alarm at me with all this dried blood on my legs.

A woman old enough to be a grandmother calls to me: 'Boy, have you been in the jungle fighting lions?'

I reply: 'No, grandmother, just a troubled journey. Where can I find the house of Sheikh Abdullah?'

'The honoured man? You stand by his house at this moment.'

Even before I turn to see which house the woman is talking about, a voice calls to me. 'Is it Abdi, from the great city?'

It is Sharifa. She beckons with her hand for me to enter her house. Once inside, she stands back with her hands stretched out to my shoulders and studies my appearance with many tut-tut sounds and deep sighs and the 'Aiee, aiee, aiee!' cry that all Somalis utter when something distresses them.

'What catastrophe is this, my Abdi? Three years since I last saw you when you were fresh and clean, and now you are like someone who has fought his way through a forest of thorn bushes! Aiee, aiee, aiee!'

Sharifa – who is much older than I am – prepares a big basin of warm water and, using a clean white cloth, washes away the blood on the cuts that cover my arms and legs, even my face. Each cut stings as it is bathed, but I am more aware of the touch of a kind hand than any pain. Sharifa's husband, Sheikh Abdullah, is not at home for the moment, and her children are away somewhere. In the quiet of the house, just the two of us, I feel as if a blessing has descended on me from above. This is the sort of care my mother would have provided, if she were here. All the time that Sharifa is bathing me, my eyes are brimming with tears of gratitude.

None of the cuts is very deep, thanks to God's mercy. When the dried blood is washed away, my limbs are left with a curious pattern, like tattoos. Sharifa prepares a fresh bowl of warm water and leaves me with a block of green soap to wash the rest of my body in private. When I am done, I wrap a long, white towel around my body and accept from Sharifa a shirt and underwear and long shorts that come down to my knees – clothing that must belong to one of her sons. And she finds me leather sandals to wear. My feet are so scratched and so sore that the sandals hurt me at first.

Now Sharifa spreads a cloth on the floor and asks me to sit. She serves me bread and flavoured rice and a thin yoghurt drink like milk. While I am eating, she asks me about my journey, and my mother and father and Jamila. When I tell her that my mother is still away in Italy, she quickly pats her cheeks in the way that Somali women do when they hear something that they don't like. I think she feels that my father and mother have not been very reliable. She says: 'And Jamila? The child, so beautiful?'

'She is with another family. I hope she is safe.'

'Such a journey, Abdi! It breaks my heart to hear your story.'

Now I am allowed to sleep. 'Here, you are safe from harm,' Sharifa says. 'My husband, the honoured man, no person would dare come here to make violence.'

As soon as I am left alone on my bedding, I tell myself that I can never sleep again in life; that the demons in my mind will plague me too much to ever close my eyes and welcome unconsciousness. But within a minute or even less I am deeply asleep and do not wake again until evening.

★

Five days I remain with my father's cousin's family. Five days of the most glorious peace and quiet I can remember in my life. It is like being cared for by angels. All the family members take part in being kind to me. This family is not threatened by what is happening in Somalia, in its change from a land of tribes that had found a way of coexisting to a perfect hell, where brother barely trusts brother and blood soaks the earth from border to border. Sheikh Abdullah is so admired that not even the drug-crazed soldiers would think of attacking him. I think if I'd wished to, I could have stayed not just for five days but five months or five years. I would have enjoyed a longer stay for the sake of feeling safe. But, you know, it is better not to exhaust the generosity of those who wish you well. And how content would I be after a few more weeks if I was doing nothing to find my mother, my father, my sister? To a Somali, a family is like the bread you eat to stay alive. You can't do without it. Just impossible.

After five days, I tell Sharifa that I must continue my journey back to Mogadishu in the hope of finding my sister, and even perhaps my father.

'Abdi,' she says, 'this home is your home. This kitchen is your kitchen. This bed belongs to you forever. Stay here, if that is the deepest wish of your heart.'

'And yet,' I say, 'I must reach Mogadishu. My mother might have returned from Italy.'

Sharifa averts her eyes, I think to hide the doubt I would see there at the mention of my mother. She does not want to seem critical.

She says: 'God's blessings on you, Abdi. If you must go, you must. In the days ahead, I don't know, maybe there is some pain for you yet, but I foresee great joy in your life in the years ahead.'

★

I set off for the great city in the early morning of my sixth day in Qoryooley. For the first time in some months, I am beginning a journey by myself, with no friends. At first I walk, but I hope that it will not be too long before I find a truck that is willing to carry me towards Mogadishu. Maybe it is the blessings of Sharifa at the start of my journey, and maybe it is just the benefit of proper sleep and good food, but I am happy in my heart. How is this possible? I have witnessed enough cruelty and depravity to make me wish to pull the teeth out of my head in anguish and yet, today I am happy. I think this: *Abdi, in this world, if you live long enough, you will see evil enough, but you will see goodness, too. It is the goodness that saves the world, surely.* Do you see how things work out? Five days of love and care is enough to overcome months of despair and violence.

CHAPTER 9

Return

I find a ride in a truck with a number of other people of my tribe who are also returning to Mogadishu. When I talk with them, it becomes clear they have no reason to expect that things will have improved in Mogadishu, but they have no choice but to believe they have. It is optimism built on nothing. Is it my task to tell them that things may have become worse rather than better? It is not. My sense of a better life in the future has persisted, and I am not about to crush anyone's hopes.

I listen to the others talking as the truck clatters along the red earth road that leads to the highway. I can follow the various dialects. Will you hear what those who are down to their last few grains of hope talk about? Football, if they are men or boys: about the West German team that won the last World Cup against Argentina; about the prospects of Somalia one day building a team good enough to reach the second round of a future World Cup (further than the second round would be considered nothing but fantasy); the Palestinians of the Middle East, and the sorrow of their struggle; whether Adidas trainers are better than Nike; jokes that make fun of the dusty people of the north-west; jokes about Siad Barre, who still considers himself president, even though he barely dares to come within a hundred kilometres of Mogadishu. And the women? The women talk about the great day that will come when a Somali housewife can expect to own a washing machine of her own, like women in America, who also have a machine for making clothes dry quicker than hanging them in the sun; and the sorrow of the murders of this relative and that, and of the wickedness of Barre. Standing or sitting in the back of the truck, the passengers chatter in the same way they would if they were standing in a group in their suburb of Mogadishu. Occasionally, I join in and speak about my mother, who might have returned from Italy, and my dad, who has spent years and years in Paris, France, and has climbed to the top of the Eiffel Tower fifty times. (This is an exaggeration.)

★

In early 1991, I reach a stopping point about ten kilometres from the outskirts of Mogadishu. Truck drivers usually ask their passengers to get down here and walk the rest of the way. They do this to avoid being stopped by soldiers for carrying people about the countryside, people who go about saying they fled Mogadishu because of the countless murders, something the soldiers do not want to hear.

And that's what I do.

A maze of roads, a couple of them sealed, lead into the city. Even from a long way out, it is usual to see all these roads and tracks full of traffic, in the African way – many battered old cars, a few shiny new ones, bullock drays, thousands of pedestrians, even laden camels. But today the traffic is light. I join a group of people on foot, mumbling a few words of greeting and trying to look inconspicuous. Those around me glance at me without curiosity. I am just a boy with scars all over his legs and arms and without any baggage to make me interesting. A woman says to me: 'You have come a long road, child.'

Whenever a military vehicle comes down the road I duck my head and walk even more closely to those around me. I don't know why I feel the need to do this. It is not as though my picture is displayed everywhere on a wanted poster. The soldiers do not know me. Perhaps I think that all the scars will make me suspicious. In any case, the military vehicles roar past too fast for the soldiers to notice anything. Nobody is even sure who the soldiers are fighting for. Maybe they are Barre's soldiers, or maybe they fight for the Hawiye, the tribe who are said to control Mogadishu now. To civilians like me, all soldiers are dangerous. We expect only grief from them.

In the outer suburbs of the city, I notice the same reduced traffic. I have never seen this part of Mogadishu look so abandoned. Buildings are deserted, shops shut, and not a single child in school uniform. I pass the first of a great number of dead bodies that lie where they fell on the roadside, flies hovering in black clouds around them, the stink of putrefaction compelling me to put a hand over my mouth and nose. I make sure that I do not glance at the eyes of the dead – as everyone knows, the horror of the victim's murder can leap out of his or her eyes and creep into your soul, turning you into a zombie. Some of the people in the group I am keeping with murmur prayers or whisper such words as 'That one is so young, what crime could she have done?' Most say nothing.

The numbers of the dead multiply as we draw closer to the inner suburbs. We even pass the bodies of small children who have been left behind. Maybe the mothers of these children were carried away to serve as slaves for the soldiers, or as prostitutes. Or maybe the parents simply could not stop for a burial; maybe they were running. I feel shame for my own country. For it to have come to this, that a child of two or three years should be left to rot away in the sun, chewed at by rats and dogs.

More people are to be seen here in the suburbs closer to the heart of Mogadishu, but still the number is greatly diminished since I left. I have spoken before of the sense of walking into one fresh hell after another – first, the Mandera refugee camp, then the site of the boiling tar, where people wailed and wept and pleaded for mercy. Mogadishu is a new hell and, in its way, the worst of all. The corpses, the daunted looks on the faces of everyone I see, the eerie silence, the abandoned shops. Why is it worse? Because in my own memory live images of these very streets bursting with life and laughter; of women calling to each other across the streets, trading saucy stories; of men shouting out the virtues of whatever they were selling, flattering whoever walked by with such prepared compliments as 'If I live a thousand years, will I see a more handsome fellow than this one who comes my way?' The streets of Mogadishu were a carnival of life and colour and rich aromas and when I walked down them on my way to school or to the beach to swim and play football I breathed in the culture of a thriving people and felt nourished by it. What is wrong with us, that we have turned away from life towards death? What good can ever come from shooting a child with a Kalashnikov simply because your gun is loaded and the child is there in your sights? Life for many of the people I knew in Mogadishu was a struggle, but it was a worthwhile struggle, one that gave us rewards as well as hardship. I remember a day when I was walking towards the beach after school – actually, not walking but running – and my friends were all around me, shouting and jeering and making jokes and whooping with the sheer joy of what was awaiting us – the waters of the Indian Ocean, then an hour of rowdy football, then more of the Indian Ocean and a drink of Fanta. I remember traipsing home with my friends, reliving the game we had played, congratulating, taunting playfully, calling each other brother or Pelé or Diego (meaning Maradona) or numbskull or moron. We walked west towards the sunset, and I stopped for a moment and gazed at the colours, which seemed more intense than ever before. My mother would have dinner ready for me when I reached home. Jamila would say: 'Abdi, in our school you are the most famous. Abdi, you are the only one who knows Australia.' How old was I? Ten? This is what I thought as I stared at the sunset: *In all of Somalia, I am the happiest.* And I remember that I laughed to hear my own voice say that inside my head.

★

Another hour's walk and I am in Medina. I stand in the middle of the boulevard and gaze down at the ruin of what was once a street full of delights. Rubbish is left uncollected in heaps on the footpaths, in the street itself. A dog with a surly look breaks off from burrowing into a rubbish heap to snarl at me. Something in his unfriendly manner makes me run at him and shout 'Get out of here! Get out!' The dog hurries away, maybe shocked to find anyone who cares about the behaviour of animals. People are still hanging about, but so few. No one waves, no one calls a greeting. In their eyes there's the look you would expect in zombies, the living dead – a blank, loveless gaze. I am showing defiance by walking down the middle of the street and, to tell the truth, it isn't sensible and is in contradiction to the wariness I have relied on for months now. But I need to feel some pride. I need to show that I am a person who can remember the Medina that was. People shrink away from me, perhaps because they have forgotten what a boy looks like when he strides along fearlessly.

I pause as I approach my family's house. I don't know what to expect. I know very well what I hope for, but that is probably a fantasy. I hope to find my mother and my sister in the kitchen, eating from bowls of savoury rice. I hope to see my mother show me one of her rare smiles and say, 'It's my boy, it's my Abdi, my Nuurow, the Shining One! Come to my arms!' But, as I say, it's a fantasy. My father is who knows where. My mother is likely still in Italy. And Jamila? I have heard nothing.

I walk cautiously towards the front door, which is closed (so often it was wide open in the old days!) and push against it. It is locked. I raise my hand and knock on the door. Not a sound. I knock again, and this time a voice calls from inside: 'Get out of here! What do you want? Get out!'

I call out: 'This is Abdi! This is the home of my father!'

Silence. Then the sound of voices whispering. The door opens and a man of about thirty years stands there, a man I have never seen before.

He is smiling, welcoming. 'Please to come in, Allah's blessing, come in.'

A few paces behind this man a small crowd is gathered, men and women and even children, all of them staring at me, most of them smiling.

I step into my family's house, partly baffled and partly resentful. How many people can I see? Maybe fifteen. More are standing in the room beyond.

The man who opened the door ushers me forward with a certain amount of ceremony. 'You are wondering who we are,' he says. 'So long since I have seen you! I am Liban, your father's cousin's cousin. And my family. All here are your relatives from the other side of the city. All.'

Now, I have explained that Somalis keep a detailed map in their heads of their relatives, both near and distant. But on my map, nothing is recorded about a man by the name of Liban who is supposed to be my father's cousin's cousin. It's not impossible that he comes from some obscure branch of the family that my father has never got around to talking about, but I have my doubts. Also, Liban and all of the others occupying my family's house are just a little bit too friendly. In Somalia, the friendliness of those near and dear to you is different from the friendliness a stranger might display. Family members greet you warmly and embrace you, but they do not go overboard with the smiles and the enquiries after your circumstances and so on. And none of these people appear to be certain of my father's name. One thing I do know is this: if I were to accuse them all of being crooks who had invaded my family's house, I would be asking for trouble. If it were true, and all of these people are indeed strangers, they might kill me or, if not kill me, hurl me out into the street. The best thing to do is to take them at their word, smile back, bide my time.

So I set aside my suspicions and play along and, before long, any tensions fade away. All in all, it appears that about thirty of these 'relatives' have settled into the house. It takes a few hours before all of them have learnt my name, but not one of them knows that I am usually called 'Nuurow'. When I ask about Jamila, Liban is vague. 'Jamila? Ah, Jamila. No we have heard nothing about Jamila. Alas.'

I ask Liban: 'Any sign of my mother?'

'Your honoured mother? Hmm. Let me see. No, I haven't come across her. Alas.'

One of the women prepares food for me in the kitchen – okra soup, and a little *surbiyaan hilib adhi*, lamb and rice, not so much lamb. Some of the fifteen or so kids in the place sit around watching me eat.

One of the boys says: 'Have you been to Baidoa, Abdi?'

'I saw Baidoa,' I say, 'but I didn't go in.'

'My father is in Baidoa.'

'Your father? I thought Liban was your father?'

'Yes, he is. I mean my uncle.'

I can't help but notice that many things in the house – things that were there when I ran away – are no longer here. Kitchen utensils, items of furniture, bedding, ornaments, most of my and Jamila's clothing have been stolen or sold.

I am waiting patiently for a chance to check what I came back to the house for, but with thirty people around, it is difficult to do anything unobserved. I find an opportunity in the evening and slip into a bedroom where I hope to find a small chest of drawers. I don't know why I need to go about this task so secretly, except that I am on edge with so many strangers nearby.

The chest of drawers is where it is meant to be. On a day before she left for Italy, my mother showed me this place and told me what she was concealing under a cloth covering the bottom of one drawer – a US one-hundred-dollar note that I found in the street three years earlier, my passport, and a big, fat pile of Somali shilling notes.

When I say that I found a one-hundred-dollar note in the street, I know it sounds most unlikely, but that's exactly how I came by that note, lying on the footpath in the main street of Medina, unnoticed by anyone until I came along. In Somalia, the moon shines so brightly that it is possible to read by its light, and the moon was shining especially brightly on that evening when I looked down and saw it, a US dollar note with the number 100 printed on it on the left side and again on the right, also a picture of a man in old-fashioned clothes whose hair was long except at the front, where his head was bald, and the words 'Federal Reserve Note' above the man in the strange clothes, and the words 'The United States of America' at the bottom, and a long number. I could read the English writing, but didn't know what it meant, except that it seemed important. It was a greenish colour, like all the other American money I had ever seen. It was as if it was meant for me, and that's exactly the thought I had in my head when I picked it up: it was meant for me.

When I showed my mother, she drew in her breath and made a clicking sound with her tongue as she always did when something surprised her. 'We will keep it until we are in need,' she said.

As far as I was concerned, I was in need as soon as I picked up the note. I was in need of a pair of Adidas football boots and many other things but, in Somalia, children always defer to the wisdom of their parents, even when their parents have no wisdom. I thought I should show my mother how responsible I was, so instead of talking about football boots I said I would use the money to start a business one day.

And yeah, Mum was impressed. She said: 'What sort of business?'

I had my answer ready. 'I will buy a donkey and a cart and carry things for payment.'

My mother looked at me in horror, or disgust, probably both. She said: 'What are you? A peasant? A donkey cart? Dear God! Listen to me, fool. I am an educated woman. Do you think I want my son to ride about in a donkey cart like a nobody? Think!'

I felt humiliated, even though it was my sincere desire to own a donkey cart, and I averted my eyes and apologised.

There is a special tone that a Somali parent, a father or a mother, will put into his or her voice when it is important to show that great wisdom is being dispensed. Your mother or father will speak more deeply than normal, use few words and never bother with explanation. 'We will keep it until we are in need,' my mother said again. 'Don't talk to me of donkey carts.'

And, indeed, my mother was right. It was best that we kept the one-hundred-dollar note for a time when we were in need. I lift the cloth and find the one-hundred-dollar note, my passport and the great heap of Somali shilling notes. I must tell the reader that a miracle is being described on this page. Anything that could be sold has disappeared from the house and yet here, under a cloth (not the most careful disguise), lies more cash than everything in the household is worth. None of the nimble thieves in the house had noticed a bulge under the cloth? Really? I am embarrassed for them in their stupidity. But I grieve too. Because I know now that my mother hasn't been back here since I left. Dad probably hasn't either – he would have guessed Mum's hiding place and taken the money. I am alone.

I tuck the shilling notes and the big American note and my passport between my skin and the belt of my trousers, and it stays there when I settle down to sleep for the night.

This is my bedroom, this room I am sharing with six other boys tonight. I once slept here by myself. And here, in this room, so very many dreams, so very many mornings waking with a type of joy in my heart, school awaiting me, then the beach, football, the sunset, dinner. I will not wake in the morning with my heart full of joy. At the same time, I do not wish to weep – nothing like that. I should not be lying in bed in this house that has been stormed by a gang of relatives who may or may not be real relatives. I should be dead, three or four times over, or crawling around in a village outside Buurhakaba covered in hot tar, wishing I was dead.

Why some people survive the shocking things that bad people prepare for them I cannot say. Is it all chance? The bullets that were fired at me and my friends when I lay on the ground two months ago – why did they not strike me dead as they struck dead my eight friends, four on each side of me? A guardian angel? What have I done to deserve a shield from heaven? Questions like this can never be answered. But I can say this: if ever I reach a place of safety in a land outside Somalia, I will live my life both for myself and for those I knew who were not so lucky. The family I make, the children I father, they will be for me and for those who died. This is the only way I can make sense of my good fortune, the only way I can repay God.

★

I'm heading for the airport on foot. This will be my bid to escape Somalia, to find a new home. I don't know what I'm doing but, at the same time, I do. What I mean is that my big plan is to find a new country. My short-term plan is to get on an aeroplane. Everything in between I don't know anything about. I will have to learn everything as I go along.

But it is a hard, hard thing for my heart to accept that I have not been able to find Dad, Mum, Jamila. *Nuurow*, I tell myself, *if you are dead, you will never find them. If you are alive, then maybe, maybe, maybe, some day in the future, not even in Somalia, you will see their faces again.*

On the way to the airport, I experience something that confirms my desire to get the hell out of Somalia. As I'm walking through the outer suburbs, gunfire sounds from somewhere close. I crouch and look around. Everyone I can see is either wailing at the tops of their voices or running or lying flat on the ground. A voice nearby calls: 'Hey kid – get down!'

I see twenty metres away the man who has called out.

'Get down, kid! Crawl!'

I flatten myself on the ground, squeeze my eyes shut. I'm thinking: *Please, God, no. I've been through this already. Not a second time.*

The gunfire has stopped. Still flat on the ground, I open my eyes and try to work out whether it's safe to stand up and run. Fifty metres away down a rubbish-strewn, unpaved street I spot a number of people lying much stiller than I am. I can glimpse bright blood. I remain exactly where I am and a few minutes later an ambulance comes roaring into the street, its siren blaring. I stand and glance over to where the guy who told me to get down was a few minutes ago. He's gone. I crouch over and hurry from the scene, and don't stand upright until I'm at least two kilometres away. A type of anger has flared in me. How can it be acceptable for men with guns to ride around in Toyotas and stop every now and again to shoot people dead? For what reason? To make people terrified? People are already terrified! And I think: *Let me out of here. This is madness. Let me out.*

The airport of Mogadishu was once such a fancy place, with classy shops staffed by young women who would look at you as if you were too insignificant to even address a few words to unless you were rich, unless you were wearing a general's uniform, unless men in black sunglasses were standing each side of you – your bodyguards. There were also lots of other shops where you would be served no matter who you were. The airport was an advertisement for Somalia. It said: 'What a happy, prosperous country, Somalia! Yes, we are going places! Buy this, it's made by Prada!' Rich Arabs in their spotless white robes would sweep past you, Arabs from

Saudi Arabia, from Dubai, from Bahrain, from Quetta, a couple of wives following them in expensive black garments, their faces partly hidden. All this I saw when I went to the airport to meet my father when he returned from Paris for a visit. Now, the airport is shabby and many people live in shanty towns on its fringe, waiting to find a people smuggler who can get them to Europe or at least to some Middle Eastern country where they can work for next to nothing as labourers, which is an improvement on not working at all in Somalia.

Strangely enough, a shanty town builds up industries that service it. People sell bottled water to the people living under cardboard and sheets of plastic; they sell them cheap food, medicines, clothing and bedding; they take away their laundry and return it clean; they act as couriers and exploit them in every way possible.

Those in the shanty towns are frightened that if they go back into Somalia, they will be killed or, even worse than being killed, they will lose their place in the queue. Only a few of them are completely destitute – many have sold everything they own in the hope of finding a man in black sunglasses who will sell them a ticket on the right 'line'. For there are a number of lines that are being advertised. You can take the Cairo–Tripoli–Tangiers line fairly cheaply since, in Morocco, you will still be living in a shanty town, although you will not be killed unless you are truly unlucky. Or you could buy a ticket on the Cairo–Istanbul line and find yourself stuck in a camp in the east of Turkey, despised by the guards. Another line is Cairo–Bucharest, which might not sound all that promising since the Romanian dictator Ceausescu, said to have been worse than Saddam in Iraq, has recently been tried and executed, and the country is in a complete mess, although people are a little happier than they were before Ceausescu was executed.

I am writing this as if I knew much more at the time than I really did. I didn't know the name of the Romanian dictator, for instance. But when you wait at Mogadishu airport, you learn new things every day – a type of telegraph brings you news of this country and that, of this line and that, of what Cairo is like for Somalis, what Moscow is like. Waiting to meet the people smuggler, I fall into conversation with a stranger who is a little older than me. 'Moscow, no good,' he says. 'Forget Moscow. You know what? If you end up in Moscow, catch the train to Finland. It's much better in Finland. They're not allowed to shoot you. In Moscow, if they want to shoot you, they shoot you. That's what I've heard.'

It happens one morning that I am in a group of people of my Rahanweyn tribe, all hoping for a ticket on a good line, and everyone in the group – six people – are making their quick additions to the airport news, like this: 'Cairo, in places, okay, they don't hate Somalis.' And 'Romania! If you get to Romania, kill yourself.' And 'My cousin is in Helsinki. It's a nice city, Helsinki, the best.' And 'You know the best? I tell you where. Australia. The best.' Because I know about Australia, I say: 'More animals than people. Maybe there is the best place for me.'

I am wearing my *macawis*, one of the few garments of mine I could find in my house. A *macawis* is a sarong, very comfortable. Mine is blue and white. It is held up by folding the top of the garment over and over to form a type of belt, but I also wear a proper belt under it – and my shorts. Beneath the folds of the *macawis* and my proper belt, I keep my passport and money safe. I sometimes sleep in the shanty town with my belt drawn tight around my middle. Any sound wakes me. Later, gangs of crooks will steal from anyone in these shanty towns who has money – a new industry. But at this time theft is not such a problem. But still, my belt is tight, very tight, every time I sleep.

The shanty town is not my home. Sometimes I walk back to my house in Medina and sit around, a little resentful of these people who have taken control of the rooms that were once so familiar to me. Some of these squatters are very polite to me; some barely acknowledge my presence. All of them know that I go to the airport each day looking for a way out of my homeland. They think: *No need to worry – soon we won't see him at all.*

I wish with all my heart that I could get into contact with my dad, but the barrier across the middle of the city makes that impossible. And I don't want to think about my dad too much, because I'll feel that he will fix everything and take this burden from my shoulders, when I know that he can't. I know it's important to accept that it is only me who can keep me alive.

CHAPTER 10

The Romania Line

The process of getting a ticket and a visa for some European destination is complicated. You cannot walk up to a kiosk and say to the man behind the counter: 'Moscow line.' The men who control the line trade, the Mokalis, are like gods. They dress stylishly and carry themselves regally. It is the Mokalis who distribute line tickets to a lower level of operators, who accept the money and hand out the tickets. I see a Mokalis at the airport but from a distance, striding along in his white suit and black sunglasses with bodyguards slinking behind. It would be out of the question for me to approach him. He's probably only walking about here to display himself, to 'show off', as the English expression goes. I watch him in awe. Imagine having such power! Imagine, too, a country in which the most powerful people are those in the business of getting people *out* of the country.

On the third day of my quest for a good line, or any line, I run into a kid I knew at school. Mehti is a couple of years older than me. His parents are with him, searching high and low for a good visa to a good country on a good line. We strike up a conversation, Mehti and I, sharing our experiences in this seething airport-clearing station. Mehti's mum and dad are taking a very close interest in me, listening courteously as I chat with their son. Before long, I realise something: Mehti's mum and dad have big, big doubts about their son's ability to negotiate the whole business of making a home in some new country. They think he is hopeless. And they think it would help him a lot if he kept me close and listened to what I have to say. I realise something else, too: that I have changed so much over the past six months that people can see what I have learnt in my face. Being a kid has gone for good. I've escaped killers and torturers and drug-crazed soldiers, and all of that has taken away the soft look in my eyes that I was once famous for. Mehti is still a baby. Nobody has put a knife to his throat; nobody has made him carry bags of rice on his back through the burning heat of afternoon. I'm two years younger than Mehti, but so much older. And I suppose it would be true to say that I am more confident than he is. That's probably what people can see in my face – the confidence of a boy who has become resourceful. Not that being resourceful has made me happy – just the opposite. The more I learn how to cope by myself, the deeper the pain of not having my mother or my father close by. Let me confess something here. When I picture myself now in the airport, I see a kid who is nimble, wary, clever, determined. But I also see a kid who gave up something important in order to stay alive. Those nightmares I spoke about that come to me at random times – they are the ongoing price of my survival. Do you know what those nightmares truly are? They are a type of mourning for the leap I made from boyhood into adulthood, grief for the tenderness that I could not afford to keep. I toughened up too quickly.

It will do me no harm to hang around with Mehti. He has money. He knows a Somali woman who is going to university in Bucharest, a woman who will help him, he hopes, if he ends up in Romania. Indeed, I needn't worry about looking out for Mehti, keeping an eye out to make sure he is not talking to the wrong people – people who will fleece him – for he is there constantly like a shadow. Even when he goes to talk to his parents, they bring him back to me and say: 'Stay with Abdi. Do you see? Stay with Abdi.'

After a few days of enquiring and following up leads, I meet a Mokalis who says that he can get me a ticket on the Cairo–Romania line. He can also get me a visa for Egypt and for Romania.

This Mokalis is not one of the big shots – one of the lords. He's more humble, maybe a beginner. Mehti and another guy, Jabriil, are with me when I settle down to negotiate with the Mokalis. They are wary, unwilling to trade with him, but he seems to me an okay guy and my instinct is to trust him. We hunker down in a corner of the airport where not too many people are crowded and discuss the deal.

He says to me: 'Abdi? That's your name, Abdi?'

'Yes, Abdi.'

'Like I said, I can arrange a visa for Egypt, a visa for Romania and a ticket to Romania with a stopover in Cairo.'

I say: 'Why do I want a stopover in Cairo? I know nobody in Cairo.'

'Sure, but the flight is not direct to Bucharest. You know Bucharest? That's the big city of Romania. That's where you get out. But you have to wait three days in Cairo for the flight to Bucharest. Do you understand what I'm telling you? Three days in Cairo. Okay, you don't want to be sleeping on the floor in the transit lounge in Cairo. You can go out into the city, sleep maybe in a hotel, not expensive.'

'Romania is dangerous for me? Romania has bad guys? Some people tell me Romania has a lot of bad guys.'

The Mokalis lifts his shoulders and holds out his hands. 'Bad guys? Sure. They get a chance, they take your money, hit you on the head. Sure. But you don't let them. You use your brains.' He taps himself on his head with his finger. 'Some guy says, "Hey, Somali kid, I got a nice hotel for you, nice girl for you, plenty to eat, not far away." You know what you say to him?'

'No, what do I say?'

'You say, "Sorry, I'm in a hurry," and you go the other way fast, fast, fast. Bad guys in Bucharest, sure. But they don't shoot you. Here in Mogadishu, they shoot you. Which one is best?'

I tell the Mokalis that I will give him two thousand dollars in Somali shillings for a Cairo–Bucharest ticket and two visas. But he says that he must pay for the visas in US dollars. The people who sell the visas will only accept US dollars; not UK pounds, only US dollars. If I had to buy one hundred US dollars, it would cost me maybe one-third of my Somali shillings. But I have my one-hundred-dollar note. Can you see what I mean about destiny? In the street two years earlier, there it lay, one hundred dollars. It's today that I need it. Best not to think about destiny until it has revealed itself. This is something I've learnt in life, even by the age of fifteen. If you say: 'Ho! It is my destiny to find the key to a palace and sleep on a golden bed!' you will never find that key. But if you let destiny please itself, there is some hope.

★

The flight to Cairo takes only three hours. I am in a daze of misery and fear the whole time. Part of the fear is to do with the fact that it is impossible for this aeroplane to stay up in the sky. In the back of a truck with twenty other people, you can see the road that the wheels are travelling along. In the sky, nothing.

When we land at Cairo, it is difficult to grasp that I have covered more distance in these few hours than in all the months of my desperate journey around Somalia. I step into Cairo airport still baffled by what's happening in my life. My visa allows me to leave the airport and wander around Cairo. It's a huge mess of a city, sort of interesting but a little bit frightening at the same time. I stay at a cheap hotel for two nights, a complete slum, then return to the airport on the third day to resume my journey.

On the flight to Bucharest, I am the youngest person not in the care of a mum, a dad or some adult to act as guardian. It has become my habit to avoid looking suspicious in any situation, and on the flight I try to give the impression that I am with a family seated in the two rows across from me. I lean towards the mother and smile whenever a hostess is watching, or I whisper something across the aisle, such as 'Is this a long flight?' or 'Are we flying over the ocean now?'

The family thinks of me as mentally retarded, and they answer me kindly, and this helps with my act. In all honesty, the hostesses probably couldn't care less whether I'm too young to be travelling without an adult, but such disguises have become ingrained in me. You learn new habits very, very quickly when you risk having your throat cut if someone doesn't like the look of you.

So I am heading to Bucharest. In my previous career as a normal human being, I studied the atlas closely without ever bothering much with Romania. It had a shape like a soccer ball that had lost half of the air inside it – a lumpy circle. It was stuck over there in the south-east of Europe with a couple of other countries I couldn't be bothered with – Bulgaria and Yugoslavia. My interest in countries diminished as my eye moved east across Europe. France, where my father lived, was my favourite, with its magnificent capital city of Paris and its famous Eiffel Tower and its boulevards and shining Seine River. And even before my mother flew away to

Italy, I had revered Rome, where the Romans made themselves so legendary and staged games in the Colosseum – spears and bows and arrows and swords and wild animals and interesting sports that saw Christians chased by bears and lions. I felt a little bit sorry for the Christians, but not so sorry that I wished the Romans would play some other sort of sport. I knew that the days of bears chasing Christians went back to a time before the Prophet Mohammed had written the law of Islam in which He told us to respect the followers of Jesus, so it seemed to me okay for the bears to feed themselves in that way. Also Italy had the best pasta in the world, and I was a boy who adored good pasta. And pizza, too, which I considered the prince of dishes.

But when my journey of study took me as far east as Russia, I became confused. Back then, in 1986, 1987, 1988 and 1989, the huge area that included Russia was called the USSR in my atlas. (It was an English-language atlas.) My very blurry understanding of this term, the USSR, was that it meant the Russian Empire, which in a way was right. But I also knew that things had changed in the world in 1989, and that the big wall that the Russians had built around their empire had collapsed.

Mehti and his friend, Jabriil, are also on the aeroplane. Mehti makes a nervous traveller. He expects trouble even though he has paid for his ticket with honest money and has a visa for Romania. When I look down the long aisle, I see him glancing back towards me. He should have no fear that I will desert him. I have no wish to see him floundering about in Bucharest.

The hostess brings us food every few hours; either a snack, or a hot meal. It is not of the quality that my father would prepare, but would I complain after spending months in the wilderness so hungry that the leaves on the thorn bushes began to look inviting? When the food is served, I don't even bother with such important religious matters as halal and haram. I have known people on the verge of giving up their life to starvation who still concerned themselves with such matters as halal and haram. It goes very, very deep in many Muslims. When I was younger I heard all the halal and haram laws from the lips of mullahs, and they are very complicated, I promise you. Few Muslims know them all. For example, it is a fact that the flesh of any animal that has died of electrocution is haram – we Muslims are to avoid such flesh. This is a modern law, since the only form of electrocution known of in the time of the Prophet was death caused by a lightning strike. And indeed, Muslims were forbidden to eat the flesh of any animal killed by a lightning bolt. The mullahs of our day have reasoned that the electric shock used to kill animals in abattoirs is a form of death by lightning. Also, it is forbidden to eat the flesh of any animal that was beaten to death. With that law I can easily agree. Muslim, Christian, Jew – all should avoid such flesh. But there are numerous other categories of flesh that are haram – forbidden – and no Muslim I know could recite every law. My family made use of flesh that was said to be halal – that is, killed in a ritual way after the blessing of Allah has been sought – and left it at that. Yet I know for a fact that I have sometimes eaten flesh that I could not swear was halal. Should I fear for my soul? I am such a practical person, when it all comes down to it. The God I imagine most easily is a practical God. He would say: 'Halal, haram, whatever. Don't let yourself die of hunger, please.'

★

Most of the time on a big aeroplane you are not aware of speed. The machine is flying very fast, for me faster than I have ever travelled in my life, but how would you know it? You can't look out the window at trees and bushes and people being rapidly left behind. But a big screen halfway down the aisle shows all of us – the passengers – how far we have gone, how far we have to go, how high we are (higher than Mount Everest, which I happen to know is 8848 metres) and how fast we are travelling in kilometres. I read the figure of our speed: 820 kilometres per hour, and I compare it with the figure on the speedometer in a car that once picked me up from the roadside in my wilderness time: 130 kilometres per hour. That was the fastest I had ever travelled before I boarded this aeroplane: 130 kilometres per hour. At that time, I though the car would fall to pieces – it was not new and it shuddered and shook. I didn't mind the speed. It was thrilling. It felt as if we were going somewhere astonishing. How could a car go this fast and end up in some desolate place in the middle of nothing? It was heading for a palace, for some place where all of my troubles would turn into mist and float away. Well, the truth is that the car stopped in a desolate place in the middle of nowhere and I climbed out and continued on my way at a slow walking pace. My troubles bore down on my shoulders so heavily that I wept with disappointment. But this aeroplane is travelling at six times the speed of that car, and the little dots on the screen show that we have left Cairo far behind. We are flying over the legendary Mediterranean Sea, and ahead of us, not so far, lies the bright red dot of our destination, Bucharest.

Two forces are at work in me as I gaze at the screen: fierce exhilaration and stark terror. They swap places every minute or so. I think: 'Oh, Abdi, God bless you for escaping from the jaws of hell!' And I think: 'I want to get off! I can't do this!' When I am trembling with dread, I lean forward in my seat and stare at the screen with my eyes wide open. When I am congratulating myself on my escape, I lean back in my seat and smile so hard it hurts my face. The man next to me is frowning; he thinks I am insane.

It is hours into the flight before I simply slump back, ready to face whatever the outcome of this journey might be. I pray softly, I look through the magazine in the pocket of the seat in front of me. What I come to accept is that I have not truly escaped. I have traded one situation that was likely to end in my death for another that is also likely to kill me.

I think to myself: *Stay alive. Use your wits. In two years, in five years, sit in a big chair in some comfortable place and laugh about your fear, Abdi. Laugh about it. You are the Shining One.*

CHAPTER 11

Bucharest

We're waiting to pass through Immigration, Jabriil, Mehti and I. Jabriil and Mehti have been told to slip a US ten-dollar note into their passports before handing them over to the Romanian immigration officer. It was suggested to me, too, but I don't have any dollars; I have nothing at all.

Mehti has a fair bit of money, and could maybe pay my ten-dollar mini-bribe, but the fact is he's lost interest in me. At Mogadishu, he accepted the advice of his parents to keep me close by, but that was when I was pretending that my parents were there at the airport and would join me. My parents didn't appear, of course they didn't, and I think Mehti now regards me as a deadbeat. Jabriil is still friendly enough, but he seems more and more willing to be led by Mehti. I'm in trouble. I hold my chin high and try to give the impression of supreme confidence, but my heart is pounding away so rapidly I'm amazed people can't see that I'm struggling badly. I'm trying to think no more than one step ahead. And the one step ahead I'm concentrating on now is getting myself in between Jabriil and Mehti in the queue, hoping that the immigration officer will consider that two ten-dollar bills out of three is a good return.

The officer, who looks bored half to death, takes our three passports in one batch. He opens each at the photo page, finds the two ten-dollar bills, glances at me and seems to be considering my case. Then he leaves his desk and goes off to consult with a guy I assume is a more senior officer.

Here's what I'm counting on: that the officer can't actually come out and ask for a bribe. If someone like me has failed to include the ten-dollar bill, it might be difficult for him to say: 'The two of you who gave me a bribe, okay, you can enter Romania, but the kid who didn't include a bribe, you have to go back home to Somalia. That's the rule.'

My gamble pays off. The officer returns from his consultation with his boss, stamps the three passports and waves us through.

★

The Bucharest airport is something like the airport at Mogadishu, but sadder. The walls have not been painted for a long, long time and all the airport stuff that could be found in Mogadishu airport in its happy days is just junk here. Junk trollies, junk kiosks, junk vending machines. And the Romanians look like they all have the flu – their faces are grey, their eyes sleepy. Under a glass-topped box there's a model of what the airport will look like after some planned big improvements are made. But the model itself is beginning to fall apart.

I have a bad feeling about the whole place – not just the airport but all of Romania. Many of the men with grey faces look to me like bad guys, even the cops and the army people. Later in my life – much later – I will read about the theory of association. It's like this. You take a man and show him a picture of an apple. At the same time you give him an electric shock. He says: 'Yow!' You show him the picture of the apple again. You give him an electric shock: 'Yow!' And the man begins to associate a picture of an apple with an electric shock. You show him pictures of ten different fruits, no electric shocks. But as soon as the eleventh picture appears, the picture of the apple: 'Yow!' For maybe many years to come, whenever the man sees not just a picture of an apple but a real apple, he begins to sweat, and his heart goes bang bang bang. He wants to run away from the apple as far as he can go. And it is said that people with their amazing brains can make associations even with very, very small things that they remember. And so it is with me. When I was in the hands of the men who wanted to murder me and torture me in Somalia, I must have noticed a hundred little things (also a few big things) that tell me when a person is capable of murder and torture. In the faces of some of these cops in the Bucharest airport and in the faces of some of the army guys I can see many of the things that tell me to beware – in their eyes, in their mouths, even in the way they tilt their heads, in an expression that settles on their faces for just two or three seconds. Sweat runs down my chest under my shirt. My heart goes bang bang bang.

Romania, I think to myself, is not going to be a good experience for a Somali boy like me. I'm impatient to be happy again, to feel my heart swelling in my chest. I won't be happy until I see Dad and Mum and Jamila once more. I've spent all these past months without a family and it's been too much for me. My boyhood is not yet over. I hope and pray that Mum and Dad are praying for me, making plans for us to reunite. Of course, they don't even know where I am. In Bucharest? How could they possibly guess that I'm in Bucharest? Let their prayers begin: 'Beloved son, wherever you are, may the sun shine on you ...'

★

We're in the arrivals hall. It's pretty grim and also very cold. All the cops and army guys are wearing enormous thick coats and fur hats. I stick close to Jabriil and Mehti, spooked out of my brain as I am. Okay, it's good to have escaped Somalia, but Romania? What on earth? Mehti plans to find a taxi and meet up with a Somali woman who is studying at Bucharest University, someone from his tribe who will let him and Jabriil stay for a few weeks. As Mehti and Jabriil stroll towards the taxi rank, I tag along. Mehti stops and says, rudely: 'Where do you think you're going? With us? Forget it.'

'I can't come?' I say.

'No, you can't come.'

'I have nowhere to go.'

'Is that my problem? Beat it.'

But I follow them – I won't take no for an answer. Mehti stops and makes a motion with his hand as if he were chasing away a fly. 'Didn't you hear me? I said beat it!'

'Let me come into the city with you. Then I'll find my own way.'

'Bullshit! Get out of here!'

Now we've attracted the attention of a cop in an especially bulky coat and a great fur hat. He raises his head and stares at us.

Jabriil says: 'Let him come. The cop's watching us.'

Mehti shrugs, not pleased, and we leave the arrivals hall.

Outside, snowflakes are falling steadily, drifting down in slow motion like the snow storms in the glass domes I have seen in the bazaar in Mogadishu, those little paperweights you might buy as a novelty. I have never before seen actual snow. It covers everything: the parked cars; the eaves of the buildings; the ground itself. In the dim winter light it has a magical appearance, and even in my frightened and trembling state I can't help but smile.

I say to Mehti: 'Snow! Look at it!'

'So what? Shut up,' Mehti says.

I am permitted to join Mehti and Jabriil in the battered, box-like taxi outside the airport. Although I've got no right to suggest anything, I do. And what I suggest is that we go to the Somali embassy. The whole idea of coming to Romania is to get out of it as soon as possible and find a home in some more prosperous European country, like Germany or France or England. I know from the gossip back at Mogadishu airport that the Somali embassy here in Bucharest sometimes helps Somali citizens get into Western Europe in various sneaky ways. Well, that was gossip, as I say. It might just be fantasy stuff.

The taxi driver catches the words 'Somali embassy', which are the same in Somali as in English. He speaks a little bit of English. He waves his hands and says: 'Somali embassy, no.' Then he says: 'Somali embassy shut.' And then: 'Holiday.'

Mehti, who probably had no interest in going to the embassy, anyway, says: 'University.' The driver nods his head and the wreck of a taxi grinds through its gears as we bump and lurch out of the airport.

★

The university seems to be in the middle of the city of Bucharest, or that's what I'm guessing, since we first pass through parts of the city that seem to be suburbs made up mostly of houses. I have to tell you, Bucharest is no Paris, of which I've seen so many pictures. It's all gray and white, and the white part is snow. Big tower blocks of concrete, people on the footpaths leaning forward against the cold wind.

It's now about midday, but the sun casts little light. I gaze out the window in a trance of unhappiness. All I'm wearing is a shirt and singlet and thin cotton trousers so, on top of my misery, I'm half frozen.

Next to me, Jabriil and Mehti are chattering away cheerfully. They can see a future ahead of them, maybe a few weeks in this grim city, then an escape to Germany, jobs, a reunion with their families in a year or so. I keep to my plan of thinking no more than one step ahead, or I'm trying to, but I can't properly imagine even that next step. *Stay alive, Abdi* – that's what I repeat to myself silently: *Stay alive, boy.* I'm like a cheer squad for myself. *Listen to me. The soldiers in Somalia wanted to kill you, but they failed. More than once, they tried to kill you. The bullets didn't hit your body, okay? That means something. Here you are in Romania, still alive, how is that possible? God knows! But you are.*

Now we are in an older part of the city. Some of the buildings are grander but sad, still. Here's the university, the buildings like the pictures I have seen of the Sorbonne in Paris or the famous Harvard University in America. Some of the buildings have tall pillars rising above stone steps. A few of the buildings of Mogadishu are like this – those built by the Italians in the old days. But why does the whole place, old and new buildings alike, look so sad to me? It's not just because of the fear and trembling in my chest, and not because of the weak sunlight and the cold winds. This is a city that has forgotten how to smile. And I recognise in the sadness of the city something that is happening in my own country of Somalia, where people have also stopped smiling, stopped laughing.

The taxi stops. Mehti pays the fare. Jabriil has a piece of paper on which the address we are looking for is written. He shows the paper to one person and another until a man points in the direction we must take. Each person Jabriil stops looks at me shivering in my thin shirt and frowns.

Before we head into the thicket of buildings that make up the university, Mehti says to me: 'Where do you think you're going?'

'With you,' I tell him.

'No way,' he says, and he picks up his suitcase from the footpath. 'You go your own way, kid.'

But I follow Mehti and Jabriil, and ignore Mehti when he hisses over his shoulder: 'Go to hell!'

I can't think of any alternative to following Mehti and Jabriil. I swallow my pride and keep at it, my feet inside my sneakers like blocks of ice as I crunch through the snow. Soon my two fellow countrymen decide to ignore me, as if I am a stranger to them.

After more inquiries of people I assume to be students, we arrive at a building that looks like a hotel but is actually (as I find out a little later) one of the university's accommodation blocks. Mehti consults his piece of paper as we stroll down a long corridor with numbered doors on each side. He finds the number he's looking for and knocks. The door is opened by a tall young woman, maybe in her early twenties, very attractive, immediately recognisable as Somali.

'Mehti, all the way from Mogadishu,' says Mehti. 'Aiee, aiee, what a journey! You are Fartuun?'

The young woman, glancing at me as I stand shivering at the rear, says: 'Fartuun is away for a few days. I am Aasiya. She told me you were coming.'

She stands aside and lets Mehti and Jabriil enter the apartment, with their suitcases. I try to follow but she blocks the way.

'Who's the kid?' she asks Mehti.

'He followed us. We don't know him.'

Aasiya says to me: 'What tribe are you?'

'Rahanweyn,' I tell her, knowing that she is not going to like what she hears. She is not Rahanweyn. Mehti is not Rahanweyn. Nor Jabriil.

'He's not coming in,' Aasiya tells Mehti.

Mehti says: 'Okay by me. I don't know him.'

'Please, let me stay just for a short time,' I plead. 'Only for a short time. Until I meet some other Somalis.'

'I don't want Rahanweyn in my place. You go away now.' And she closes the door.

I stand there in the corridor with my bag at my feet – a fabric bag with a shoulder strap, containing all my possessions in the world: a second pair of trousers, a shirt, some biscuits and a piece of cake from the aeroplane, wrapped in cellophane. I am so sick of this whole tribal culture of my country: you are this tribe so I hate you; you are that tribe so I welcome you. I want to shout out: 'Do you know what tribe I am? I am the tribe of fifteen-year-old boys who long for some warmth. I am of the tribe of people from a country gone mad with the hunger for blood. Is it too much to ask that you see me first as a human being?'

I pick up my bag and walk on down the corridor. Along the way I pass young men and women from Africa, students who must have come to this university in Bucharest on scholarships. They are not from Somalia. I cannot even guess what countries they come from. I also pass students speaking Arabic, not the same Arabic that Somalis speak. They may be from the Middle East. I catch the aroma of food being cooked in the apartments – familiar aromas. I feel as if I could burst in on these people cooking rice and lamb and throw myself on the floor and say: 'I will not leave until you feed me. Show mercy, in the name of God!' But of course I do no such thing.

I wander down to a small park we passed on the way, where tall trees, bigger than any I have seen before, stand with their bare branches reaching up to the winter sky. I clean the snow off a park bench and sit down, my arms wrapped around my shoulders to prevent myself shivering to pieces. I gaze up at the beautiful patterns of bare branches and twigs against the sky. From the position of the sun – a faint, yellow blur behind the clouds – I estimate that it must be mid-afternoon. My purpose in sitting here is vague. I hope to see Somali people from my own Rahanweyn tribe – I will know them if I see them. Since the young woman who has just refused me shelter is from Somalia, surely there are more Somalis about. It's a faint hope, isn't it? But if I were to see a Rahanweyn, at least I know this: he would not deny me help. So many times in the past year I have grown sick to death of the tribal allegiances of my native country, where a person from one tribe pretty much denies the humanity of a person from another but, at this moment, a fellow Rahanweyn would be a gift from God.

So I wait, my whole body quivering with cold. I am probably the only person in Bucharest this day who is not wearing a big coat and a fur hat. People – Romanians, and students from Africa – glance at me as they pass, sometimes with pity, sometimes with curiosity, sometimes without any reaction at all. At last I can sit on the bench no longer without dying of cold – such a way to perish for a boy from Somalia! In the snows of a land in Eastern Europe! – and I get to my feet and head out into the city. I can no longer feel my feet. I tramp along the footpaths, past shops, most of them dingy, the lettering on the windows a complete mystery to me. Outside some shops are long queues of people stamping their feet to chase away the cold, their breath rising from their mouths like steam from a boiling kettle. It is bread they are queuing for, and milk, too, by the look of it. Shortages in this freezing land, just like in Somalia, a land of burning heat.

The snow is now coming down in swirls and the light is fading. It will soon be dark. I shuffle back towards the university, still hoping to meet a Somali of my tribe. I scan the faces coming towards me on the footpaths, looking for someone with my skin colour and the tall, erect posture of my people and a kind gleam in his eye. I see a number of people from lands outside Romania, people with *keffiyehs* on their heads rather than a big furry hat, but no Somalis. There are quite a number of drunks in Bucharest, I notice, leaning against walls with a bottle sticking out of a coat pocket, or wobbling along the footpath, sometimes singing or mumbling. Do they drink to keep warm? I have never had a sip of alcohol in my life, but I know people who have and they say it warms them up – an odd condition to seek in a country where the sun can cook bare flesh on a living body. In the dying light of the day, I wander into the lobby of a cinema, hoping for a little bit of warmth to thaw my feet. The people in the lobby gaze at me as if I am part of the entertainment and, indeed, the woeful expression on my face probably looks like something you'd expect to see on the stage. Some people even smile. I want to burst into tears and cry out: 'What do you want me to do? Juggle balls in the air? Tell jokes?' I drink some water at a fountain in the foyer, close my eyes and make my short, fervent prayer to Dad and Mum, but this time I add something more urgent: 'Do you want to see me alive again? Surely you do! Send me a Rahanweyn, that is my prayer!' Finally I leave the warmth of the lobby and trudge back to the university.

Earlier at the university I'd noticed a room with an open door, and inside a row of washing machines – a laundry. When I return to the university, I find the room again, and the door is still open.

Nobody is inside at this time – it's about seven in the evening – so I creep in, climb up on a bench, put my folded hands under my head as a pillow and try to sleep. If I'm found, I might be thrown onto the street, but I don't care so long as I'm out of the cold.

Without making any decision to do so, I have somehow adopted a fairly reckless attitude to survival. I'm not the goody-goody I was in Mogadishu when I was growing up. Back then, the first thing I used to think about was good manners. Now, I'm ready to take advantage of any opportunity that comes my way. Perfect manners – that was a luxury, and I can't afford perfect manners anymore. If someone had left a plate of hot food behind in the laundry – not very likely, I know – I would probably eat it without a second thought. Hunger, cold and loneliness change you.

When I think back to that time in Bucharest, I realise that I was learning how to be a refugee. You are not a refugee simply because you have no home and no country. No, you become a refugee little by little. It's not that things become more hopeless with each passing day, it is that you adapt to the hardship and, in a way – this will sound mad – you become an expert in hardship. You learn to sniff out relief, a free meal, a place of shelter that is available only for a day, and from kilometres away you seem almost to pick up the scent of kind people, perhaps of your faith, perhaps not, who are prepared to provide you with a coat and a big furry hat. You accept the status of a beggar. You search out other beggars from your homeland, and comfort each other, listen to stories of escape. 'Did you ever meet Mahdi (or Farxaan, Fowli, Habane, Guhaad)? He made it to Vienna. It cost him five hundred Romanian leu. He went in a truck with a compartment underneath.' And stories of people who went even further, to Anchorage, Alaska, in the United States, after travelling across Russia to Vladivostok – amazing!

And of people who one day gave up and jumped off a bridge into the Danube. You become ready to do things so dangerous that you wonder if you have gone mad and don't yet understand that you're mad. Some Somalis hide underneath trains and hang on for ten hours as the train rushes along at great speed towards Germany, and if they happen to fall asleep or lose their strength they are found the next day on the railway lines, so much as is left of them.

I am sorry to say that you learn to tell lies, too, when it is unavoidable, just as I did in Somalia, where my education as a refugee began. Back there, people might ask me if I was Rahanweyn, intending to kill me if I said yes. So I would say that I was not Rahanweyn, except for that one time, when my pride refused to let me lie and I was taken prisoner. Do you see the lesson? Your pride can kill you. In your education as a refugee, telling the truth on every occasion is not only unwise, it is suicide. In the part of my story still to come, you, the reader, will see me tell lies to survive, but I ask you to believe that such lies do not make an untrustworthy person of me. In the life of comfort and happiness that awaits me (eventually!) I make sure that the period in my life when I was, can I say, 'inventive', does not influence me any longer, and I hold the truth to be sacred, as my wife and children know.

If I catch one of my sons fibbing, he might say: 'But Dad, you told plenty of fibs when you were a refugee.'

And I say: 'Okay, if a time comes when you have no food and no shelter and you are weeping with hunger, I give you permission to tell fibs if they will save your life. But now, when you have everything you need and more, absolutely not.'

A refugee comes to know every little niche in which he can hide, all over a big city like Bucharest. He knows when to smile and when not to smile. If a policeman is anywhere within a kilometre of him, he knows. If he has to drop everything and run, he takes about a half second to reach top speed. The number one rule is this: stay alive. Things might get better one day. Stay alive.

It's not as cold in the laundry as it is outside in the snow, but it's still pretty cold, I promise you. I struggle to stay asleep. I hear footsteps on the walkway, and prepare to jump down from my bench and act as if I am waiting for the washing machine to finish its cycle. If security people find me, I will say: 'I lost the key to my apartment. I will get a new one tomorrow.' Or I will say: 'A visa? Sure I have a visa.' Or 'I'm lost. Can you tell me the way to the Somali embassy?' How I will say this when I don't speak a single word of Romanian, I don't know. I will have to rely on the inspiration of the moment.

But nobody comes into the laundry all night. It is not until the early morning (or so I judge it to be) when a man steps into the laundry and looks at me in a puzzled way. He's maybe twenty-five, something like that. He's not Romanian, so far as I can tell. He looks more like someone from Yemen or Palestine – I have seen Yeminis and Palestinians in Mogadishu. And, sure enough, he asks me in Arabic what I'm doing here. My native language is Somali, really a dialect of Somali called Maay, and I also speak Northern Somali and the Benaadir dialect. I can understand Arabic if it is spoken very clearly. And this man who has come into the laundry is speaking slowly and deliberately.

'What are you doing, kid?'

'Nothing.'

'You don't have a coat? You die here without a coat.'

'Pardon?' I say, though I understood quite well.

'My name is Yusuf,' says the man. 'You understand. Yusuf.' And he pats his chest.

'Yusuf?'

'Yusuf. Okay? You understand?'

I don't feel in any danger. He has a kind face – exactly the sort of face I was looking for. If he was Rahanweyn, even better, but a kind face is welcome, whatever the nationality or tribe.

'Abdi,' I say, also patting my chest.

'Abdi? Good. What country, kid? Somalia?'

'Sure, Somalia.'

'In Romania how long?'

I say: 'Two years.' Then I change my mind, and decide to honour this man's goodwill. 'One day.'

Yusuf smiles. 'One day. That I believe. You have nowhere to stay?'

'Nowhere.'

'Abdi, come with me.'

Yusuf leads me into the accommodation block and up some stairs to his apartment. I'm so happy to be inside, and I'm also hoping and praying that I'll be permitted to stay for a few hours, long enough for the freezing cold in my bones to fade away. Yusuf gestures with his hand towards his blue sofa, and I sit. It is a simple place, just the sofa and an armchair, also blue, a television set, a CD player. His kitchen is part of this one big room. I can see a toaster on his kitchen bench, and also what looks like a jaffle iron.

From another room a second man appears and for a moment I stiffen. This second man looks at me, raises his hands and shakes his head, as if to say 'Who the hell's this?'

'Abdi, that's his name,' says Yusuf. 'Somalia.' Then he looks back at me. 'This is Abdullah. No problem. Abdullah is a good guy.'

Abdullah laughs and claps his hands. 'Somalia,' he says to me. 'A lot of shit in Somalia now. Bad guys. Pow pow! Right?'

'Very bad,' I say.

Yusuf says: 'From Jordan, me, Abdullah, Jordan. You know Jordan?'

I answer in my rubbish Arabic: 'I know Jordan, yes.'

Abdullah and Yusuf smile at my accent, not unkindly.

'So, not long in beautiful Bucharest, Abdi?' says Abdullah, who seems to be a cheerful guy. 'A bit colder than Somalia, is it?'

'Colder,' I say. 'Sure.'

Yusuf is going about the business of making breakfast, an omelette by the look of it. The sizzle of the mixture in the frying pan reaches right down to some potent pleasure-centre in my brain and saliva surges in my mouth. I say to myself: *Don't look at the frying pan, Nuurow. Show some manners. Don't assume that Yusuf is going to ask you if you want some breakfast.*

And Yusuf can see what I'm thinking. A big grin spreads over his face. 'Hey, Abdi. What do you think? Are you hungry enough to eat some breakfast?'

'Please!' I say. It is almost a shout.

I'm served omelette and bread on a plate, and a glass of orange juice. I try to eat as slowly as I can but it's impossible to deny my hunger. In the space of maybe three minutes I gobble my way through what is in fact quite a big plateful of omelette and two slices of bread. Abdullah and Yusuf watch me as they eat from their own plates.

'That's better?' says Abdullah.

'Thank you, thank you.'

The experience of a good feed when you have been desperately hungry puts you into a trance. And that's what the omelette does to me. I'm thinking: *Tomorrow? Who cares! My stomach is full.* This is also part of your education as a refugee: you take a short-term view of everything. Somewhere in the back of my brain, sure, I want security, I want a new country, I want a roof over my head. But mostly I'm thinking: *What good luck! I'm doing so well!* As a matter of fact, if someone should come along now and say: 'Abdi, my friend, I have a home for you in Germany, a house, a job – but only for a week, then you're out on the street again,' I would say: 'Suits me!' This will only last until I again become hungry and tired, of course. Then my spirits will tumble and I will think of Mum and Dad and Jamila and weep like a baby.

CHAPTER 12

Refugee

Yusuf tells me that I can stay until nine-thirty in the morning – a bit over two hours away. The two of them leave me watching their old black and white television. I'm happy to sit in the warmth and stare at the screen – it's Whitney Houston looking gorgeous, some sort of concert, lots of dancers and flashing lights – without worrying about what I will do when the two hours are up. I'm still in a trance. Every few minutes this thought comes to me: *Is this really happening? I'm in Romania, right? In Bucharest? And a few days ago I was in Somalia at the airport?* I find it difficult to keep hold of my own story. It's as if another person, also named Abdi, is playing a part in a drama that I, the real Abdi, am watching, thinking, *What will this other Abdi do next?* And then I think: *Abdi, Abdi! Listen to me! People go mad when they think in this way!*

Abdullah and Yusuf return at nine-thirty, just as they said they would, and I am compelled to leave the apartment. I wander around the campus of the university in an aimless way, trying to keep the accommodation block in sight in case Mehti and Jabriil appear. They won't be pleased to see me, but they are Somalis and, right now, the only relief I can imagine is to be with Somalis, even Somalis who are sick of the sight of me. And sure enough, I eventually catch sight of Mehti and Jabriil leaving the accommodation block with the young woman, Aasiya. They are now dressed in big, waterproof coats and fur hats of the sort that the Romanians wear. Where on earth did they get those? I hurry to catch up with them. When Mehti catches sight of me, he waves a hand at me, meaning, I suppose, 'Go away!' But I don't go away. I tag along behind them to the tram stop, and even hop aboard the tram with them. They pretend they don't know me, but I keep close and finally Jabriil buys me a ticket to show the conductor.

'Where are we going?' I ask, as if we are all one big, happy family heading off on an adventure.

Mehti says: 'Shut up.'

To the main post office of Bucharest, that's where we're going. Soon I'm shuffling about with a hundred or more other Somalis in the courtyard in front of the post office building, trying to work out what the deal is here. I wanted to find other Somalis and, okay, now I've found them. What next? By listening, I begin to piece together the story. People come here, so it seems, to enquire if any messages or letters are waiting for them at a place called 'poste restante' inside the post office. They're also here to see if money has been transmitted to them or to make telephone calls to Somali friends back home. All of these people are refugees, just like me, but I think every single one of them has more resources to draw on than I do. I stand beside a group of three Somalis, each of them a Rahanweyn, and try to look casual and innocent as I listen in on their conversation. It seems to be all about disappointments – money that hasn't turned up; friends in Germany who haven't yet made contact.

One of the group notices me and grins; he can tell that I'm Rahanweyn. 'Hey kid, how's it going?'

'Yeah, good,' I say.

'Where's your daddy?'

'My dad? He's in Mogadishu.'

'Yeah? Where's your mum?'

I don't know the answer to this question. In Italy? Or has she returned to Mogadishu?

'Mogadishu, maybe.'

'Maybe? You're here by yourself?'

'By myself,' I say. 'Sure.'

The guy gives a long, low whistle. His two friends have now taken an interest in me.

'Where you hanging out, kid? You got some people here, maybe?'

'No,' I say. 'No people.' It seems to me better to seem pathetic and lost. And as a matter of fact, I *am* pathetic and lost.

'Listen, kid, my name's Saahid. This guy's Kaahin, this's Wardi. Okay? We have to be somewhere else now but, tomorrow, you come here, we'll fix you up. Okay? Tomorrow.'

'Sure. Tomorrow.'

The three of them hurry away to wherever they're going. I feel elated. I say to myself: *You see, Nuurow? Don't give up. Good things happen.*

I now recognise my three new friends (I want to think of them as friends, even though I've known them for only five minutes) as part of the first wave of young men who fled Somalia in 1991. That first wave was made up of the sons of big shots in Somalia. Their families saw the way things were going when the country began falling to pieces, and they had the money and connections to get their sons well out of the place. When I was travelling around in Somalia months earlier, I'd hear stories of these fortunate guys who headed for Europe. We called them 'golden boys'. Will they keep their word and meet me tomorrow? I think so. Deep down they are still of my tribe.

So much of the time you spend as a refugee is taken up with nothing, with standing in one place for an hour, then moving a short distance and standing in another place for an hour. You see around you in the city – in this city of Bucharest – people on their way to work, shopping, catching trams and buses, driving their cars; people on their way home with a family to greet them, and all the while you are standing still. For me, waiting in the square outside the Bucharest post office, it is as if I am watching from the sky like the moon, while on the earth below life is swarming in every country. I am the lonely moon. Do you think the moon is calm and at peace in its place in the sky above the earth? No, the moon is so lonely that it wishes it could fall down and crash into the earth and be closer to the place where life is being lived. The moon is thinking: *Here nothing happens. In a million years, nothing.*

★

I sleep in the laundry again that night. I am the laundry boy. What if my Somali friends don't return to the square as they said they would? This laundry in Bucharest could become my permanent home.

The next day I go back to the post office square – again I have tagged along with Jabriil and Mehti, accepting a ticket from Jabriil. It doesn't cost much at all, but Mehti resents Jabriil paying for me.

I think: *What a miser!*

Sure enough, my three new friends, Saahid, Kaahin and Wardi, make an appearance nice and early.

They recognise me the minute I show myself. Saahid puts his arm around my shoulders; Wardi rubs the top of my head with his hand.

Saahid says: 'Hey, little buddy. Good to see you.'

Kaahin says: 'You know what's wrong with this kid? This Somali kid? He's too skinny. Aiee! Too, too skinny! We're going to feed you up, kid. What do you think?'

I say: 'Beautiful.'

'You hear what he says? He says beautiful! Of course it's beautiful! You came from Moga to starve? What shit is that? No way! We're going to feed you up.'

I hang with my new friends all day. I've become their mascot – is that the right word? A mascot? Like a kid who becomes a symbol? I think it's right. I'm a mascot. I get introduced to the friends of my friends, and I'm always joked about, like this: 'This is our little buddy from Moga. Bad guys wanted to kill him.'

And the guy I'm being introduced to says: 'No way! Kill this kid? No way!'

'Yes way. They wanted to kill him. Arseholes. Nobody's going to kill you here, little bro.'

These guys – Saahid, Kaahin and Wardi – they're very like my dad. They're cool in the same way, pretty relaxed. Here they are, from out of the Somali disaster, jiving about in a square in Bucharest, but they're not scared. Snow on the ground, grey buildings all around, cops and soldiers with Mk 48s and pistols, but they stay loose. I'd like to be cool in the same way. I never will be, I'm too conscientious, too concerned to get ahead and become the owner of a house very like the one I will come to purchase with my wife, Angela, one day. But I wouldn't mind being able to let go just for a day or so and put on some Ray-Bans, try out a few Rasta moves like Bob Marley, rub knuckles with other cool guys. Not going to happen.

I'm invited back to Saahid's place in the afternoon. It's in the middle of the city, a tower block divided into a hundred apartments, and one of the apartments is his. It's on the sixteenth floor. We take an elevator that shudders and rattles – the first elevator I've used, although I've heard about them. Also, this is the highest I've ever been above the ground, except on the aeroplane. I watch the flickering numbers on a little screen above the door. It's like magic. When we reach the sixteenth floor, the number '16' shows on the screen and the elevator stops with a jolt.

I make a big deal out of the ride and the jolting stop because I know Saahid likes to think of me as a naïve kid who's likely to get excited or spooked by modern technology. And I am naïve, sure, but I've read about elevators in the big, big buildings of New York City that can zoom up fifty, sixty, seventy floors in ninety seconds. I say: 'Whoo! Aiee!' and Saahid, Kaahin and Wardi laugh their heads off.

The apartment is crowded with Somalis, men and women, all of them young, although not as young as me. It's like being back in Mogadishu. The air is full of the chatter of my native language.

Saahid introduces me around, and the first comment anyone makes is to do with my age: 'Little guy, where's your mum, where's your dad? Aiee! So young! I can't believe it!'

Some of the men add politics to their comments: 'You see? Kids leaving the country now. Who will be left? The government is so corrupt, it can't even protect children.'

I smile as I'm taken from group to group, and of course there's plenty of hugging, plenty of head patting.

Saahid says: 'This apartment, this is a piece of Somalia in Romania. Okay? You say to me: "I am safe here with my friend Saahid." Say that.'

'I am safe here with my friend Saahid.'

'That's good. Very good. Get yourself something to eat.'

I'm left to work out the whole situation myself, while Saahid sails off to get friendly with all the other Somalis. I wander into the kitchen. A woman preparing food at the cooker gives me a big smile and a hug and hands me a plate of pasta swimming in rich red sauce. 'Bread, take it,' she says. 'Here's a fork. Hey, so skinny, little guy! Don't starve to death!'

'What is happening here?' I whisper. 'All these Somalis.'

'Yeah,' she says, 'all these Somalis, it's good! Everyone's waiting for Germany. Lots of jobs. Me too. Germany, Berlin, Frankfurt, Hamburg, wonderful for us Somali people, maybe. Big Europe. Germany, Netherlands, France, Belgium, also Yuna Kinum, very good for us, maybe.'

'United Kingdom?'

'Sure, Yuna Kinum, good for Somali people. Okay, sometimes not so good in these countries. Sometimes they put Somalis in jail. Sometimes send them back to Somalia. We need some good luck. Hey, you know where you should go? Denmark. Go to Denmark, Go to Volvo. Sweden. Not Russia, no way.'

I wander off with my plate piled high and another plate piled with bread. I find a corner, sit down on the floor and fill my stomach. I'm thinking and thinking with every mouthful, listening from my position on the floor. All the people here are so optimistic that it's difficult to stay realistic. But in the conversations I overhear there's talk of people – Somalis – found dead in truck compartments, and of people being ripped off. Why is everyone smiling? It must be because we are all Somalis here. People here must feel that something good will happen, simply because they can speak their own language and behave as they would back in Mogadishu. This is a party, and, at a party, nobody wants to frown. Some of the people here must have been smiling for six months, a year, always believing that they will finally, one day, go to Germany. As I eat, I tell myself that I should make sure that I don't become a party Somali. I must find a way out of this cold country. The future won't come looking for me – that's what I think. I have to go out and find the future.

Saahid notices me in the corner, looking cautious. 'Hey, Abdi,' he says. 'You having a good time? Sure, have a good time. Give me a smile.'

CHAPTER 13

The Kid

My stay in the apartment goes on for weeks. I'm 'the kid'. Visitors to the apartment are always introduced to me as if I'm a type of pet to be patted and hugged and sometimes kissed. 'Come here, you poor little darling. Oh, look at his big brown eyes!' It's embarrassing but, I must confess, I play along with it. People have all sorts of theories to explain why I am alone, without my parents. Often, they go over these theories while I'm standing there, as if I would be the last person who could tell them anything. 'Maybe his mum and dad are dead. Maybe his whole family was murdered, except for him. Maybe he stowed away on a jet. You can do that. You can hide in the place where the jet's wheels fold up. Except that you get really, really cold. Maybe he was kidnapped.'

I stand there grinning my head off like a lunatic. But what I want to say is: 'Just ask me.'

I've said a number of times in this story that I am a very practical person. I never make up what in English are called 'fairy stories' to believe in. I never say: *Hey, Nuurow, people love you, you're so beautiful, just relax and let it all come to you.* I can never feel easy with fantasies. Another thing: today these nice people are kind to me, but they could easily get sick of me. And then I say: *So, Nuurow, work.*

I help each day with the housework. To tell the truth, if I didn't do any housework, there would be no housework. I wash the dishes.

I pick up the newspapers that have been left about – Bucharest newspapers, yes, but some of the Somalis have taught themselves to read a little Romanian. I take the rubbish out. I do the shopping at the market. Saahid gives me money and tells me what to buy. Not always Saahid – any of the people staying in the apartment. I make sure I spend as little as I can, and I return every tiny coin to the person who's paying. Some of the items I'm asked to buy are not halal, but to Saahid this doesn't matter at all. He is not religious. You could set down a plate of roast pork in front of him and he would finish it off without any comment at all.

In the markets of Bucharest, on the streets, I learn more each day. But I am not learning what a tourist picks up – I don't know anything about the sights that Bucharest is known for. I don't look at the buildings and think: *Hmm, fine examples of nineteenth-century architecture.* All that my eyes see is what a refugee sees. I notice what time in the morning the cops come on duty, and whether they are alert or drowsy. (Mostly, they're drowsy.) If I see a flock of pigeons, I know that I will find tourists feeding the birds from small packets of breadcrumbs. And I go in the opposite direction, because tourists attract not only pigeons but crooks, thieves, con men. Sooner or later, one of those tourists will cry out: 'My wallet is gone!' and I don't want to be there when a cop starts grabbing the collars of suspicious-looking people like me, a refugee.

When I'm shopping, I sometimes wait until evening then go down to the bakeries where bread that was fresh in the morning is not so fresh now and sells at half price. Another thing I know is to keep away from the Romanian street people. I shouldn't feel that way because the street people are permanent refugees – I should think of them as my brothers. But I can't. Some of those guys can pick your pocket from five metres away. I see how quickly their eyes move, just a glance that lasts half a second. In that time they make a plan and in another half second they carry it out. I feel a shudder of fear when I watch them at work, these sharp-witted homeless people who have made a career of crime, because I never want that to happen to me. I am clever, I am quick, but if I remain a refugee for long enough, I might start using my good brain to do bad things. Who knows? It might happen overnight. I could wake up one morning and think: *You know what? I'd make a good crook. I could be a genius amongst crooks.* If that ever happens to me, let me at least have enough shame to go and jump off a bridge.

Another thing I have learnt is to keep away from the river bank – the Dambovita River – and the alleys and lanes down there, because that's where the prostitutes of Bucharest gather, and the bad guys who own the prostitutes get refugee kids like me to run errands for them, deliver drugs, that sort of thing. So I'm told. That's another way you can suddenly find yourself being beaten over the head with a policeman's club. And they say that you can't say no to those bad guys when they tell you to run an errand. Okay, I better come clean and admit that I know what those bad guys are called. Pimps. I keep a long way away.

I'm building a mental map of Bucharest. After three weeks, I know where every bus goes; where the trams go. I know all the stops, and in my head I carry a timetable. I know the roads and streets and highways, too; the lanes; the squares; the big buildings that I use as landmarks. If I was not a refugee, it would take me a year to learn what I've picked up in three weeks. If somebody dropped me off on the outskirts of the city, I could find my way back to the apartment where I'm staying without one false turn. It's not that I'm a genius; all the Somalis here in Bucharest can do the same. These are the skills of those without a country.

Saahid makes a present of a big winter jacket to me. 'A bad thing if a kid from Moga dies of the cold,' he says. 'The heat, maybe. But not the cold.' So I now get about looking like that cartoon guy in the advertisements for Michelin tyres, except for my skinny legs. I wear the jacket gratefully, but at the same time I hope I can give it away as soon as possible. More and more I miss Moga. More and more I'm getting sick of this city of Bucharest where the sun is always behind the clouds.

On the weekends I'm invited to the houses of Somalis. Not those from the apartment on the sixteenth floor, but Somalis who have set themselves up in Bucharest for a long stay. They visit the apartment from time to time, give one of those hip handshakes to Saahid – you know, where you tap your knuckles against the other guy's knuckles, hook your thumbs together, clasp wrists, then a high five. They say to me: 'Hey, little Abdi! Little Nuurow, the Shining One! Hey, stay with us for a couple of days, kid. We'll take you to a movie, maybe a soccer game, what do you think?'

'Yeah, sure, thanks.'

These hospitable fellow countrymen live in apartments themselves, always a bit shabby, but a couple of them have houses out in the suburbs. I have to tell you that the suburbs of Bucharest are pretty dreary. The people in the suburbs try to make their houses and front yards look like those of suburban people everywhere else: a garden, a tree or two. But the houses still look sad.

I notice flowers beginning to bloom in the parks – the flowers of early spring. I love to see flowers. Not so many flowers in the gardens of Mogadishu these days. A flower does some good for your heart. The snow covers the ground for months, and you can't believe anything will ever put out bright leaves again. But the leaves come, and the early flowers appear, so I have to thank this grey city for at least giving me a few flowers to enjoy.

★

Now and then, people from the apartment who have at last found a new home in Germany or France or Sweden remember me and a five-dollar note will come in a letter addressed to Abdi. The letters say: 'Abdi, thinking of you kid, can't afford much but maybe this money will help you.' I'm always grateful – of course I am. At the same time, I know that five dollars is not going to pay my way to London or Paris or Frankfurt. I have to believe that my mother or my father will hear of where I am from someone – I don't know who – and make a big plan to save me. I am beginning to feel as if I am – I don't know how to say this – as if I am 'un-owned', as if there is nobody now who will look at me and say: 'That's my son. That's Abdi. He belongs with me.' I have begun to float like a balloon that has been let go with a string trailing down. I want someone to catch the string and hold me in place. I've even thought of going back to Somalia. That's a crazy, crazy idea, but I have such a longing to see the country that is in my blood.

★

Refugees are like people living through a drought, listening for the sound of rain on the roof that will make life possible. Like farmers who search the sky for clouds, we are full of hope, and even when the rain doesn't fall, we think: *Maybe tomorrow.* The farmers finally lose hope, and smiles vanish, and refugees lose hope. At the apartment, people are becoming gloomy. Very little laughter now. People need to build. They need to feel that they are making something. Here, we are making nothing at all. Down at the post office square, the Somalis are talking of a protest. They want to march to the office of the United Nations High Commissioner for Refugees to demand to be registered as refugees, maybe given visas. They say: 'Okay, so this is not our country. But we don't have a country in the world. Help us, that's all we're saying. Help us.' I feel anxious. Maybe the Romanian police and the army guys will run at us with their clubs and beat us. Maybe they will say: 'You know what? We didn't ask you to come here. You don't like it, go to Russia. In Russia they'll shoot you.' But the Somalis, my countrymen, they are convinced that they must do something. The guys who are doing the thinking say: 'Come here tomorrow. All of you. We're going to march to the UNHCR office. The cops can't arrest all of us.'

I can't speak up. Nobody is going to listen to a kid. Some of the people I know see the worried look on my face. 'Hey, Abdi,' they say. 'Lighten up, brother. We're doing something good. You want another winter in this dump?'

So I'm there at the post office square the next morning when we start our march to the UNHCR office. I've never done anything like this before. This is 'political activism'. I don't know a thing about politics. I feel like I want to say: 'Hey, you know what? Let's just send them a letter.' I take my place amongst all the Somalis, I try to look optimistic, I shuffle along the boulevard to the UNHCR office, when all the others shout out in English and French and Somali: 'Help us! We are refugees! We are human beings!' I shout out the same things. The guys in charge say: 'Shout louder!' and we all shout louder.

Lots of Romanian cops are pouring out of vans wearing helmets and carrying those riot shields made out of Perspex. The army guys come roaring in and leap down from the backs of trucks. They wade into the crowd, blowing whistles. But the guys at the front of our protest crowd have pushed their way into the UNHCR office and they're lying down on the floor, refusing to budge. Somebody screams at me: 'Abdi! Get in there! Don't let them drag you out!' I'm so small and skinny that I can wriggle my way past adult bodies and into the lobby. I curl up in a corner and watch the battle in a state almost of panic. I don't like it. I can't see what good will come of this. When we're out on the streets again in a day or two, the cops are going to pick on us more than ever. Let's face it – if you're a Somali in Bucharest, you stand out. Somali protesters are hanging onto anything that is fixed in place – the desks, the counter, the door handles – while the cops try to drag them back out onto the street. Other guys try to stop the cops from getting at us. So much shouting, so much fighting, whistles blowing, cops issuing warnings through megaphones. And now, tear gas. The canisters are fired from guns and come whirling through the air and burst into white smoke. I pack myself more tightly into my corner and pull my jacket up over my face, my eyes shut. I have never had tear gas in my eyes, but I've seen it on television back in Moga and I can guess that it's painful.

After an hour or more, the cops withdraw. I'm thinking: *What the hell?* No more tear gas. The fifty of us – maybe more – inside the office look at each other puzzled and confused. Some guy from the UNHCR is announcing that the new president of Romania has ordered the police and army to back off. But why? I'm not complaining, I just don't understand. I can see the cops outside the office, keeping to the far side of the street. Some of them have a grieved expression, as if they resent not being allowed to beat the living daylights out of us.

And we're still there at night. I'm huddled up in my corner, a place I've colonised, waiting for another change of strategy by the Romanians, maybe along the lines of dragging us all outside and shooting us in the head, which is what would happen in Somalia. Then one of the guys I know from the apartment crawls up to me and rubs my head with the palm of his hand. 'Hey, little guy. You look worried. Nothing to worry about.'

'How do you know?' I ask. I'll be really happy to hear some good news.

'Hey, listen to me. This new president the Romanians have got themselves, he doesn't want trouble. You hear me? He wants the rich Europeans to love Romania – the Germans, the French, the English. He wants them to love him like crazy, okay? He wants his shit country to join the Europeans, okay? So he's being nice. The rich guys, they don't want to see pictures of Romanian cops hitting us on the head with big sticks. Take it easy, kid. Nothing bad is going to happen.' Then he crawls away.

So I'm left thinking: *Is he right?* I want him to be right. But I am wary, of course I'm wary, I've come out of a country where you can't count on anything. When I was travelling around Somalia, I'd meet people all the time who had optimistic tales to tell. They'd say: 'Hey, the war will be over in ten more days. Trust me. Ten more days.' And they'd say: 'Barre has handed the government over to his deputy. The deputy is a good guy. He doesn't want any more killing. No way. Trust me. Things are going to get much, much, much better for us in a few weeks.'

I'd listen to these people and nod my head, but I didn't believe a word they said. You know, most times, things are what they look like. If people are being shot in the head all around you, you're likely to be shot in the head yourself. So you always have to act as if the thing you most fear is likely to happen. Sometimes you'll be wrong, okay, but at least you'll be alive to see that you're wrong. This is all short-term stuff. In the long run, sure, I think things will get better, or at least I choose to believe that things will get better eventually. But right now, trying to sleep on a hard floor inside an office in the middle of Bucharest, I'm thinking that the thing I fear most – being murdered – is very likely to happen.

Throughout the night small political meetings are going on in whispers all over the lobby. Listening to the whispers, I begin to understand that some of the Somalis who are my brothers and sisters have a shrewd idea of what is about to happen. They are not guided by blind violence, and they are not as desperate as I thought. They lean their heads together and attend to what first one then another person has to report. I wriggle myself a little closer, full of curiosity. The guy I'm trying to overhear says: 'They won't attack, not tonight, not tomorrow. Reporters from Big Europe are out there now. Frenchies, Volvos. They'll send buses and take us to a camp. We'll be recognised as refugees. Trust me.' The others murmur together, then one person from the group walks in a crouched position across the carpeted floor to another group, maybe to pass on the message. The 'Volvos', by the way, are the Swedes, as I'm sure you have guessed. And I should say, too, that when the Somalis talk about Big Europe they mean the rich European countries – Germany and France and Britain and the Netherlands and Belgium and Denmark and so on.

The guy in the whispering group, the clever guy, he notices me listening and gives me a smile. 'Hey kid, you're not a spy for the Romanian cops, are you?'

'Me? No.'

'That's good,' he says, and gives me a smile. 'I would have had to shoot you.'

This is new to me – this idea of having a strategy, and I'm fascinated by it. I've made use of simple strategies at times over the past year, sure, like sometimes denying that I'm Rahanweyn because, if hadn't denied it, I would have had my throat cut. But what the clever guy is talking about is much more sophisticated. It's as if he could always see beyond all the shouting and all the slogans and all the demands and the fighting and the tear gas. As if he knew that there was a process that you have to go through to reach your goal. What an amazing thing! This is going to stay with me for a long time, I can feel that. I think: *Nuurow, use your brain, always, use your good, clever brain.*

And in the morning, early, the buses come, just as the savvy guy said they would. An official from the Romanian government reads from a document as we all listen. He says we will be taken to a camp outside Bucharest, and that we will be accepted as refugees. He says that the UN will find new countries for us. Then he says that the Romanian government is committed to assisting refugees in their genuine struggle for security. He says that the Romanian president, Ion Iliescu, has been very moved by the struggle of the Bucharest Somalis. He says that the Somalis are the friends of the Romanian people. The minister speaks only one sentence at a time before a Somali guy in a business suit beside him translates the Romanian into Somali.

While the official is reading from the document, I stand as close as I can to the clever guy and his friends. I hear the clever guy saying: 'Okay, we cooperate. This way we get registered. If we fight them, this Ion guy will say to Big Europe: "Hey, we tried to register them, they punched us in the face." So, go, show them your documents, get on the buses.'

So we go. Government people with clipboards take down our names, look at our documents. I'm nervous, scared. The thing that keeps me under control is knowing that the clever guy said we should do what we're doing. All the times in the past when I've seen Somalis herded together like this, it was the start of a massacre. I keep telling myself: *Abdi, listen to me. If they wanted to kill you, they would have done all this in secret. Look at all the people from the media. Look at the Volvos, look at the English, look at the Germans.*

★

The buses take us through the suburbs and further still to a camp beyond the outskirts of the city. I stare out of the window at the scattered farms of this country that is so different from Somalia. It's March, and the snow has disappeared from the ground now and everything is green and lush. A sudden pain makes me wince. I miss my homeland. A crazy plan takes shape in my mind. I will wait until this bus reaches the camp, then I will run away and find my way back to Somalia. If I am killed, too bad for me. I want to be in a land in which the sun at midday stands right over your head and burns you like a piece of toast. I want to walk down the main street of Medina and call out to all the shopkeepers. And especially – especially! – I want to take a soccer ball to the beach and kick it around the sand. My hopes are not fairy story things. I don't expect to suddenly find a diamond as big as a camel and build a magnificent palace in Moga. My hopes are small and humble. Just a chance to live my life in Moga, and eat my mother's cooking, *hilib ari duban*, *macsharo*, *surbiyaan hilib adhi*, tuna *sambusas*, *soor*. And I want to watch my father playing cards with his friends. So, so simple – and so impossible.

The pain settles into an ache in my chest and my stomach. I brush tears from my eyes. I don't want to be strong anymore. I glance around at other people in the bus. A few seem quite excited about what's happening, but most look sad, as if they are thinking the same thoughts as me. People need a home. Some Somalis are nomads, and never settle in one place. But the truth is that the routes they follow with their cattle and the places where they camp and light a fire and the line of hills they see when they look up at the horizon – it's all their home, just as surely as mine is Moga and the main street of Medina. It is only when people find a home that they build – and I don't mean only houses, I mean that they dream and build what they dream, a family that they cherish, children, a beloved wife, a kitchen full of the aromas of Somali food, a university education, a job that gives them pleasure. I am a nomad at the moment, but without familiar places where I can make a fire, without hills on the horizon I can gaze at with joy in my heart.

Then, for the sake of relief from sadness, I think of the clever guy – I think of his strategy. I say to myself: *Nuurow, surely for anything to happen, you must have a strategy and stick to it. Don't be a cry baby! Think, with your clever Nuurow brain. Think.*

And I do think. The bus is taking us to a camp. I will have a refugee number. I will tell the UNHCR people where I want to go to live. I will say: 'Send me to Germany, to the big city of Berlin, to Frankfurt. Send me to Paris. Send me to live with the English. Send me to the land where the Volvos live – Sweden. Send me there.' I will come to the UNHCR office every day until they are sick of me. They will say: 'Oh, not you again, Abdi.' And I'll say: 'Yes, it's me, Abdi, and I will be here again and again and again until you send me where I can make a new home. Again and again and again.'

This is a strategy. It gives me relief from sadness. I look at the clever guy, who is three seats behind me.

He sees me turning to look at him, and he sees the smile on my face. He says: 'Hey, kid, we did it, yeah. A clean getaway.'

I nod my head. I'm still smiling. The clever guy begins to sing a song in English, a song I have heard my father sing, 'I Shot the Sheriff' by Bob Marley – Rasta Bob.

'You know that song, kid? You know that song by Bob Rasta?'

I say: 'I know the song.'

'Listen, smiley boy, you're going to be okay. You get it? You're going to be okay.'

'Sure,' I say. 'I'm going to be okay.'

I turn around again in my seat and softly sing the words of 'I Shot the Sheriff' to myself.

CHAPTER 14

Abu

The bus enters the camp through tall, wire gates. The whole compound is given over to wooden huts with iron roofs, each with a number on the door and a few letters that must mean something to the Romanians. Beyond the compound, you see the countryside, fields, trees. The camp looks like a place that has been forgotten. You wouldn't want to stay here too long.

The UNHCR official on board the bus tells us to get off and assemble in the area between the rows of huts. Some of the passengers are muttering in Somali that the place looks like a concentration camp. One man says: 'Believe me, brothers, they will kill us here and burn our bodies, I tell you this for certain.' But this man has been complaining for the whole journey and is generally considered half mad. In any case, everyone cooperates and we form a crowd where we're supposed to. The UNHCR guy stands in the middle of the crowd with another guy from the Romanian government and a policeman. On the outside of the crowd, two more policemen keep watch. They have automatic rifles, but the guns are slung over their shoulders, not pointed at us.

Now the Somali interpreter turns up. He's been driven here in an SUV. He's still wearing his beautiful suit and stands beside a guy from UNHCR, ready to translate. The UNHCR guy looks very serious. He's short, with grey hair and big spectacles. He has this to say, in English, translated into Somali by the guy who arrived in the SUV: 'You have been brought here for your own protection. I don't need to tell you who we are protecting you from.' He means the police and the army. 'You have a perfect right to demonstrate, but you must remember, this is a country that has a long history of coming down hard on demonstrators. However, the Romanian government, under the leadership of President Ion Iliescu, wishes to avoid any … any unpleasantness. You will remain here while the UNHCR office looks into the possibility of your refugee status being recognised and you being issued, so we hope, refugee registration. This may take a few weeks, perhaps as long as a month, possibly two months.'

A mumble of unrest comes from the crowd. Somebody calls out, in English: 'This is shit!' Another voice calls out, in Somali: 'Hey, mister snake man, you told us we get refugee status immediately!'

The interpreter tells the UNHCR guy what the Somali means in English.

'We are doing everything in our power to expedite your registration,' says the UNHCR guy. 'I urge you to show patience while we deal with the Romanian government, on the one hand, and a number of European governments, some of which may be willing to accept you under their humanitarian resettlement programs.'

I should say before I go any further that I do not have a memory that can recall the exact words spoken this day. But what I've provided here is very close to what the UNHCR guy told us – certainly the sense of it. I have a good enough memory for that.

I don't have enough experience in life to judge whether the UNHCR guy with his big spectacles is telling us the truth. I glance at the clever guy to see what sort of expression is on his face. He seems pretty calm about the whole thing, as if he expected the

UNHCR guy to say exactly what he said. I think: *Okay, if he's cool with all this, I'm cool, too.*

But then the clever guy does say something. He doesn't even have to shout. He just raises his hand to show that he wants to speak. Everyone falls silent. He says, in English: 'Can we leave the camp during the day and go back to the city? Or are we prisoners?'

The UNHCR guy consults with another guy from the Romanian government. He's wearing a suit, but it's not nearly as smart as the translator's. Then the UNHCR guy says: 'You will be free to leave the camp each day, and return when you wish. Buses will travel to the post office square in Bucharest every morning. You are not prisoners.'

The clever guy nods his head. 'Good to hear,' he says.

Even those who are upset and angry don't look as if they're about to march out of the camp or anything like that. Something I don't know at this moment but will come to learn in the future is that there is always someone in any crowd of protestors who can move things in the way he or she wishes to. The clever guy doesn't want to shout out: 'We've been shafted!' He or she is the guy who could change things: who could start a riot, even, if that seemed like a good idea. And you know, in years to come, I myself will be in a position to influence the way a crowd or a group feels. It will be me with my convictions that people will listen to. And why will they listen to me? Because they know my story, they know about Somalia, and they think: *This guy isn't just talking about things he's seen on television. He was there.*

So we accept the deal the UNHCR guy is offering and we stay in the wooden huts with their rows of bunk beds. It's not uncomfortable, but it's boring. Beyond the camp are trees, fields, grazing animals – a horse, five or six cows. We walk about without any purpose, hands in our pockets because of the cold, the sun a blurry yellow glow behind the clouds. Wandering about, I see Somali guys standing in a group, talking about nothing, and I think: *Look at them, tall and black and slim. They don't belong here. This is crazy – Somalis from the hottest part of Africa shuffling around in Romania.* And these cows that I can see in the fields are nothing like the cattle of Somalia, which carry their heads low, never grow fat and are forever swishing their tails to chase away the flies. Somalia seems to me a much older part of the earth than Romania. The colours of Somalia are stronger, the sky the deepest blue you will ever see, and the sun so golden that it looks as if it is melting itself in a huge furnace. Sure, there is more greenery in Romania, but it looks soft. In Somalia, the greenery is hard and bright. I think: *This country of Romania is fine for the Romanians, but us, Somalis, we can't live here. It's madness.*

I take the bus to the post office square in Bucharest each day, run errands for people to make a few coins, listen to everything. And, really, nothing has changed since before our demonstration. The UNHCR hasn't yet given us registration numbers; nothing's happening. I say to myself: *Nuurow, do something. I'm sick of you waiting for other people to save you. Save yourself.*

My mother has a friend in Rome, a fellow Somali woman named Lula. I'm able to contact her by calling the same number that used to be my mother's number. I've been phoning Lula in Rome whenever I've made enough money from running errands. My question to her is just the one question, each time: 'Any news of my mother, Lula?' And there is only ever one answer: 'Abdi, no news. I don't know where she is, aiee! I don't know.' But then there is a change. When I next phone Lula, she says she has learnt that a guy by the name of Abukur, who works at the Somali embassy in

Bonn, is an old friend of my father's. He was badly injured when Somalia was fighting the Ethiopians years ago, when I was a tiny kid, burns over seventy-five per cent of his body, and it was thanks to my father that he survived. My father at that time was a head nurse in Moga, and he saw to it that Abukur was not left to die. Later – this all comes from Lula – my father pulled some strings and got Abu transferred to a hospital in Germany for treatment, and also called in a favour to have Abu given a diplomatic post of some kind at the embassy. So, according to Lula, Abu owes my dad big time. And Abu has made a name for himself over the years as a guy who can get you a visa, get you a ticket to Big Europe, maybe also Canada, the USA.

How Lula knows all this is a mystery to me. So what? Abu's a friend of my dad, and he's in the right line of business for me. But one thing Lula doesn't know is Abu's telephone number in Bonn. I could ring the embassy, but would that be a good idea? What he's doing is pretty much illegal, so maybe he wouldn't be able to talk over the phone from the embassy. I need his home number.

Now, one thing I do know is that somebody in Bucharest will have Abu's home number. It's not possible to have a Somali in Bonn with the ability to wheel and deal without other Somalis in Europe knowing him. It sounds crazy, but every Somali in Europe is connected to every other Somali. There'd be Somalis in Finland or in Siberia in Russia who would know me in some way, friends of friends who know my dad. If I somehow ended up in Helsinki, the big city of Finland, and I put my mind to it, I would sooner or later meet the friend of a third cousin who knew a friend of my father, Isak. Here in Bucharest, sure, there are people who know my dad, or who know someone who knows my dad. They are powerless, and can't help me, but they are here.

So I ask around, I ask everyone, I ask the clever guy. I say: 'In the Somali embassy in Bonn, there's a guy called Abu, a Rahanweyn. Maybe you know him?'

When I ask the clever guy, he says: 'What do you want from him, kid?'

I tell the clever guy I want Abu's home telephone number so I can talk to him about a visa.

'Tomorrow,' the clever guy says. And sure enough, he has Abu's number the next day.

I phone the number in the evening when Abu might be home. He is home. I say to him in Somali: 'Sir, maybe you don't know me, but I am Abdi Aden, the son of Isak Aden.'

And Abu says: 'So what?'

This doesn't sound so friendly, but I push on. 'I am in Bucharest, if you know of it. I had to escape from Somalia.'

'Everyone has to escape from Somalia. The place is shit.'

He sounds harsh. My country has its problems, but I don't like to hear Abu saying Somalia is 'shit'.

'But you know my father? You know Isak Aden?'

'Maybe. What are you calling me for?'

'Sir, if it is God's will, I hope to find a new home for myself in Big Europe, maybe Canada.'

'I see. In Canada.'

'Or in Big Europe, sir.'

I would not normally have said 'if it is God's will', but I am trying it out in case this Abu is religious. In the Australia I will come to know so well, non-Muslims assume that all Muslims are crazy religious. But the truth is that there are about a hundred shades of belief amongst Muslims, ranging from complete devotion to a type of indifference. Two Muslims who don't know each other might start out assuming that the other one is devout, then gradually work out where he belongs in the catalogue of belief. After ten minutes, it might be accepted by one that the other is sort of serious about religion, but not always, maybe more on Fridays, but only certain Fridays, while the other can see that this guy he's talking to is actually only a man of faith when his wife is nearby. It's best to begin, always, with a few phrases of faith, since you can always back-pedal when the other guy signals the degree of his devotion, if any.

Abu says: 'I'm coming to Bucharest in a few days. I'll see you then.'

I don't want to give my address as the refugee camp, so I tell him I'll meet him at the train station.

He agrees.

'Let me take you to dinner,' I say. I want him to believe I have money. I don't have anything, of course, but you'll remember what I said about becoming educated as a refugee. Complete honesty would find you starving in the gutter. You have to be clever. You know what they say in Australia? It's a phrase I hadn't heard before I went to Melbourne: 'Play your cards close to your chest.' That's what I'm doing – playing my cards close to my chest. A very difficult thing to do when you don't actually have any cards.

'You want to take me to dinner?' For the first time, Abu is interested in me. Not much, but a bit.

'Sure. At a restaurant.'

How in God's name am I going to pay for this?

Then I say: 'How will I know you?'

Down the line comes a laugh, like a grunt. 'Isak told you about me? And you want to know how you'll recognise me?'

Then he hangs up. I'm puzzled for few minutes, then I remember what Lula said about his face, so badly burnt, with the rest of his body. *Abdi, you fool of a boy!* But there is nothing to be done.

I tell the clever guy that I'm to meet Abu in a few days, and the clever guy smiles then rubs his thumb and his index finger together, meaning 'money'. Yes, well that's the big problem, isn't it? I've borrowed enough money for a meal in a restaurant, but the three thousand dollars I'd need to get to Canada or somewhere – well, that's impossible.

I wish with all my heart that the clever guy, who is so like my dad, so cool in the same style as Dad, would just take over the negotiations with Abu and work out some way that I can get to Big Europe or Canada. But he doesn't. It's as if he trusts me to work it all out, as if he thinks I have the same kind of savvy as him. I wish!

Abu comes to the station on the day he said he would. It's easy for me or for anyone to pick him out from all the other Somalis because half of his face is burnt away. I go up to him and say in Somali: 'Sir, it's Abdi. We spoke on the telephone.'

Abu looks at me with a frown – or as much of a frown as a man with half his face missing can manage. He says: 'How old are you?'

'How old? I am twenty. Yes, twenty, for certain.'

Abu says: 'Twenty my arse.'

'I look young for my age, sir.'

Abu is now looking over my shoulder, not paying me much attention. I glance behind me to see who he might be looking at. And sure enough, another guy is approaching us, a guy years older than me. Abu stretches out a hand to greet this new guy, and within a matter of seconds the two of them are whispering together like old buddies. I'm hurt and disappointed that Abu finds this new guy more interesting than me. Then it dawns on me that Abu has come here from Bonn to meet this guy, not me. I'm just incidental.

After a few minutes, Abu glances over at me. 'This is Abdi,' he says. 'He's taking us out to dinner.'

What the hell? How am I supposed to make my borrowed money cover three meals? I'll have to make do with bread for myself.

In the restaurant, the other guy stuffs the food down his throat as if, where he comes from, there's a time limit for eating dinner. Then he's gone, without saying a word to me.

Abu is beginning to make a move himself, but I plead with him to listen to me.

'Okay, say something.'

'Sir, it's most important for me to get to another country. It's no good in Bucharest. If I'm here next winter, I'll die in the snow.'

A month ago, there was a story on the news about two Somalis who had frozen to death in the snow in Romania. Maybe Abu has heard about it.

'Keep warm,' Abu says, and he turns to leave.

'Sir,' I call when he is halfway to the door. 'I can get money. I can pay.'

Abu stops dead in his tracks, turns to me and gazes at me for a full minute or more. Then he comes back to the table and sits down again. He sits side-on so that the left half of his face is only partially visible. This is his habit, to sit or stand with only the right side of his face – the undamaged half – showing to whoever he's talking to.

'Go on,' he says.

'Sir, my mother's friend in Rome, Lula, she has money that my mother gave her. It is meant for me, to help me.'

'And how long has she had this money?'

'How long? Three months, maybe.'

'And how long have you been here?'

'Seven months. No, eight months.'

'So for the past three months you've stayed here in this pisspot country, where every man's dick is frozen, just because you felt like it, eh?'

I had to think quick. But I can think quickly, thank God. 'I've been looking for someone who can help me,' I say. 'You're the first one I've met who knows what to do.'

'Is that right? Aren't I a lucky man.' Abu continues to study my face.

'I can ask Lula in Rome to call you,' I tell him. 'She will tell you the whole story.'

Abu says nothing at all. And yet, I can see that he's interested. 'Get her to phone me in Bonn. You know the number.'

He stands and prepares to leave for the second time. Before he goes, he says: 'Your father is a good man.' Then he leaves.

The next day I phone Lula from the camp.

'Abdi! Aiee! I knew in my heart that you would call me! Aiee!'

'Lula, listen to me. You must telephone Abukur in Bonn and tell him you can get the money I need for a ticket and a visa. Will you do this?'

'What?'

I repeat what I'd said.

'I don't have that sort of money, Nuurow! Maybe three thousand dollars, maybe more! Aiee! How can I get so much money as this?'

'Just tell him you can.'

'Just tell him?'

'Sure.'

Lula is quiet for a short time. Then she laughs, a deep, gurgling laugh. 'Abdi, my baby boy, you're playing this Abukur guy! Aiee! You're playing him!'

I want to deny to Lula that I'm doing any such thing. The word she uses in Somali for 'playing' has just the meaning that 'playing' has in English (that is, it means leading someone along, deceiving that person for your own ends). I am not a con man, I am not a crook. But if I'm not a con man, why do I want Lula to pretend that we can get the money we need to pay Abu? It's a question I don't want to deal with on the telephone to Lula. I don't feel ready to accept that what I'm doing is dishonest. Looking back, sure, I can say straight away, yes, I was playing Abu. But as I've explained earlier in this story of mine, I think dishonesty is acceptable in certain circumstances. Maybe. I'm not sure. Probably.

Lulu rings Abu. I know the time she intends to ring him, and I call her an hour later. She says that he told her to find the money, or it's no deal. She told him she could get the money, no problem, but she needed time. Meanwhile, she would cable him one hundred and fifty dollars to get me out of Romania and into Germany.

'Really?' I say to Lula. 'You have one hundred and fifty dollars?'

'Yes, I have. And that's all I can get. But he believes that I can get the rest, three thousand dollars. That what he thinks.'

Lula's deep, wicked laugh comes down the phone line. She says again: 'That's what he thinks.' She's enjoying this.

Lula's one hundred and fifty dollars will not only get me to Frankfurt, it also convinces Abu that Lula has much more money at her disposal. And so the day finally comes when I am able to get the hell out of Romania. Considering that at various times over the past eleven months – and it is now early in 1992 – I thought I would die in that dreary, sunless land, this is a happy day. Better to be a refugee in Big Europe than in Romania.

On the aeroplane to Frankfurt, I am exhilarated. This is progress. Something has happened. Human beings, many of them, live in hope that something they desperately desire to happen will actually happen, but when it does happen, they are amazed, disbelieving, flabbergasted. They say: 'I can't believe it! I can't believe it!' And yet this is what they prayed for, so why do they say 'I can't believe it'? Because they didn't believe it. They didn't deep down believe it would ever happen. It's a miracle. Hope is a form of fantasy and, really, that's how we should think of hope, as a type of fantasy. For every hope that becomes a reality, another million do not. My hope has been one picked out of a million. When I lay on the ground in Somalia and men with Kalashnikovs fired two rounds at me without so much as wounding me, that was one chance in a million. I'm a lucky kid. That's why I have such a big smile on my face as I fly to Frankfurt. I'm a lucky, lucky kid.

Abu is flying with me. I am travelling on his passport as one of his sons. Somali passports include all the children of the family. Nobody is likely to say that a picture of Abu's son is not me. If Abu were a white guy, maybe. But white immigration officers will only look for the skin colour. That's good enough for them, Abu has informed me. The kid in the passport is black, this kid is black – not a problem. I've left my own passport behind in Bucharest – Abu told me to.

Abu doesn't say much, but he seems a bit more sympathetic than he was. 'Look at the pictures in the magazine.' And 'When they offer you a sandwich, say yes. Don't say: "Is it halal?" Okay? Eat it.' I nod my head and do whatever he suggests.

Frankfurt is not our true destination. We're going to Bonn, where Abu lives with his family. It's much cheaper to fly to Frankfurt than to Bonn. Once in Frankfurt, we'll catch a train to Bonn. And then? And then I don't know. Certainly Abu will ask me for the three thousand dollars I need for a visa, and I won't have it, and he will be angry, and so on and so on. I don't care for the time being. I will use my wits.

Frankfurt airport is like a hundred airports all pushed together. And so many shops! I didn't know that in the world there were so many shops. Imagine the money that must be in Germany for people to need all these shops! This is my first look at the wealth of Big Europe, and it dazzles me – more than that, it frightens me. I didn't understand that there is such a difference between Somalia and Big Europe. Sure, I knew that Big Europe was rich, but this rich? No, no. When can Somalia be as rich as this? In a thousand years? That's what's so scary. Right now, our main industry is murder. Or maybe I'm too pessimistic. A few decades ago, Germany's main industry was murder, too – more murders than in Somalia, many, many, many more. And the whole country was smashed to pieces, like Somalia. Maybe there's hope for us.

★

The train to Bonn is streamlined, like a sports car, and very fast. I watch the German towns and countryside flying past. I have to say, Germany looks much more prosperous than Romania. So much of it is brand new, except for the smaller towns, which look like pictures in books from two hundred years ago. Germany is further north than Romania and for that reason it should be a bit colder. But the sun, instead of being hidden behind clouds as it was in Romania, is shining. I think the Romanian clouds are there permanently, the same clouds.

I am shy about talking to Abu, not that he gives much sign of wanting to talk. I am shy, but at the same time, I'm not. The shyness that people saw in me a couple of years ago – that's all gone.

That was when I was a kid. The Somalis in Bucharest used to call me 'kid', but I'm not a kid anymore. If I let myself, I could feel sad about that. I have mentioned this before, I know, but today, on the train after the flight to Frankfurt, I feel it more than ever. I'm not a kid. The people in Somalia so happy to murder people like me, they took away all of my kid stuff. And, you know, there are kids in Somalia even now, younger than me, and they're not kids anymore, either. They are eight years old, even younger, seven years old, and they've seen too much, throats being cut, people set on fire. Once you've seen that, you can't go back to thinking that your mum and dad will save you no matter what. You know that your mum and dad have no power when it comes to stopping a soldier on amphetamines from taking out his knife and going insane. Looking out the window at the land of Germany, I promise myself that if I have kids, they can stay kids for as long as they want to, until they're twenty or thirty, fine by me. It's the best thing in the world if you can say to yourself: *I could grow up, I suppose, but this is so much fun, so I won't.* If my kids still want a cuddle when they're thirty, I'll say: 'Sure, come to Daddy.'

CHAPTER 15

Germany

From the main train station in Bonn we take a taxi to Abu's house in the suburbs. Nice suburb, nice house, a little garden. There are no such suburbs and houses and little gardens in Moga – Abu has become a black German.

He has four kids, two of them sons, and one of the sons is about my age and size. This kid's cast-offs are offered to me. In fact, they're not even cast-offs, they're the next thing to new – black trousers, a shirt, a jacket and some brand-new black shoes. Before I change clothes, I'm introduced to Abu's wife and kids. They're all courteous to me, but pretty much indifferent to my existence, and the kids go back to the television once they've said hello, while Mrs Abu returns to the kitchen to prepare dinner.

'You can take a shower if you wish,' Abu says, and he shows me to the bathroom, gives me a fresh towel and a new toothbrush and points out the soap and shampoo. It takes me a few minutes to figure out how the shower works – the chrome taps have indicators on them to show how much hot is to be mixed with the cold. But once I get the mixture right, oh, man, it's terrific, the best shower I've had in the whole of my life! The bathroom is full of steam but I don't want to stop. I wash my hair with shampoo then notice another plastic bottle with writing on the label in German: '*haar-conditioner*'. *Why not?* I think, and smother my hair in the creamy stuff from the bottle. I dry myself slowly with the fleecy white towel, get into my new clothes and shoes, scrub my teeth like a crazy person with the toothbrush.

By this time the mirror has cleared of mist and I'm able to take a good look at myself. I say aloud, in Somali: 'Nuurow, you're a handsome boy. Very handsome.'

Back out in the dining room (I came to know later that such rooms are called 'dining rooms') the family is getting ready for dinner. I give Abu and his wife and kids the chance to take a proper look at my smart clothes, my hair shining with shampoo and *haar*-conditioner, my teeth gleaming. They barely notice me at all.

The next day, Abu takes me to his office in the house and asks me about the money. I say: 'Lula will take care of it. Ring Lula.' And so he does. When he puts the phone down, Abu stares at me for an age before speaking. 'She says the money is coming.'

'The money is coming?'

'She says it's coming.' He takes an envelope from the drawer of his desk and takes out what I recognise as a Somali passport. He opens it and displays the page on which a visa is stamped. 'Commonwealth of Australia,' he says. He points to the date. 'We have to use it very soon. You understand?'

'Very soon?'

'Six days from today. Lula can send the money in time?'

'Certainly, certainly.'

What do I mean 'certainly'? There is no money.

Abu sits in his office chair and gestures for me to sit in a second chair on the opposite side of his desk. He stares at my face fixedly. I want to return his gaze, but I can't be as unblinking as he is. His face is badly scarred. It would be rude to stare. But between his steady stare and mine, during which I occasionally lower my gaze, a

SHINING

sort of contest is being played out. He wants to know if I am lying. I want to prevent him from guessing that I'm lying.

Abu says: 'You are sure that you can get this money?'

'Lula can get it,' I say.

'Lula can get it. Okay. But do I believe you?'

'You can believe me.'

'Really?'

'Really.'

'On your mother's life? On your father's life?'

Sorry, Mum. Sorry, Dad. 'On my mother's life. On my father's life.'

Abu leans forward and continues to stare at my face, his head resting on his joined hands under his chin. 'Okay,' he says. 'I believe you.'

I think: *Do you? Well that's good.*

The thing I recognise is this: Abu badly wants to believe that I either already have the money, or that Lula has the money, or that either Lula or I can get hold of the money. He can't believe that I am on this journey without the backing of my mother and father. My dad, his friend, has worked in Paris for years, so he must have heaps, Abu thinks. My mother went to Italy, so she must have heaps. I flew from Mogadishu to Bucharest, so I must have heaps. But here's the thing: at the same time that he believes I can get three thousand dollars from Lula or my mum or my dad, he has his doubts. He has to sell that visa for Australia that's due to expire. He can't afford to listen to his doubts. He would have paid someone for that visa, 'under the table', as they say. Behind my innocent gaze, I know all this. I am playing a part, taking the short-term view once more. The money won't come, but maybe Abu will keep me here and feed me until it becomes clear that the money doesn't exist. That's okay.

Three days, four days, then I get thrown out. I can eat and rest a lot in three or four days.

And I do. I lounge about Abu's house for the rest of the day, sleep comfortably at night (sharing a room with Abu's two sons), eat everything I'm offered. When Abu is away at the embassy, I watch television. The four kids are at school. I'm here alone with Mrs Abu. I smile at her in a friendly way every so often. I think she wants to be rid of me.

The next day, Abu takes me to another house in Bonn, one that is rented by a friend who is away for the time being. It's furnished, it's comfortable. I'm told that I'll stay here until the money arrives for the ticket to Australia. I say: 'Sure!' but even as I'm saying it, I'm trying to come up with a strategy for the coming week, a strategy that will have to include what I'm going to do in Bonn after Abu kicks me out, as he surely will.

But my strategy for the moment is to do nothing but watch television. Abu intends to bring me back to his house each day for the main meal, and for other meals I can rely on what's in the refrigerator. Whenever I get anxious, I counsel myself with these words: *Abdi, don't worry. You'll be dead in a year, certainly within five years. Take it easy.* This is therapy – pretend there is no future, therefore nothing to worry about. But I also have another plan which does not include being dead anytime soon. This other plan is to find a big, happy new country and live there forever, to find a nice job, buy a nice house, meet a nice lady, arrange a nice marriage, have some nice kids. This second plan is a fantasy, I know that; the other plan – to die – is more realistic. So for the moment, I'll watch German television, which is quite interesting, even though I don't understand any words other than *ja, nein, dummkopf* and *mein Gott*, which sounds like the English 'my God', something I heard a tourist at the post office say.

Five days into my 'holiday' in Bonn, and Abu is getting more and more frustrated with me. The money hasn't come. He's talked with Lula another three times. 'Be patient,' she says.

I make out that it's all in the hands of Lula.

Abu says: 'Your family has two houses in Moga, is that right?'

'I think so.' Strictly speaking, we do have two houses in Mogadishu, if you count the house in which my father lives, which may or may not be his.

'So where is your mother? In Italy? I'll take you to Italy and we'll get the money from her.'

'To Italy?' This has an appealing sound. At least I could stay with Lula. 'Sure,' I say. 'Let's go to Italy.'

'Where? Rome? Milan? Where?'

What I don't know at this time is that my mother is, in fact, in Kenya, looking for me on the Kenya–Somali border. She's searching through the refugee camp, asking everyone if they've seen me. She has a photo. If I had known, I would have been hysterical. I would have been breaking my neck to get on a flight back to Somalia. I would have been praying day and night. So it's a good thing I don't know.

'Actually, that I don't know,' I tell Abu. 'But maybe we could find out. Maybe we could put an advertisement in the newspaper.'

Abu snorts in disgust. 'Advertisement my arse,' he says and stalks out of the house.

Then he stalks back in. 'Okay, let's go to Australia. Pack your bag. I'll be back in three hours.'

It takes about five seconds to pack my bag. A few items of clothing and that's it. I'm thinking: *Australia? Unbelievable.* It's as if I'm playing the part of a kid from Somalia in a television drama. At each stage of the process that ends with me sitting on a lie-back seat on an aeroplane to Australia, my mind is telling me that I am an actor in the role of Abdi Aden. This whole thing isn't real, it's a show, it's for an audience.

Two hours later, we're at the train station in Bonn, where I expect my performance to end. Someone is going to say: 'Okay, kid, that's it, thanks for your time.'

Three and a half hours further along, we're at Frankfurt airport. I'm in a daze. I can't remember my lines. Another two hours and we're on a Lufthansa aeroplane, waiting to take off. Surely this can't go on any longer! Abu is going to say: 'No money, so you get off now.' But now the plane is in motion, heading for the runway. If we actually get into the air, then okay, I'll rethink this whole thing, I'll concede that it isn't a television show. But that won't happen – we'll never get into the air, never. Except that we do get into the air, way, way up in the air above Frankfurt, above Germany.

I say aloud, in Somali: 'Incredible! Madness!'

Abu, next to me, gives me a look full of suspicion. 'What is madness?' he says. 'What are you talking about?'

I give him a huge smile. 'Me? Nothing. Aiee!'

I begin to hum the tune of 'I Shot the Sheriff'.

I'm travelling on Abu's passport. I'm supposed to be his son. I'm in a crazy mood. First Bucharest, then Bonn, now a city with the name of 'Melbourne'. Seated here beside Abu, feeling no guilt or shame whatsoever for conning him in this way, I try to recall all that I know about Australia. First, it's a long way from Bonn. A very, very long way. Secondly, it's big, much bigger than Somalia, and most of the people are white, except for some black people who were there a long time before the white people. I've seen pictures of the black people of Australia. They were holding spears, almost naked, and they didn't look happy. I also happen to know that the great weapon of the black people of Australia is the boomerang. None of the black people in the picture I saw was holding a boomerang, but another picture showed a boomerang all by itself. And I have seen a picture of the most famous man in the whole of Australia, a man who wears steel armour to stop bullets killing him. I don't know his name. I don't know why people want to shoot bullets at him. Another picture showed this man without his steel armour. He looked nice enough; he had a big beard, like a mullah from Iran or Yemen.

The food on the plane is okay – I've chewed on acacia bark and eaten flying insects on my Somalia travels, so no complaints from me. The magazine of the Lufthansa company is full of pictures of beautiful wrist watches made by the Pierre Cardin people, also Rolex, jewellery for women, diamonds and gold. There's something called Microsoft, a big mystery, and a phone you carry around with you made by the Motorola company of America, as well as gowns for women and suits for men by Armani, which I happen to know about because one of the ministers in the stupid government of Siad Barre was criticised for spending money that was meant for immunising babies on Armani suits.

There are movies on the plane, a new one each two hours. I watch one about a man with a bow and arrow from the old days of England. Kevin Costner is the hero – I know him from *The Untouchables*, which was shown in Mogadishu with Somali language instead of English. And there's one about a pirate with a hook for a hand and a boy who can fly, and, best of all, *Teenage Mutant Ninja Turtles II*. In Bucharest I saw *Teenage Mutant Ninja Turtles I*, the best film ever in the world.

The aeroplane stops at Singapore, but only for two hours. The last part of the journey will take another eight hours. And then?

And then I have no idea. But once we return to the plane and take our seats, I know that I must tell Abu that there will be no money, not from Lula, not from my mother and father, not from me. Why do I want to tell him? I haven't been honest with him and now, after feeling completely free of guilt, I have a bad conscience.

Having said that, I make sure the plane is in the air and on its way to Australia before I mention anything about the money that is never going to come into the hands of Abu. I say: 'What happens when we get to Melbourne?'

And Abu says: 'We go to a hotel.'

'To a hotel?'

'Yes, to a hotel. And we stay there until the money comes.'

I look away for a few moments. Then: 'Sir, I have no money.'

'What?'

'I have no money.'

'Lula will send it.'

'Lula has no money.'

'Listen to me,' says Abu, twisting himself around in his seat, 'you told me that you could get the money. Your family has two houses in Mogadishu, maybe three houses. Lula said she'll get the money.'

'She can't get any money. There is none.'

Abu lifts his hand, as if he intends to hit me. Then he lowers his hand. He puts his face close to my ear. 'Hear me, you little rat. I'm going to call the steward. I'm going to have you thrown off the plane!'

Can he do that? Is it possible?

'Now, are you still going to tell me there's no money?'

I'm silent for a minute or more. Then I say: 'There is no money. I'm sorry.'

Abu hisses swear words in Somali and also, I think, in German. He lies back heavily in his seat, shaking his head. Every minute or so, he shoots me a look full of anger. What he says in Somali is too filthy to put down in these pages, but what he means is that I am the lying, thieving cub of a hyena and that I will go to hell.

Now we sit in silence, and the silence lasts for the rest of the journey.

CHAPTER 16

Australia

At Melbourne, we pass through Immigration without any trouble, although one officer does cast a questioning look in my direction. At the time, I could see no reason for any suspicion (except for the fact that I was not the son of Abukur mentioned in the passport) but, when I think back now, it must have been because of the colour of my skin. Other than Abu, all the people around me are white. I'm going to learn in the years ahead that the whole of this continent of Australia once belonged to people whose skin colour was much darker than my own, and that they were considered (for the most part) to be of no importance by the white people who took their ancestral lands from them. And I will learn, too, of what was known as the 'White Australia Policy' and slogans such as 'Australia for the white man'. But I come from a country where everyone is black or brown, coffee-coloured, chocolate-coloured, some blacker than boot leather. There is no colour discrimination in Somalia, not against dark-skinned people or fair-skinned people.

My first reaction when I came across discrimination against people with my skin colour was: 'Are you mad? You think I'm some sort of bad guy because my skin is dark?' But I know nothing about all this when the immigration officer eyes me with suspicion. If I had known, I would have been baffled. Black people from America, they know all about discrimination, but not people from Somalia.

The first blond-haired, fair skinned people I ever saw – this was in Mogadishu – made me want to clap and laugh. I'd seen such people in magazines but I'd never seen one in the flesh. I thought: *But this is crazy! How can a person live with such pale skin? It's unnatural! Surely they should be in hospital!* At the same time, these white people were fascinating. I followed them for a while, sure that they would soon collapse and be taken away in an ambulance.

Once we're through Immigration and Customs, Abu says: 'That's it.' He heads away towards a line of maybe twenty taxis at the rank outside. I watch him go with a twinge of regret. He was trying to make some money, and instead he cost himself a big pile of dollars. And yes, I suppose it would be a bit much to expect him to help me get to the city of Melbourne on top of helping get me from Bucharest to Australia. But I have a telephone number I can ring. Lula gave it to me. It's the number of a Somali guy who lives in a place called Brunswick, close to Melbourne. And apart from the telephone number, I have a US fifty-dollar note that Lula sent me in Bonn, which I have kept secret from Abu. It's hidden inside my belt. I haven't even allowed myself to think about it since it arrived from Italy. I thought: *Nuurow, forget it. If you think of it, you will spend it. So it's not there, okay? It doesn't exist.* But it exists now. I take it to the exchange and I'm given sixty-four Australian dollars and forty cents for it. In Bucharest, I could have found food and shelter for a week with a fifty-dollar note. In Australia, I don't know.

Now I should ring the Somali guy. I can't ring him *collectico*, as I would have if I were calling Lula. I have to use coins. I go to Tourist Information (I know the English words) and ask the lady there for help in calling the number. She points to a telephone booth, an open one, no door, and describes very carefully what I should do. I have just enough English words at my command to work out what she is saying. She writes the local number on a slip of paper for me, without the international numbers before it.

She's very helpful, and smiles a lot, and asks me something I don't understand. She leans towards me over the counter and says: 'Mama? Papa? Where?'

'Mama, Papa?' I say.

'Where? Mama, Papa?'

Now I get it. I also realise that it would be a bad idea to say that my mum and dad are in two other countries, on two other continents, and do not know that I'm in the city of Melbourne, Australia. So I put my clasped hands to the side of my head and make the sign of sleeping.

'Ah. Mama, Papa tired?'

I nod my head, without knowing what 'tired' means. Then I go over to the booth, study the dial for a minute or so, put a coin with a '20' on it into the slot and dial the number.

A woman's voice says something I don't understand; the line makes a buzzing sound. Then nothing.

I go to the woman at the information desk and act out a little pantomime to make her understand that the telephone isn't working. I shrug my shoulders, point at the telephone, point at my ear. The woman is kind enough to come over to the telephone. I still have a 20-cent coin worth of credit. She dials the number on the slip of paper, listens, hangs up then performs her own pantomime. She shows me the number on the paper. 'No good, no good,' she says.

I understand what 'no good' means. 'No good?' I say.

'No good.'

I say in my best English (I know maybe twenty words): 'I thanking you, madam.'

She is very pleased, and pats me on the arm before returning to her desk.

What I'm thinking is: *What the hell?*

I telephone Lula *collectico*. It is goodness knows what time in Rome. In Melbourne, it's five o'clock.

Lula answers.

'Where are you, baby boy?'

'I'm in Melbourne.'

Lula gives a shriek that nearly makes me deaf. 'In Melbourne? You got to Melbourne?'

'Sure.'

Again the shriek.

'Nuurow, I bless God for this amazing thing. I bless God, and also the god of the Australians. I bless all the gods of the world.'

And the shriek.

'Okay, listen Lula. That number you gave me. It's no good.'

'No good? How come?'

'I don't know. There is no answer.'

'Nuurow, listen to me. Ring me again in half an hour. I will find out.'

'Half an hour?'

'You can wait half an hour, baby boy? Aiee! In Australia! Such a good thing.'

Then she's gone.

The information lady is watching me. I give her a big smile. 'Okay,' I say. 'Okay. Good.'

She smiles and sighs and puts her hand over her heart.

To fill in the time for the next half an hour, I stand outside and watch what's happening. Lots of people waiting for taxis, but not Abu. He's gone. Lots of young people with backpacks, maybe having a holiday. Two pretty girls with shorts made by cutting the legs off jeans are chattering rapidly, I don't know in what language, maybe German. I want to look at the long, beautiful legs of the two girls, but I am too shy. So I look at the sky, which is very, very blue, almost the same blue as the skies of Somalia. And the weather is hot. It's near the end of the afternoon, but still hot. A great many cars come to the edge of the road and stop and pick people up – people who have just arrived from other countries, maybe, like the people on my Lufthansa aeroplane. A car comes and picks up the two pretty girls. I watch them put their backpacks into the boot and kiss the boy who is driving the car. I'm thinking: *The people in Australia are not shy. I should be like that. Not shy. Here, a man kisses a pretty girl while everyone is watching. Is this a good thing? I don't know. Maybe.* I think something else, too. I think: *I like it here. Australia, I think, will be a happy place for me. The sky is the right colour.*

When I call Lula back (*collectico*, once more), she says that the guy who had that number has changed it. 'I telephoned someone in Mogadishu. She says that too many people were ringing that guy up, so he changed his number. Somalis ringing him up from Germany and Romania. They want to come and stay with him. He changed his number.'

'So what do I do now?'

There's a worried sound in my voice, I know it.

Lula says: 'Baby boy, don't cry, don't cry. I have his new number. Aiee! Be brave in Australia, Nuurow! Be brave in Australia!'

I ring the new number, and this time a girl answers in Somali.

I say: 'I am calling from the airport in Melbourne.'

'Who the hell are you?' she says.

'I am Abdi. My friend gave me this number to call.'

'Your friend? What friend?'

I have to think quickly. 'Isak,' I say. My father's name is the first one that comes to mind.

'Isak? Really?'

'Sure.'

'And what do you want? Did you call yourself Abdul?'

'No, Abdi. I need somewhere to stay for the night. Just one night.'

'Yeah?' says the girl. 'Maybe one night is one year.'

'No, no. One night.'

'How old are you? You sound like a kid.'

'I am sixteen,' I say.

'Sixteen? Where's your mother? Where's your father?'

'In Mogadishu.'

'You're here by yourself?'

'Yes, by myself.'

'You poor kid! Stay where you are. I'll come and get you. Listen, I'm driving a red Honda. You understand? Wait near the taxis. I'll come and get you.'

It sometimes pays to be a kid. This girl I've just spoken to – I still don't know her name – was full of suspicion until she heard how young I am. Even so, I only have one night's shelter – my first night in Australia.

Back in school in Mogadishu, I knew two or three facts about this Australia I've come to, and those two or three facts meant I probably knew more about this country than anyone else in Somalia. So here I am, I know about the ratio of humans to animals, but what good is that going to do me? This is the third continent on which I have been homeless in the space of a year. Is it my fate to visit every continent on earth, and find myself begging for shelter?

Because that's what I am – a beggar. A very well-travelled beggar, but a beggar nonetheless.

A red Honda. Okay, I know what a red Honda looks like. I've seen Hondas in Mogadishu and in Bonn. I always look for the name of a car when I get the chance. I know what most of the Toyota range looks like, also Mitsubishi. Volvos I know immediately. And Cadillacs – there were a few Cadillacs in Mogadishu, owned by people high up in the army. It's either a Cadillac or a Rolls-Royce for you if you've succeeded in robbing the Somali people for a few years. But okay, a red Honda. I stand near the taxi rank and wait.

Sure enough, the red Honda appears, driven by a young woman with a man in the passenger seat. I raise my hand, and the Honda pulls up close to me. The young woman motions to me. It is very strange because the driver's seat is on the wrong side. Then I understand. I've been watching the traffic without realising that all the cars are driving on the left side of the road instead of the right, which is normal. If I were back in Mogadishu, in Siad Barre Government School, I'd be able to say about Australia: 'They drive their cars on the wrong side of the road. They're insane.'

Once in the car, the young woman introduces herself as Iishe. The man, older than Iishe, is Mohammad. Iishe drops Mohammad off at another house in Brunswick before continuing on to her own place.

Iishe's apartment in the suburb of Brunswick is fairly new and comfortable. I'm shown where I'll sleep, I'm fed, I'm asked if I want to take a shower. Iishe shares the house with her three children, two little boys and a girl. After I shower, I sit on the sofa with her and answer a hundred questions about Mogadishu and the political situation in Somalia. What can I tell her?

She asks if it's dangerous in Mogadishu and I say: 'It's very dangerous.' She asks me if things will quieten down in a few months. I say: 'Not in a few months, not in a few years.' I think she wants me to say something hopeful, but I would have to lie. The truth is that we Somalis no longer have a country. It's just a patch of earth where people are murdered by the hundreds each day. Even talking about it, answering Iishe's questions, makes me depressed.

At eight o'clock in the evening, when Iishe is studying, I take myself outside and stand by the gate. The light is fading from the sky, but it is still warm. I can hear the sounds of the traffic from a main road not so far away. I can hear the rattle of a tram. The grey wooden lampposts, I notice, still reveal the shape of the trees from which they are made. On the wires sit four birds, black and white, unlike any I have seen in Somalia. When they throw back their heads and sing, their song is so musical you'd think they had been taught to make this sound by a master teacher. The houses across the street from me are older than Iishe's apartment block. This apartment block of Iishe's is pale blue. The two houses closest to me on the far side of the street are both white, and each has a letterbox. In the front yard of one house, a child's toy car has been left on a concrete path. It's an orange car, metal, with stripes down the sides. There's also a football, but not like any football I have seen before, sort of stretched out rather than round, a reddish colour. In the front yard of the other house, a child's bike rests against the stone side of an ornamental fountain. No water is coming from the fountain for the time being. A car is parked in the driveway of each one. Even from where I stand, looking at the boot of each car, I can tell that one is a Mitsubishi Magna, dark blue, a fairly big car. The other car is a make I haven't seen before, not in Mogadishu and not in Bonn.

A little distance away, three small children and two women who may be their mothers are standing on the footpath talking to each other, waving their hands about, laughing every now and again. Two of the children are playing a simple game of tag, circling the two women with shrieks of delight. As they circle the women, they sometimes bump into them and one woman or the other reaches down and shoves the child away, not roughly. The third child, the youngest, is sitting on a grass strip between the kerb and the footpath that runs the whole length of the house – it's the same in front of all the other houses. This child is talking to a dolly with red hair, sometimes smoothing the dolly's hair, sometimes holding her up and shaking a finger as if angry with it. The three children are girls, as far as I can tell from the length of their hair. They are all wearing pants that are not really jeans but like jeans.

The thing that interests me so much is that one of the women is white while the other is black. The black woman is not Somali, more like a Kikuyu from Kenya, to judge by her features and also the English she is speaking – many more Kenyans than Somalis speak English. The black woman is dressed in Western clothes – a bright summer dress, thongs on her feet – except for her scarf, which is Kenyan, a red and green scarf tied up so that it sits high. It's not a Muslim scarf but one that probably tells what clan she is from in her Kikuyu tribe. And of the children, two are black. It gives me a strange pleasure to see the two mothers speaking together and the three children playing happily. As I have said, I haven't had much experience of racism in my life, but I know from television how much of it there is in the world. I know that black people in America came there as slaves, at least their forefathers did, and that for many years, centuries, the black people of America suffered badly and had no rights, and could be hanged from trees by their necks by the white people, who feared no arrest. I have seen all this on Somali television. I have seen a television show called *Roots*, which was dubbed into Somali, about the black people of places such as Carolina and Georgia and Louisiana. And something else I know is this: that some of those black people may have been captured in Somalia and taken to America and lived the rest of their lives as slaves. It could even be that some of my ancestors were amongst them. So a person with skin my colour knows that white people are capable of looking at them with contempt, for no reason or for reasons too stupid even to talk about. When I see the black children of the Kenyan woman and the white child of the Australian woman playing games together, and the women themselves so friendly with each other, I think: *I will stay here in this country of Australia. This is where I will make my stand. I have a good feeling about this place. I am not going to find a fourth continent to try my luck. Here, this is where I try my luck. In Australia.*

The two women notice me standing by the apartment block letterboxes, and both of them wave to me. Maybe they know Iishe and believe I am her relative. I wave back, and smile.

★

The next day, Iishe takes me to Mohammad's place, also in Brunswick, where I'm to stay for a few days. Mohammad is a factory worker, not a student. I ask him what I'll need to do to remain in Australia, but he's evasive. 'Just stay,' he says. 'Do nothing.'

'But I want to go to school. I want to get a job.'

'You can get a job maybe.'

'How?'

'How? The same as me,' he says. 'You work for the right people – they don't ask you any questions. Tomorrow I take you to a place near here. It's a charity place. It's run by Christians, but they help Muslims, no problem.'

I think for a minute. The idea of a strategy comes back into my head. I say to myself: *Abdi, do what is clever. This guy, he's not thinking straight.*

'I want to go to Immigration,' I say.

'No, not now,' says Mohammad.

'Why not?'

'Why not? Because it's not the right time.'

'Why is it not the right time?'

Mohammad shakes his head and waves a hand at me.

'Tell me, please, why is it not the right time?'

'Listen to me, kid. You want to stay here in my house, you listen to me. It's not the right time.'

So I shut up. But I'm concerned. There's something a bit shifty about this guy. What it is, I don't know, but my instincts tell me that he's, well, like I say, a bit shifty. The thing is, I'm serious about this country of Australia. I want to stay. I don't want to be living in the shadows. I don't want to be a ghost. I want to go to Immigration and say: 'My name is Abdi Aden. My country is Somalia. But in Somalia they want to kill me. Believe me, they've already tried. So let me stay here. I'm clever, I can work hard. Also, I'm good-looking. Keep me.'

Next day, Mohammad takes me to the place he was speaking about, the charity. It's called City Mission. It's in the suburb of Brunswick, not so far from us. It's in a street called Albion Street. Mohammad makes me remember the name. As I write this, I am spelling 'Albion' as if I knew exactly how to pronounce it in English. But at the time, I could barely say the name. 'Albion' is difficult for Somali speakers. I pronounced it 'Yarrby Yam' Street'.

At the City Mission there's a lot of activity. On the walls are posters, some showing people who are dark-skinned, some showing Asian people. The writing everywhere is in English mostly, also some Asian languages, maybe Chinese, maybe also Vietnamese, I'm not sure. A number of Asian people are here today, too. From where, I don't know. And some people who look Asian, but may not be.

I ask Mohammad: 'Where are these people from?'

'The country of Burma,' he says.

I nod towards some of the Asian people. 'What about them?'

'Them? Vietnam.'

I can see some Kenyans, too. And some dark-skinned people who are not Somalis and not Kenyans.

'Them?'

'Zimbabwe.'

'In Africa?'

'Of course in Africa. What do you think?'

'Where are the Somalis?'

'The Somalis come on Tuesday. Different countries come on different days.'

'Do we have to come back on Tuesday?'

'Tuesday' in Somali is *Talado*.

Mohammad looks at me in an annoyed way. 'No, we don't have to come back on Tuesday. You're such a *doqon yahow*.'

Doqon yahow means 'idiot'.

'You think I'm an idiot?'

'Sure. You know nothing. You should have stayed in Somalia. Listen, in Australia, so many different people from one hundred countries. More. Maybe two hundred. They can come any day they like. But some of them organise themselves so they are all here on one day. Do you see?'

'Yes. Certainly.'

I feel stung by being called a *doqon yahow*. I take pride in my brain. 'What now?' I ask Mohammad, who is himself an idiot, as far as I'm concerned.

'Now you wait to see the lawyer.'

'A lawyer? Yeah?'

'A lawyer. And maybe he'll help you. You don't want to go to Immigration until you see a lawyer.'

'Why do I need a lawyer?'

Mohammad rolls his eyes. 'Why does he need to see a lawyer?' he says, as if he's talking to the wall. *'Ilahey amarkis badanaa.* How did you get here? On your own passport?'

What Mohammad said in Somali means 'God give me strength'. It's what you say when someone is driving you crazy. Me, I'm only trying to understand.

'Not on my own passport,' I say. 'I left it in Europe.'

'Okay, not on your own passport. That means you've broken the law, idiot. Why don't you just go to the police and say: 'I'm Abdi Aden. I broke the law. Better you put me in prison! You talk to the lawyer.'

A couple of the children of the women here from Zimbabwe come over to where I'm sitting on a bench against the wall. They stand before me and stare at me. One, a girl, is about six; the boy is about eight. The older one says something to me I don't understand. I think he's speaking English. About Zimbabwe, I know nothing. Maybe they speak English in Zimbabwe.

'What's he saying?' I ask Mohammad, who speaks much more English than me.

'He wants to know if you play cricket.'

'If I play what?'

'Cricket. It's a game they play in Australia, also in Zimbabwe. Wherever the English went, they took cricket with them. The English were in Zimbabwe. You know that, don't you?'

'Of course,' I say, but I didn't know it at all.

Mohammad says: 'It's an insane game. The Australians play it all through summer. Let me tell you the most insane thing. They play a game that lasts five days. Five days! Maybe after five days, no one wins. Ridiculous. This kid doesn't know where you are from. He thinks you might be from one of these cricket-playing countries.'

Mohammad speaks to the boy in English. The boy makes a face, as if to say 'What are you talking about?'

'What did you say?' I ask Mohammad.

'I said the game of cricket is for morons. And I said if he plays the game, then he is a moron.'

That seems harsh. I smile at the boy. I say: 'Cricket good, very good.'

He's pleased, and goes back to his mother satisfied.

'This is what you have to understand about Australians,' Mohammad says. 'The people are like children. They have never seen anything bad. They think only about sunshine and sport. Children.'

The people at the City Mission are kind and cheerful. I haven't met many Christians face-to-face, but if these people are like all the other Christians then let me meet more. What I know about Christianity makes no sense at all – people who can walk on water and make one fish feed a hundred people. But the information I have comes from here and there, little bits and pieces, so maybe I've got it wrong. Who cares? Christians, Muslims, Buddhists, Hindus – all fine by me, so long as they're kind and they're not interested in murder.

The mission people give me chocolate biscuits called Tim Tams to take home, and tins of spaghetti (very strange – I have never before in my life seen spaghetti in tins), also something called baked beans, and rice, pasta sauce already made in a jar, a carton of cow's milk, bananas and oranges and, craziest of all, a plastic package containing what are called frozen peas. I am very grateful and say in my poor English: 'Very good, thank you everything.'

As it turns out, the City Mission is not the place where I am to meet the lawyer. That is at another place called Legal Aid in the city called Fitzroy. Mohammad takes me there two days later. The lawyer is a good man. He is fairly young, his fair hair is messy and his collar is a little bit too big for his neck. None of this matters. He's a good man and he wants to help me if he can. The only ID I can show him is my birth certificate. He says the Australian government needs photo ID before any claim for political asylum will be considered. All of this is translated for me not by Mohammad, who sits beside me saying nothing, but by an interpreter who works for the City Mission. He is Somali, but not from my tribe. His accent sounds like he might be from the north.

'Can you obtain photo ID?' the interpreter asks me.

'Only on my birth certificate.'

'How old is the picture?'

'Seven years old. Eight years. Maybe ten. More.'

'Hmm. Too bad.' He speaks to the lawyer for a minute or so then addresses me once more. 'It might be possible to lodge a claim for political asylum without photo ID,' he says. 'This gentleman will make enquiries. And he will make an appointment for you with Immigration in three months from now.'

CHAPTER 17

Temporary

I am moved the next day to another house in Brunswick. Mohammad has had enough of me. The guy at this new house is called Rashid. He is also Somali. It is not difficult to move me to a new house. All I own in the world is a small bag with a few clothes in it. There is a term in English that I didn't know at this time I am speaking about now, but which I came to learn years later. It is 'travelling light'. That is me. I travel light. If I was travelling any lighter, I would barely exist. Isn't it an astonishing thing that we can at one stage of our lives own nothing, just our skin and eyes and brain and bones and, at a later stage, live with ten thousand items we've purchased – house, sofa, armchairs; drawers and cupboards in the kitchen overflowing with all manner of things; and then there's the refrigerator, the dishwasher; in others rooms a great monster of a television set and a CD player and a DVD player, and more rooms with beds and bedding and chests of drawers and wardrobes bursting with clothes for hot days, cold days, every day in between, not just one pair of shoes but thirty between all the members of the family; toys galore, gadgets, goodness knows what; and outside a car, maybe two cars, a garage packed with things you no longer have a use for, swings in the back yard, garden tools, on and on and on. In Somalia, my family lived a happy life (for a time, at least) with

about one fifth of what we own in Australia. But I'm not going back to the Somali way of life.

Rashid is friendlier than Mohammad. He's also more encouraging. He says: 'Sure, go to Immigration. Everyone knows what's happening in Somalia. Everybody knows people want to get the hell out of there. And look at you. A kid. Why would a kid be going all over the world unless he was afraid of what he's left behind? You know what they're going to say? They're going to say: 'Okay, kid, we believe you.' They're going to give you a big house for yourself and maybe your girlfriend. Have you got a girlfriend? No? Too bad. In Australia you need a girlfriend. Nice Muslim girl just for you. I'll fix you up. I'll talk to this guy I know who has thirty daughters, each one more beautiful than the next. You like that?'

I'm smiling, of course. 'The Australians are not going to give me a house. And you don't know anyone with thirty daughters.'

Rashid says: 'Did I say thirty? I meant forty. Forty beautiful daughters. Believe me.'

While I'm waiting for the three months to pass before I go to Immigration I wander around the neighbourhood, just taking an interest in what I see. Not so many people in Australia. On the footpaths in Mogadishu, there are thousands of people. You learn to walk in a special way in Mogadishu, weaving around so you don't bump into anyone, taking quick steps to the side. There's no such thing as just walking straight ahead. But here in Brunswick, there's no need to weave, no need to jump out of the way when you're on the road. People in Australia drive their cars in straight lines, the same as when they're walking. In Mogadishu, if you cross the road you have to be an athlete. Nobody will stop if you're in the way. Australians are – what can I say? – Australians are very well behaved. In the cafes, the customers wait near the counter to place an order. If somebody is about to be served before it's his turn, he points to the person who was there before him. And at the tables in the cafe, the customers talk softly or read a book or a newspaper. In Mogadishu, you walk into a cafe and shout above the noise of the radio, maybe the television, also the CDs that the cafe boss is playing at top volume. You say: 'Hey Bilaal, bring me an espresso, my man! Hey Bilaal, play that Madonna song, you know the one I like. Hey Bilaal, what's the matter with you? I'm still waiting for my espresso after five hours! Hey, you want me to go across the street? Is that what you want? Hey, put on that Bon Jovi song, my man!' I didn't say things like that – of course not, I was just a kid in Mogadishu – but that's what my dad and his friends would say.

It's very quiet in the cafes of Brunswick. Too quiet. I miss the noise.

While I'm out walking I see a couple of Somali guys, older than me. And they see me. I wave my hand at them – they're on the other side of the street. And they wave back. I wait for a tram to go past, then I go over to talk to them. They are not Rahanweyn, but Yibir, from the north. It doesn't matter so much in Brunswick if you're Yibir or Rahanweyn – it matters a little, but not much. The Yibir make up one of the poorer classes of Somali society – many Somalis consider them outcasts. They have a secret language that they never speak to anyone but another Yibir, but they speak Somali too. Like I say, it doesn't matter so much in Brunswick if you are Yibir, but in Mogadishu, if you are Yibir, people won't speak to you. One of the guys is called Yaquub and the other is Hanif. Both are very tall, like the northern Somalis. Many Yibir are strange, but Yaquub and Hanif must have spent time in the big cities because they are cool, like my dad.

Yaquub says: 'How you like Australia, my brother?'

I say: 'I'm staying.'

And Yaquub and Hanif laugh out loud. 'We know you're staying, little brother!' says Yaquub. 'What do you think, you go back to Somalia? Whoo hoo! That's crazy!'

'This is the place,' says Hanif. 'You been to Big Europe?'

'Sure. To Germany.'

'Better than Germany. Sunshine, little brother! Here you get sunshine. Germany, your eyeballs freeze in your head. You got your protection permit?' Hanif says 'protection permit' in English. I don't know what he's talking about.

'What?'

'Protection permit, my brother. You know that? You been to Immigration?'

'Not yet. I've been to a place called Legal Aid. I go to Immigration in two and a half months.'

'You better get your permit, kid. Then you go to Social Security. You get money, dollars, every two weeks, one hundred and forty dollars. You go to school, maybe get a job. Plenty of jobs here, I promise you. Maybe you can be a waiter. Each week, four hundred dollars, six shifts. You know what is a "shift"? Okay, I tell you for when you get a job. You work one day, that's one shift. You work six days, that's six shifts. Pretty good.'

And off they go, Yaquub and Hanif. One thing I can tell you for sure, Hanif and Yaquub were not as happy as this in Somalia. Even before the war, the Yibir had a hard, hard time. Some Somalis say the Yibir are not true Muslims. They say the Yibir come from the Jews of Ethiopia. And a lot of them are fortune tellers and magicians. Sure! Lots of them. A strange thing I have to tell you now. Even here in Brunswick, I feel a little bit of that superiority to the Yibir that I would have felt in Somalia. I think Somali culture is so deep in me that it will be there even if I live in Australia for a hundred years.

My life becomes that of a nomad, but a nomad of the city. I move from one Somali household to another. Giving shelter to a fellow Somali, whatever his or her tribe, is a strong part of Somali culture, stronger, in fact, amongst Somali refugees than it is in Somalia. Back in my native land, if I turned up on the doorstep of Somalis of a tribe that had some grievance against my Rahanweyns, the wife or husband of that household would say: 'Rahanweyn? Get out of here!' But in Melbourne, all Somalis feel as if they are in the same boat. Well, up to a point. The members of some families I stay with still look at me with suspicion, as if they want to be rid of me as soon as possible. Some say: 'Two days you can stay, kid, then you move on.' But I must also say that many Somali families are very generous to me, and share the little food they have without scowling.

Apart from the food I'm given by the City Mission, I get other food from the Red Cross office in South Melbourne. The people there are just as kind to me as the City Mission people. 'Learn English,' says a woman there who is as old as a grandmother.

'English?'

'Yes. Learn English.'

Okay, I'll try to learn English. When I'm watching television at the many houses I go to for shelter, I try to understand a few words. I ask the Somalis who can speak some English what the people on the television are saying. 'Who is "mate"?' I ask.

'"Mate" is "friend",' I'm told.

'Friend?'

'Sure. "Mate" is friend. It is only for men, not for women. A woman is not a "mate".'

Then there's an argument between two of the Somalis. One is saying that a woman can also be 'mate'. The other says, no, a woman can never be 'mate'. The first one says that a wife is a 'mate'. The other says that the first one is insane – a wife is not a 'mate'.

But I manage to learn a few words, then a few more. I can speak sentences – not so many, but some. I can say: 'I am going to the shops' and 'It is nine o'clock' and 'Do you want something from Maccas?' and also 'Does this tram go to Melbourne?'

I see more of the city, too. Flinders Street station is magnificent, so many trains going and coming and going and coming. I see the department stores – Myer, mostly. So much for sale, like the shops at Frankfurt airport, only more. In the place for men's clothes, I try on shirts and trousers and jeans and jumpers, but I can't afford any of them. I have to say I look pretty good in these new clothes. I say to my reflection: 'Nuurow, you are a handsome devil.' I make a promise to myself: when I have a job and money, I'll buy ten pairs of jeans, ten shirts, ten new pairs of shoes.

It's a strange thing, but it's when you are mixed in with a great big crowd that you really know who you are and where you belong. In Mogadishu, when I was mixed up in a big crowd at the market or in the street, it felt natural. I was one of these people, I was Somali, I was the same. When I'm amongst a crowd of Australians in the big Myer department store, for example, it's then that I know I don't yet belong. People glance at my face and I know they're thinking: *Who's this kid? Where's he from?* It's not just that my skin is dark while most of the Australians around me are fair-skinned. The other people can feel that I am an outsider, that I don't understand a thousand things about Australia that they have known all their lives. When you belong to a society, you are tied to it with many, many invisible threads. It will take me years – ten years, twenty years – before I understand even a small part of what an Australian who is born here knows in his bones, deep in his heart. It would be the same if a native Australian came to Somalia. He might live in Somalia for decades and carefully study everything in Somali culture – he might learn twenty dialects of Somali – and still he would be a stranger.

One of the things that I will come to know in the years ahead is that one people can have a great deal of sympathy for another people – Australians for Somalis, say – but we can never truly know what it is to be Australian, we can never know what it is to be Somali. Even today, Australians will say to me: 'You must have been so happy to get out of that hellhole and find safety in Australia.' 'Sure!' I say. But let me tell you the truth. I still love Somalia. The bloodshed, the violence, the drug-maddened soldiers with their guns, the poverty – all of that is horrible, but I love Somalia all the same.

★

When I take the tram to the Red Cross office, I can see the beach at South Melbourne from the window. It's not summer anymore, and not so many people are in the water. But it's a nice beach. The beach at Mogadishu is a little bit better, but the South Melbourne beach is okay. Everything I see in Melbourne makes me want to stay, but I have to say that I feel anxious about my appointment at Immigration and whether they'll *let* me stay. The other refugees I meet in Melbourne tell me to behave like a proper refugee. 'Tell Immigration that they tortured you with a big knife,' they say. Well, I'm not going to do that. Some lies are necessary, some are not. And one refugee who is not from Somalia but can speak Somali and has a temporary protection permit says: 'Kid, you have to look like a refugee. You have to sound like a refugee. I'll tell you something. No matter what Immigration says to you, don't laugh, don't smile. You understand me? Talk about the bad things that happened to you. Okay, you don't want to say you were tortured. What about starvation? You were starved, right? Talk about that. You saw dead people? Okay, talk about dead people, lots of dead people. You see?'

I say: 'I'm not going to do that.'

After almost three months, I have a lot of experience of the refugee scene in Melbourne. The refugee community is really three communities: those who desperately want to remain in Australia and spend every day worrying themselves half to death; those who expect to be thrown out of Australia and have given up worrying about it; and those who are very confident that they will be given permanent residency in time and don't worry at all. Each of these communities is made up of a number of nationalities: Somalis; Kurds from Turkey, Kurds from Iraq, Kurds from Iran, Kurds from nowhere; Iraqis; Iranians; Sudanese; Ethiopians; Eritreans; Burmese; Cambodians; Chinese; Vietnamese; Afghanis. And more. The members of each nationality believe that they have suffered more than the members of every other nationality. The Iraqis think: *This woman from Sudan, some bad guys set fire to her village and shot a few people. So what? In my village they killed everyone except me.* Each group of refugees keeps count of the permits that have been given out to other groups. Often people get jealous if one group is getting more permits than another. They say: 'The Australian government loves the Iranians. You're from Iran, they give you a permit if you feel a little bit depressed. We Ethiopians, we just about have to hang ourselves before they pay any attention. The Iranians can go to hell.'

All this jealousy and anger – I don't want anything to do with it. Nothing. I hated the tribal and clan rivalries in Somalia, and I hate what goes on here. I can truthfully say that I give every Somali my support in his or her struggle for a new life. I am happy, very happy, when someone succeeds in getting a TPP or permanency. Many of the Somalis are big-hearted, generous people, and I try to hang around them more than those who have hours and hours of complaints. I think: *I was spared death, I was saved, I should be dead. Have I come all this way to Melbourne, Australia, to argue and complain? Is that why I was spared?*

I am watching too much television. I see *Hey Hey It's Saturday*. I don't understand any of it. A lot of laughter. People sing and dance; some of them do tricks. I don't understand. The Somalis who are watching it with me, they know much more than I do. They laugh their heads off. They say: 'He's a bad guy.'

'Who's a bad guy?' I ask.

'Red. He's the bad guy. He's the best.'

Sometimes I laugh just to be polite.

Another show is called *Doctor Who*. This, I understand a little bit. But not much. Best is *Neighbours*, about Australian people talking and arguing and kissing. It's easy to follow, even without knowing English. Also, *A Country Practice*, which is about doctors and a hospital. Everyone talks and argues and kisses. Not bad.

But I have to do something else. I can't sit around watching television and waiting for a letter from Immigration. The next time I am at the Red Cross office, I say that I want to be a volunteer. That means you work without any pay. That's okay, I'm happy to work without any pay. The Red Cross people give me a job in the tracing department. It's like this: you send out information to other Red Cross offices all over the world. The information says: 'Feysal Rahim from Somalia is looking for his wife, Isra, and his children, Galaal, Calas, Amran and Aamino. If you have any information, please reply.' This is just an example. My job is to check the replies that come back from Somalis.

The English is difficult for me, but I can deal with the replies from Somalis without any trouble. I usually do ten checks a day, then I do one for myself. I have sent out a message for my mother and father and sister, Jamila. I have some hope – maybe not all that much – that I will be sent a reply. But I check each day that I'm at the Red Cross office. It would be such a day of joy for me if I heard from my mother and, if by some great miracle, that my sister was still alive in the world, such a day of joy that I am afraid to even think about it, because really, it won't happen. It won't happen. Or it might. Sometimes I whisper: 'Abdi, Nuurow, please, please don't give up hope. It might happen.' But it won't.

Other Somalis ask me about my family and when I speak of my mother and my father and my sister, I usually say that Isak and Aalima are still alive, but that Jamila is dead, that she died in the war a year ago. I don't know any details, but that's the account I usually give. When I say that Jamila is dead, I am asked if I have held a *tacsiyo* for her – a *tacsiyo* is a Somali ritual gathering honouring the passing of a relative. I have to confess that I haven't yet held a *tacsiyo* for Jamila, which is shameful. So finally I do.

Jamila's *tacsiyo* is held in the house of a Somali friend in Brunswick. Singing, food, prayers. That's a *tacsiyo*. Since I can't even be certain that Jamila is dead, maybe I shouldn't be holding a *tacsiyo*. But really, it doesn't matter. If you honour someone with a tacsiyo and that person turns out to be alive, nobody minds. People just think: *No problem. We'll have another tacsiyo when you die next time.* During Jamila's *tacsiyo*, sure, I sing, I pray. But I also weep. I will never have another sister. I weep.

CHAPTER 18

A Place of Safety

The day finally comes when I am to take myself to the Department of Immigration offices in King Street and make my claim for asylum. I know what 'asylum' means. When I was at Legal Aid, the lawyer explained it to me through the interpreter. It means that I have run away from Somalia because bad people want to murder me. It means that the bad people are still waiting to murder me if I go back to Somalia. The bad people have the guns. People like me have no guns. That is the meaning of asylum. Also, I know what the word 'asylum' itself means. It means what in Somali we would call *meesha quduuska ah*, meaning 'sanctuary', a place of safety. That's exactly what I'm looking for – a place of safety. Over centuries and centuries, probably thousands of years, people in different places in the world have left their own lands looking for sanctuary, for safety. I am at the end of a long, long line of people who ran away from murder. And, you know, years later than this day of my visit to the offices of the Australian Department of Immigration, I will hear of the story of how Jesus and his parents ran away from murder in their homeland to Egypt. So perhaps Jesus and his mum and dad were asylum seekers, the same as me. My road to the immigration office also took me through Egypt.

The immigration officer whose job it is to talk to me is a man of forty or so. He wears a jumper without any sleeves over a pale blue shirt and a tie with an awful striped pattern on it. He doesn't smile much. The interpreter worries me. He's Somali, of course, but not of my tribe and with small scars on his face. He seems hostile the minute he sees me, as if I'd thrown a rock through his window back in Mogadishu. Whenever the officer asks me a question, the interpreter seems to me to be adding a bit of his own on.

'He wants to know exactly when you arrived in Australia,' he says, and then: 'Do you know how to tell the truth?'

Do I know how to tell the truth? Why does he say that?

'On 18 January 1992.'

The interpreter repeats my answer in English.

'Where is your passport?'

'I came here on another man's passport.'

'Is that right?' the interpreter says in Somali. 'On another man's passport? And how would that be possible, unless the other man is your father?'

'He isn't my father. He let me travel on his passport.'

'As if you were his son is what you're saying?'

'Yes.'

'That's dishonest.'

'I suppose so. I'm sorry.'

The interpreter turns back to the officer, who has been listening with a blank face, and speaks for what seems about three or four minutes in English.

The officer raises his eyebrows. Then he writes something on a form on the desk before him. I notice that the officer has a picture on his desk in a frame. From where I sit, I can just see that it's a photograph of the officer with a woman and two children, a boy and a girl. The boy is about my age. In the picture, the officer is wearing almost exactly what he's wearing now, except he's left off the awful tie, and the jumper with no sleeves in the photograph is different to the one he's wearing now. The woman, I have to say, looks a bit too pretty for the officer.

I am asked many more questions. My answers are short but the interpreter's answers continue to be long. I'm thinking: *Is this guy being paid by the number of words he uses? Is he trying to stretch this out?*

While the interpreter is giving his lengthy translations, I gaze around at the posters on the office walls. One is a black and white photograph of a crowd of people waving from the decks of a ship. I have seen ships at the port in Mogadishu, but ones that carry oil, not people. These people must be coming to Australia, that's what I think. They all look happy. Parents are holding up small children so the children can wave. Maybe they're waving to people who have come to meet them. Hundreds of people waving. Not one is black. I can't read the English print under the picture but I can read the numerals: 1954. I wish I had come here by ship, like all these white people.

More questions. I am asked: 'You are from Mogadishu?'

'Sure, from Mogadishu.'

'Who was the president of Somalia when you were there?'

'Who was the president? The president was Siad Barre.'

'And what colour is the main post office in Mogadishu?'

What the hell? What colour is the main post office? How would I know? It might be blue or orange or yellow or rainbow-coloured. I've never noticed. What's the matter with this immigration officer with the pretty wife? Does he think I am just pretending to be a Somali? And the interpreter knows perfectly that I am indeed Somali. He knows that I speak Somali. He knows that I speak four dialects of Somali. He knows that I am Rahanweyn. What is the use of these questions?

I say: 'It's green. The post office is green.'

Then I am asked through the suspicious interpreter: 'What is the biggest city in Somalia?'

What's the biggest city? Is this guy completely insane? What is the biggest city?

'The biggest city is Mogadishu.'

I hear the interpreter say 'Mogadishu' to the immigration officer, who nods his head.

'What language is spoken in Somalia?'

Okay, now I know the officer is insane. What language is spoken in Somalia? What language does he think? Russian? I am speaking the language that is spoken in Somalia!

I say: 'Somali. In many dialects. Also Arabic. Some people speak Italian. A few speak English.'

The interpreter says only one word to the officer: 'Somali.' And again the officer nods his head and makes a mark on the form in front of him.

The officer with the pretty wife asks me a few more questions. I am told that these questions are known as 'local knowledge'. I am asked what colour the trams are in Mogadishu. I don't say anything for a minute. I'm thinking carefully, in case this is a trick question. Then I say in English: 'No trams in Mogadishu.'

The officer seems impressed. For the first time, he smiles at me. Is it possible that a battle is going on between the interpreter and the officer? It could be that the interpreter wants to send me back to Somalia, while the officer is thinking he could let me stay.

'No trams in Mogadishu?' says the officer.

And I say a second time: 'No trams in Mogadishu.'

The interpreter is scowling.

I will be told by mail whether or not my application for asylum has been accepted. So after all the questions, I don't know what has been decided. The translator tells me the immigration officer with the pretty wife will have some news for me in a few months. A letter will be sent to me. Fortunately, I have come prepared with an address that I can use for months.

I return to the house at which I am living for the time being – not the same house as my 'permanent address'. The Somalis at the house, a husband, a wife and a couple of cousins, ask me how I went at the immigration office.

'I don't know,' I say.

'Did you tell them the truth?'

'Sure. The truth.'

'Aiee, aiee, aiee!'

Then we sit on the sofa together and watch *Home and Away*. This is a show like *Neighbours*, except set near the beach.

The wife whispers to me: 'I hope you have a big success.'

The husband, on the other side of me, says: 'They'll send you back to Somalia, kid. Believe me. A man with an AK will shoot you. Sorry.'

After a few minutes, the husband says to me: 'You know why they want to send you back to Somalia?'

'No.'

'Because your skin is brown. Believe me.'

I say: 'But your skin is brown and you have a TPP.'

'That's because I'm an electrician. The Australians need electricians. But you know nothing.'

I'm worried about the immigration officer with the pretty wife. I think he has doubts. The truth is, I didn't tell him the full story. I said that I flew to Germany from Mogadishu, then flew to Melbourne from Frankfurt by Lufthansa. If I'd told him I first flew to Bucharest, he'd have said: 'Very interesting. Why didn't you ask for asylum in Romania?' He wanted to know why I didn't stay in Germany and ask for asylum there. I told him that my ticket from the airport in Mogadishu was for a flight all the way to Australia, with a transit stopover in Germany. I had to lie. But everything else I told him was the truth.

The more I think about my interview, the more I feel that the immigration department is going to send policemen to put me on an aeroplane back to Mogadishu. But here's the crazy thing. I don't care. If the Australians don't want me, that's okay, I'll go back to Somalia and try to stay alive. Probably get shot, but until I get shot, I'll try to stay alive. The thing that frightens me is looking like a criminal. People will see me being taken away; maybe I'll be forced to wear handcuffs. Nobody who sees me being taken away will know the true story. People will think: *That kid must have killed someone. That kid must be a robber. That kid must have been telling lies to the Department of Immigration.* I would burn up with shame.

★

I want a job. I'm desperate. I try at one place and another, but who wants a Somali kid with not much English? I am always asked: 'Have you had any experience?' This means experience of pushing a wheelbarrow around filled with bricks or stacking supermarket shelves, that sort of thing, and I have to be honest and say no. I am always told: 'Come back when you've had a bit of a go.' And so, for the sake of 'experience', I accept a job from a Turkish guy who wants me to cook meat then pack it into blocks. The special thing about this job is that I am not paid a cent. The Turkish guy says: 'I'm doing you a favour.'

I accept the deal, which is no deal at all. The job is horrible. The meat stinks. But I keep going to the meat plant for weeks, and then for weeks more. The Somali families I stay with still feed me, sure, but I want to pay my own way. Getting paid nothing is not going to help me pay my way. Finally I tell the Turkish guy I'm leaving. I'm courteous about it. He says nothing – only shrugs his shoulders.

★

In September 1992, I receive a letter in the mail from the immigration people. I ask one of my Somali friends to translate it for me. I could probably read it myself, but I don't want to get anything wrong. The letter tells me that I have been awarded a temporary protection permit. I am entitled to enrol in a secondary school. I am entitled to a payment of one hundred and forty dollars per fortnight from the Department of Social Security.

The letter tells me many other things, some of them in the nature of warnings. A booklet is enclosed in which many more warnings are found. And there is a date, two weeks away, when I am supposed to go the Department of Immigration office and accept my TPP.

My Somali friend who is reading the letter jumps up from the sofa, pulls me to my feet and demands a high five. Other Somalis are gathered around me, kids and adults, about fifteen of them. All of them want a high five. A lot of shouting, a lot of laughter. A Somali called Ismail, a young man, very groovy, starts singing 'No Woman No Cry', the Bob Marley song. He's a big Rasta Bob fan like my dad. Also a big fan of dope. A woman by the name of Afraxo makes the high-pitched warbling sound that women in my country cry out when they're celebrating something. A girl called Saafi plays a Madonna CD and starts dancing to 'Like a Prayer'. People are joyful in this way because my TPP gives many others hope.

I must explain something to the readers of this book. If you are a refugee and you're waiting to learn from the immigration people if you can stay, you have all sorts of ideas. You say to yourself: *Okay, probably they will kick me out, too bad, I'll just go back to Somalia.* And that's a thought I've had. Or you might say: *Okay, if they don't want me, who cares? I'll go to New Zealand somehow. Maybe they want me in New Zealand.* Or you might have this idea: *Okay, I'll hide in the desert and live with the Aboriginal people.* But there is really only one thing you want, and one thing you are hoping for, and that is a letter from the Australian government that says: 'Sure, you can stay. You can get a job. This country can be your country, so relax.' That's your prayer. And you hide that hope deep, deep in your heart. Even when refugees are waiting for a permit and they see things about Australia that drive them crazy, like the stupid game of cricket, or if the refugees come from a very traditional country, very strict, and are always making a tut-tut sound with their tongues when they see girls and women wearing hardly any clothes out in the street, what those refugees want more than anything on earth is that letter from the Australian government that says: 'Sure, you can stay. You can get a job. This country can be your country.'

Even as my appointment at Immigration approaches, I am waiting for the police to come and arrest me. I'm thinking: *It's a trick.* Or maybe they will arrest me when I go to pick up the permit. On the day of the appointment I dress in my best clothes (not so different from my worst clothes), clean my shoes and practise smiling in the mirror. I say to my reflection in English: 'Yes, I am

Abdi Aden. Please do not put handcuffs on me.' My English is getting better, thanks to *Neighbours* and *Hey Hey It's Saturday*. Also a little to *Doctor Who*.

And now it is my pleasure to tell you of one of the happiest experiences of my life. It is a great, great pleasure to tell all those reading this story, this book called *Shining*, of the happiest of all my days. It is a very simple thing that makes it such a special day. Listen closely.

I walk into the Department of Immigration offices of the Commonwealth of Australia in King Street in the city of Melbourne. I show the woman at the front desk my letter. The woman is very busy but she takes the time to smile. 'Go to the third floor in the lift,' she says. 'Show your letter to the person on the desk in the waiting room. Good luck' – she looks quickly at the letter again – 'Abdi.'

I take the lift to the third floor. When the doors open, I see the waiting room. People – old men, young men, old women, young women, children of all ages – are sitting on plastic chairs arranged in rows. I can see straight away that some of the people waiting are Somali – maybe six altogether. And there are other nationalities, too, I am guessing but I would say Kenyans, Sudanese, Vietnamese, Palestinians, maybe, and three white people who might come from South Africa. (I have been told that many white South Africans are now coming to Australia. Since Nelson Mandela was released from prison the white people are afraid that the black people will take over. Even in Somalia, I knew who Nelson Mandela was.)

First thing to be happy about: no police waiting in the waiting room. I find an empty seat close to a Somali guy. I have never met him before today. I smile at him and say: '*Sidee tahay maanta, walaalkay?*' (How are you today, my brother?)

And he answers: '*Waad ku mahadsur tahay, waxaau ahay caafimaad wanaaagsan, Ilaah ugu mahad naqayaa.*' ('I am in good health, thanks to the mercy of God.')

He is also waiting to pick up his TPP, and he's anxious, just like me. 'I don't like to have my destiny in another man's hands,' he says. 'But what can I say? In Somalia, my destiny was in the hands of bad guys every day. Here at least they don't want to murder me.'

We sit thinking for a few minutes, then he says: 'Kid, if you'd seen the things I've seen.'

It's on the tip of my tongue to tell him about all the bad things I've seen, but I decide to say nothing. Although I don't know it as I sit with him, I have begun the process of forgetting. It is not real forgetting. It's more like refusing to look at nightmare pictures in my brain. You can do that. A picture of blood and horror jumps into your brain and you whisper to yourself: 'Go away. I hate you. Go away.' I have to do this, otherwise the pictures will come again and again and I will go mad.

I've been waiting for an hour when a man with some papers in his hand comes to the desk at the front of the waiting room and raises his head to look over the people remaining. While I've been here, this man or sometimes another, older man has called out the names of maybe five people. This man is dressed exactly like the immigration officer who interviewed me. He wears a jumper without sleeves, a pale green shirt and an awful tie. He is very skinny, and even though he's young, he is beginning to become bald.

He says: 'Mister Abdi Aden?'

It takes me a few seconds to understand that he is talking about me. Mister Abdi Aden. My chest swells with pride. Mister Abdi Aden. You know, on that day, all I could think of was how happy I was to be called 'Mister Abdi Aden', but when I think back, I know what it was that made me so happy. I was being treated with respect, I was being treated with courtesy. All that I had endured, all the poverty and dirt and blood and brutality, looking into the eyes of men who cared no more for me than they would for an animal, men who would have been happy to shoot bullets into my face – all of that, and here I am in the Department of Immigration in Melbourne, Australia, and a skinny man who has probably never had to go a single day without food is calling me in such a respectful way 'Mister Abdi Aden'. My smile as I walk up to the man with the papers in his hand is so big that it hurts my face. Mister Abdi Aden. I want to throw my arms around the man in the jumper with no sleeves and hug him.

CHAPTER 19

Abe, Father

It is at this time that I receive a letter I was not expecting. It comes to the place that I use as my postal address and it started its journey to Brunswick from Nairobi in Kenya. It is from my father, although it has been written for him by someone else, a friend of my father's. The letter tells me that my father is in Nairobi, and that he has come to Kenya to find treatment for a bullet wound. Yes, a bullet wound, for he was shot while he was involved in a political demonstration against violence and bloodshed in Somalia. By the way the letter is written, I can see that some of the comments come from the man who is writing it, and I get the impression that my father is not doing well. The letter also says that my father came to know that I am in Australia from a Somali man who heard it from another Somali, who picked up the information in his travels. It doesn't amaze me. There is a worldwide Somali network that passes on bits of information like this. A grapevine, as they say in Australia.

This letter comes into my life like a storm on a summer's day. Do you know what I'm talking about? The sky is blue, the sun warms your skin, then out of nowhere comes a great wind, rain that falls in torrents. My TPP brought happiness; this letter from my father brings despair. I think of him in Nairobi with his bullet wound and I want to fly in an aeroplane to Kenya, run from the airport to wherever my father is staying and sit at his bedside until he is well. I cannot fly to Kenya, but at least I can telephone him. He has given me a number to call.

I call the number, a landline number, and make an appointment to talk to Dad. This is the custom – ring and make an appointment, a certain day, a certain hour, and the person you want to reach will be waiting.

Oh, the emotion when I hear Dad's voice coming all the way from Africa, from my continent! Tears gush from my eyes faster than I can wipe them away.

All I can say at first is: 'Abe, Abe, Abe …'

When I ask him how he is doing, he says: 'Not so good, Nuurow, I have to tell you.'

He asks about Jamila. I tell him that I don't know where she is, but that I will look for her. I don't tell him that she is probably dead. He doesn't ask about Mum.

After the phone call, I walk up and down the footpath outside the GPO in the middle of Melbourne. I walk up and down, up and down, waiting for the pain in my heart to die down a bit.

A few days later, I cable my first fortnight's payment from Social Security to my dad, then wait a week to ring him once more to find out if he has received the money. When I call again and make an appointment to talk to Dad, the guy who answers the phone tells me that the money came. He says my dad can't talk to me just for the time being. He says: 'Ring back in two weeks, maybe.'

But before those weeks are up, a new letter comes. The Somali guy who has the house that I use as my postal address brings the letter to where I am staying with another Somali family. He hands the letter to me in a respectful way. It is as if he knows that he might be bringing bad news. Somalis are a people who can grasp things that other people can't see. From the feel of the letter, this man who has brought it to me senses heartbreak. And he is right.

The letter tells me that my father is dead. When I read those words, I lose all the strength in my body. The letter falls from my hands. I try to pick it up again, but my hands won't move, my legs won't bend. I want to cry out, but I have no voice. The other Somalis in the house are staring at me, expecting a noise to come from my mouth, some words, something. But there's nothing. It's as if I am not in a living room of an apartment in Brunswick, but in the desert of Somalia at night, the cold air pushing into my bones. My father died on my birthday, 16 March.

★

Do you remember me speaking earlier in this book about the *tacsiyo* I held to honour my sister, Jamila, who died in the war? In Somalia, we always hold a *tacsiyo* to honour the passing of a relative. It is a ceremony of mourning. Many people are invited, and even those who are not invited come along. Food is eaten, tea is served. The person who has called the *tacsiyo* stands with bowed head and listens to whispers of sorrow from the guests.

And this is what I do, stand with my head bowed.

People whisper to me: 'Your honoured father has left the earth. I grieve with you.' And: 'Abdi, you must carry this burden, but I am beside you.'

It's a strange thing to say, but it is an honour to hold a *tacsiyo*. It is as if you have shown your respect for the one who has passed, according to a custom a thousand years old. People are watching to see that you know how to show sorrow. In the months to come, in the years to come, people who are here today will say: 'The father of

Abdi Aden passed from the earth in Kenya, a great blow to his son, but Abdi did all that was right in the eyes of God.'

It would be considered acceptable for me to hold yet another *tacsiyo* for my mother, since no one has heard anything of her for a couple of years. But I am not ready to hold a *tacsiyo* for my mother. I will never be ready for that. Every day my prayer is that she will be found alive. Every day.

CHAPTER 20

My Mum Plus Nine

I apply for enrolment at Brunswick High School and I am accepted. It is now 1993, and I am eighteen years of age. This is a bit embarrassing, but I have to tell my readers that I was put into year eight for some classes, since my English is still a bit of a struggle. Abdi, the Prince of Students in Mogadishu, is now sitting in class with kids five years younger than him.

In my school in Mogadishu, I never understood what it meant to be amongst those who found learning difficult. And there were many like that in my classes, in mathematics, in geography, in history, in science. For me, every subject was, as they say, 'a piece of cake'. Those students who had a permanently puzzled look on their faces – did I sympathise? No. I thought: *They don't try hard enough*, or *Dummies*. Well, in Brunswick High School, I am the one with a puzzled look on my face. It makes me feel sorry for the way I looked down my nose at the 'dummies'. When you haven't got a proper hold on the language, it's like being thrown into deep water before you know how to swim. You think: *I'm drowning*. It's the terrible struggle with English that distresses refugees as much as the insecurity. Language is what allows us to live and make meaning and be understood. It's agony to find yourself constantly baffled and frustrated.

So high school is not a wonderful experience, as I say. On top of everything, I have a teacher in my ESL class who thinks it is

hilarious to make fun of me and other refugees. He mocks our weak grasp of English and makes jokes about our past. I can see by the look on his face that he is enjoying himself in a cruel way but I don't know why. Is it so difficult to show some sympathy? But at least I have a friend in class, a Romanian kid by the name of George. I am able to say a couple of Romanian words to him that I remember from my time in Bucharest. We try to support each other, to keep close.

When I look at George, I see the trouble in his eyes and I think: *I must look like that.* I don't mean the trouble of being ridiculed by our teacher. That's just unfortunate, not tragic. I mean the trouble that mounts up over years. In Romania, people were murdered and tortured just as they were in Somalia. I don't ask George about his suffering and he doesn't ask me about mine. Nobody who has been in the hands of people who have made you suffer wants to talk about it. Even in this book, it hurts my heart to talk about the worst things. I wish I could tell my story and never mention the bad guys, but that wouldn't be my story, would it?

I still help out at the Red Cross. It's not so bad. All the volunteers are nice people, but they don't have to worry about money like I do. The manager says to me: 'Abdi, always smiling. You make us all feel optimistic.' I know what the word 'optimistic' means, because it was explained to me by one of my Somali friends who has very, very good English when we were watching the news on television. The man who reads the news on Channel 2 said: 'There's an optimistic forecast for the Middle East conflict.' Refugees always watch the news on the ABC or on SBS, because they hear about other refugees.

My friend said: 'Do you know what this means?'

'No, tell me.'

'This is Palestine. The Israelis are having peace talks with the Palestinians. "Optimistic" means they think the peace talks will be good.'

'Optimistic?'

'Sure. If you think that things will be good, that's "optimistic".'

Now, here's something that I've noticed in my life, many times. If you do a good deed, never thinking about it, just doing it, and then you keep doing it, somehow – I don't know how – good news comes to you. One afternoon, I look at the notice board at the Red Cross and see a slip of paper with a message on it from my mother. My heart stops beating for a few seconds. I stare at the slip of paper, read the Somali writing, see that it is signed by my mum, then read it again.

It says: 'If you are Abdi Aden and your father is Isak Aden and your mother is Aalima and your sister is Jamila, then you have a right to read this message. I am Aalima. Contact me only if you are sure that you are my son, Abdi. Do not make a mistake.'

The message has been sent from a refugee camp in Kenya, and it is dated only two weeks before today. I put both my hands over my face and scream. *My mother? She is alive?*

One of the ladies who works here comes over to me and puts her hand on my shoulder.

'Abdi, what's wrong?'

I point to the slip of paper on the notice board. 'My mother,' I say.

'Your mother?'

'My mother. Not dead. My mother.'

The lady (I can't remember her name – may she forgive me if she reads this book) helps me to send off a reply to my mother's message. I say: 'Aalima Aden, I am your son. I am Abdi. I am in

Australia. I am in Melbourne. I am alive. I am by myself. Can I call you on the telephone in your camp? Send me a number. This is great happiness for me. Abdi, your son.'

I have said before at the start of this book that my mother is a difficult woman. Think of a wife and mother who is always smiling, always relaxed, always finding ways to make life easier for her husband, for her kids. Now think of a wife and mother who is exactly the opposite, and that is my mum. She is proud, she is very clever, she is one of the great women of the world, I promise you. But she is difficult. Nobody should think that my mum being so difficult makes any difference to my love for her. It doesn't. But I am realistic. She is not an angel. And when I am able to talk to her over the telephone from Melbourne, she demonstrates immediately just how difficult she can be.

First come the tears of joy for both of us. 'Abdi, Abdi, my dear boy, how did you get to Australia? What miracle is this? Oh, I bless God for a thousand years, my dear Abdi.' And so on. Then I say: 'Hooyo, I am going to get you to Australia. Don't worry, I will find a way. I have a Temporary Protection Permit. When I am given permanent residency, I will bring you to Australia.'

My mum says: 'Bring me now. You think it is a holiday in this camp? Bring me now.'

'Hooyo, I can't bring you until I have permanent residency, don't you understand?'

'Permanent residency? What is this nonsense?'

'Well, that's the way it is, Hooyo. That's what the government of Australia says. First, permanent residency, then you can bring your relatives.'

'Your relatives? You call me a "relative"? I'm not a "relative", I am your mother! Dear God!'

It's no good arguing with her. She has never lost an argument in her life. I think maybe my dad, when he was in Paris, remembered what it was like to argue with my mother and decided to stay in France.

I make enquiries. I ask people in the Melbourne Somali community about getting my mum to Australia. And I ask the people at the Red Cross. It seems my mother must go to the Australian embassy in Nairobi and apply for a permit. She must tell the embassy that her son is a resident of the Commonwealth of Australia, and they will give her a permit. Maybe. But that can only happen when I am indeed a resident of Australia. That's a year away, perhaps longer. If the horrible situation in Somalia stops being horrible and peace returns, the Australians can send me back to Mogadishu.

I know what the Australians don't know: that peace will not return to Somalia in one year or five years or ten years. I know my country, and I know the war. Once war starts, it can only end with the complete defeat of one side. But third-world countries don't know how to end a war once it begins. Nobody in Somalia has any idea of how to bring a war to an end. Too many people are counting on the war going on and on. It is the main industry of Somalia. Arms flow in for each side. Neither side has to pay for the weapons. The weapons are paid for with foreign-aid money. One side says: 'Hey, give us some grenade launchers and we'll kill all the enemy soldiers and you can come to Somalia and build factories. We'll be your friends forever.' The other side says the same thing. I will still be in Melbourne, Australia, in a year's time.

I also find out that it will cost me a thousand dollars to get my mum to Australia. I call my mum in Kenya once I have all the information I need and tell her the deal.

She says: 'Good. I'll go to Nairobi. I'll talk to the Australians.'

I say: 'It's going to cost a thousand dollars, Hooyo. I'll have to get a job and save money.'

'Good. Get a job. Save money. You'll need ten thousand dollars.'

'Ten thousand dollars? No, one thousand.'

Mum says: 'Ten thousand. I'm bringing my adopted children. Nine of them.'

'What? Are you mad? You can't bring nine children with you! Do you think the embassy is going to give you permits for nine children?'

She says: 'I am looking after these kids. Do you think I will come to Australia and leave them behind? What? Do you know the things people will say in the camp if I do that? They will say: "Aiee! She is a disgrace to her parents! Aiee! She is wicked!" That's what they will say. Ten thousand dollars you must save.'

When I put down the telephone, I feel like pulling my teeth out of my head with my bare hands. I feel like bending down and banging my head on the footpath. Nine kids she wants to bring? Just getting her to Australia will be a huge task, but nine kids? No, my father was right. Mum is impossible. Nine kids? Ten thousand dollars? Oh, God!

To white Australians – I have noticed this – family is a different thing to what it is to Somalis. An Australian mother might easily say to her son: 'Here I am, stranded in Nairobi. I don't have any money. Please, dear son, can you get me back to Australia?' And the son, who is a good boy, of course, would say: 'Sure, Mum. Sit tight.' But an Australian mum would not say: 'And also nine kids.' She would think that was unreasonable. In Somalia, when it comes to family, there is no such thing as unreasonable. So that's what I must deal with. I must save ten thousand dollars.

I study all the job ads at the employment agency. I try most of them but no deal. Then I have some luck. I see an ad for a factory in Footscray called Tontine that makes upholstery for the insides of cars. The job doesn't require any great skill.

I go to the factory, meet the boss. By this time, I can get by with my English.

He says: 'You need to be strong.'

I say: 'I'm strong.'

He says: 'You work twelve hours each shift. Three o'clock in the morning to three-thirty the next afternoon. Half an hour break in the middle.'

I'm thinking: *Whoa!*

He says: 'Can you do it?'

I say: 'How much do I earn?'

'How much? One thousand dollars net. That means one thousand dollars after you pay tax.'

I say: 'I'll take it.'

So after around fifteen weeks' work, after I pay my rent and buy my food, I can save ten thousand dollars and my mum and these nieces and nephews I've never met and have never even heard of before in my life can come to Australia.

I should have said that I now have my own apartment. It's in Ascot Vale. The Housing Commission gave it to me. I have to pay rent but the rent is not much. 'Peanuts', as the Australians would say. I love it. And so when I start work at Tontine I have a place to come home to, a nice little kitchen where I can make my meals, a shower, a living room. I even have a television set. So far, so good. But dear God, the job at Tontine is hard, hard, hard. The upholstery has to be moulded in a very hot place in the factory, hotter than Somalia on the hottest day in its history. I said to the boss 'I am strong', but I didn't know that I had to be Superman. The sweat runs off me in streams and the pace of the work never slows down.

When I reach home in the afternoon I drink glass after glass of water then fall asleep for two hours in front of the television, wake up, shower, make myself a meal, sleep until two in the morning, eat some breakfast then head off to work in Footscray. The crazy thing is, the life I lived in Somalia, when I was travelling all over the country and often had to run for my life, has prepared me for this job. When I was carrying roofing iron and big bags of rice for the soldiers with the sun beating down on me, I certainly didn't think, *Oh, Nuurow, this is good training for some future employment*, but that's exactly what it was. The job is torture, but it's a torture for which a person is well paid.

Most of the people who work at the factory are immigrants, new to Australia. We have the chance to glance at each other, to say hello, maybe smile, but that's all. I wish I could get to know these guys. At break time, all I can do is sit in a chair in the lunch room and munch on a sandwich I've brought with me. I haven't got the strength for conversation.

Other Somalis in the refugee community say to me: 'Hey Abdi, what the hell? Is your mum insane? Nine kids? Just say no.' Oh, sure. If they were in the same situation as me, they'd do what I'm doing. All of us Somalis have carried our culture with us. We can't say no. Now that I have lived in Australia for more than twenty years, I'm very used to hearing about 'multiculturalism'. I like to hear about it. I love the culture of Australia, except for cricket, which is madness. I even like Australian Rules football. I've been to a few games. Very, very skilful, those guys. My team is Essendon. So, yes,

I love the culture of Australia. I love justice. You have justice here. But I feel like I should warn Australians about some parts of the Somali culture I have brought with me. Like the need to do what your mum tells you to do when she says 'And I'm bringing nine kids with me'. Somali mothers – Aiee, aiee, aiee!

The fifteen weeks pass and just in time because all the sweating has caused me to lose weight. I have always been skinny, and now I am skinnier.

On my last day at work, I tell the boss: 'I can't do it anymore.'

The boss nods. 'You lasted longer than I expected, Abdi. You know how to work, I'll say that.'

It pleases me to hear him say that. I think about it on my way home. I brought to this country a skinny body full of strength and a good, clever brain and a heart that had not been destroyed by what I'd seen. It makes me feel rich to still have these gifts. Not rich in money, but with strength and brain and heart. In Somalia, having a good, clever brain and strength and a good heart hasn't meant anything since the war started. Plenty of Somalis with those same gifts are now dead. But in Australia, a brain and a strong body and a good heart give you a chance to build something. I don't say that Australia is a miracle. I only say that this is what I want for all the world: a place where simple gifts can be used to build something.

I now have permanent residency. The Department of Immigration has sent me a letter saying this: 'Hi, Abdi. Guess what? It is our belief that you are a good guy, also very handsome, and we want you to live in Australia forever. Yo!' Well, okay, not exactly those words, but with the same meaning, sort of. I've been confident for a long time now that I'd be granted residency. If the immigration people ever want to know if it's safe for me, or anyone, to go back to Somalia, all they have to do is ring up the Department of Tourism in Mogadishu. There isn't one. Nobody goes to Somalia, unless he's going there to fight.

Permanency means that I can now bring Mum and these nine orphans to Australia. I take thousands of dollars in cash to the Red Cross office and put it on the desk in front of the guy whose job it is to organise refugee reunions. I say: 'This is for my mother and her adopted children.' The Red Cross guy says: 'I'll get things started.'

My next task is to find another job. I'm hoping to keep away from factories. I speak to my friends in the Somali community, and all the advice is that I should get my driver's licence then get a van and become a delivery man. It's now 1994, and I am nineteen, old enough for a licence. I borrow money from Social Security. I take a few lessons, find driving easy, and get my licence on my first attempt. The loan from Social Security also covers the cost of a van – second-hand, nothing fancy. I don't want to make a career out of any of the jobs I've had so far, but being a delivery man sounds like a big improvement. I apply for a position with a delivery company, show my licence, give the boss a look at my van, and that's it. I'm a delivery man. I didn't pay a single bribe to anyone. What a country! If I was a poet, I'd write a long, long poem of praise. Not one bribe! Amazing.

Those reading this book will be thinking: *Abdi, working, working, working. What did you do for fun?* Okay, I have to confess that I like music, I like hip-hop, I like reggae, I like pop, and I like parties. In the Somali community, you get a big choice of parties. Somebody gets a TPP, there's a party. I was given a party when my TPP came through. Somebody has a birthday, there's a party. A baby is born, a party, of course. Or maybe there's a party for no reason at all. Somalis love parties. They love to make a lot of noise. Some of the noisiest people in the world come from Somalia. Right here, I should say that I don't think of any of the days and months and years I have been in Australia as tough. Hardship? No. Sure, I had to work hard, so what? Tontine was … difficult, okay. But most of the time I've been in Australia I've been happy. I think about soldiers with AKs, looking for some kid about my age to shoot through the head, and I tremble. Then I look around me at this big country I've come to, and I'm okay. I'm happy. I'm Nuurow, the Shining One. Parties, music, good food to eat, of course I'm happy. The last time I even glimpsed a soldier was in Bucharest. Where are the Australian soldiers? Haven't seen one.

CHAPTER 21

Hooyo, Mother, Mum

My English is at the stage of a breakthrough, I think. I can follow almost everything on the television, but I need more words of my own and to understand grammar better. I know all about the grammar of the Somali language, and that makes me see that grammar must be just as important in English. I don't want to go about sounding as if I have just stepped off an aeroplane from Mogadishu. I want people to say: 'Hey, Abdi, good English my man!' So I enrol in a CAE English course, and that's great, but I need more practice between classes. There's another course available to me, one in which retired people in the community hold conversations with you and correct you. So I go to these people, the 'retirees' as they're called, and get more practice. Do you know what 'conjugation' is? You take a verb, and you show how the verb changes depending on the tense and the person you are talking to. Like this: 'I am, he is, she is, we are, they are'. You can do that with all the verbs in English. It's wonderful. I can do that. I can conjugate verbs on paper, and in conversation. I love it. You see how good it is to have a clever brain? I bless my father and my mother for giving me my brain.

★

You remember I said that the Red Cross agency is looking after the migration to Australia of my mum and her nine orphans? Well, the agency wants to use the opportunity to make some publicity. A crew from *Today Tonight* film me smiling.

The lady who's interviewing me says: 'Abdi, how do you like Australia?'

'Great!' I say.

The producer stops the camera. He says: 'Can you say more than just "great", Abdi? We'll take that shot again.'

So: 'Abdi, how do you like Australia?'

'How do I like Australia? I love Australia. Very, very much!'

And the producer: 'Perfect!'

When the day comes around for the arrival of my mum and the kids – she is bringing five with her on this trip, with four more to follow, once they've completed health checks – the Red Cross lady and the film crew come out to the airport with me. The crew is filming when my mum and the kids come through the swing doors into the arrival area of Melbourne airport. I'm so full of emotion that I can barely hear what the producer is saying. This is my mum! I haven't seen her for six years.

For a moment, I'm like a baby, I just want to cry and cry and cling to her. But Mum is not a cry-and-cry-and-cling-to-me sort of woman. Sure, she's glad to see me, and we hug, but she has these five kids to look out for and they take up most of her time. I'm standing there with the *Today Tonight* people and the Red Cross lady watching Mum shouting at the kids, getting them into order. Tears run down my face. It's my mum! Then it's as if I'm an adult once more, and I remember everything about my mum's character and how aloof she can be. And I shape up. It's okay. I just had a fantasy moment. I'm cool, now.

I let Mum and the kids have the Ascot Vale apartment to themselves. What choice do I have? Mum is a bit critical about the size of the place, as if she had lived with the kids in some king's palace in the refugee camp. I want to say: 'Hey, Mum, hot and cold running water, a refrigerator, an oven, a cooktop with four hotplates, a television, cupboards full of food: isn't this a bit of an improvement on Kenya?' But I don't say anything. I let the whole lot of them settle in while I go and stay with a friend.

Lying in bed that night, I'm too amazed at the turn my life has taken to fall asleep, tired though I am. I must now add to the very, very strange experiences of the past six years the arrival in Melbourne, Australia, of my mum, who has flown here from Kenya after disappearing in Italy. The whole insane adventure of those six years has changed me; Australia has changed me. But Mum is still exactly how she has always been. Her husband has died, her daughter is surely dead too; most of the people she once knew in Somalia have been murdered; she's become a mother to a whole tribe of orphans; her son is on the way to becoming a citizen of Australia; and yet she is unchanged, just as strict, just as bossy, just as aloof, just as proud. If an atomic bomb had been dropped on Mogadishu in the years when my family lived there, my mother would have walked out of the ruins with orphans gathered around her, saying: 'Abdi, what is this nonsense! Find a house for me and these children, a big one. Don't waste time.'

★

The Social Security office is now called Centrelink. And it's to Centrelink I take my mum and the tribe of kids a couple of days after their arrival. My mum is in charge of discipline (of course!) but I find myself behaving like a parent, too. I've never been in this situation before. I'm only about five years older than the biggest of the kids, and here I am, saying to the kids: 'Hey, listen to what your aunty tells you! Hey, wait for the red man to turn green! Hey, don't run on the footpath! No, you can't have any chips, you just had breakfast!' The thing about me is that I was an adult before I was an adult. I was all about duty and responsibility and hard work even before I was a teenager. It's probably because my mum expects me to behave like an adult. She's had this expectation since I was about three. In my mum's way of looking at things, if you're the oldest son you go straight from being a baby to being an adult as soon as you stop breastfeeding. It's okay by me. I survived the war in Somalia by being an adult before I was an adult – the same as lots of other kids. In Somalia, now and for the last six years, there is no childhood.

★

Mum is given a benefit by Centrelink that covers her and the kids. It's enough for them all to live on. What has happened is that the Australian government has agreed to take ten people from a no-future, shanty town of a refugee camp in Kenya and support them in the security of an Australian suburb. Without the goodwill of the Australians, perhaps half of these ten people would have died in Kenya. As it is, nine of these ten people will become educated in Australian schools, become Australian citizens, build families here. It's true that all of this support and education costs the Australians money. Sure. But I think of it this way. One of the best things anyone with some money to spare can do in the world is to save someone else from the dirt and poverty of a shanty town. The Australians can't save everyone, but they can save some. Some is good. Some is very, very good. If in a way that I can't imagine, Somalia one day becomes as rich as Australia, and Australia becomes as poor and as violent as Somalia, I hope the Somalis of that distant time remember that Australians saved some Somali lives, and I hope these future Somalis say: 'We'll help.'

I turn twenty-one. And on the morning of my birthday, I wake in my bed and think: 'I want a house.' Sure, a house. This is Practical Abdi. He wants a house. At twenty-one? Who buys a house at twenty-one? Me, Practical Abdi, that's who. The house is not to be for me, but for Mum. She has to have a house of her own. She needs to set up her own rules for the house, because that's what she's used to. From her young years in Somalia, she has been a queen. She has the instincts and pride of a queen, and the beauty. So she must have her own place to rule.

I talk to the Somalis in the community. They say: 'The Australians will lend you money. Go to the bank. The Australians have lots of money and they will give you a loan.'

And I say: 'Just like that?'

'Sure. Just like that.'

So I walk into the bank and say: 'I'm Abdi. Give me the money to buy a house?'

'Sure. So long as you have a deposit.'

'What's a deposit?'

'Maybe five thousand dollars that you've saved up. Maybe ten thousand. Do you know what this means? This means that you know how to save money. No problem.'

A deposit. Five thousand dollars. I don't have five thousand dollars. But I'm strong, I'm intelligent; a guy like me might have no such thing as five thousand dollars one day, then have it the next.

That's one of the most beautiful things about this Australia I've come to. I don't have to think: 'No, no, five thousand dollars, no way.' I'm strong, what's to stop me working hard and earning an extra five thousand dollars?

See how I'm becoming such an optimistic person? Remember that word 'optimistic', that my Somali friend explained to me? It means you expect good things to happen. I'm optimistic. I expect to make five thousand dollars and get a loan from the bank and buy my mum a house in Australia. In Somalia at this time, if I needed five thousand dollars quickly, I might have to pick up an AK and rob someone.

I work extra shifts with the delivery company. About three months is all it takes to make the five thousand. Then I start looking at houses with my Somali friend, Denim, a clever guy, a 'savvy' guy, as the Americans say. What we're doing is something Australians love – looking at houses to buy on a Saturday and Sunday. I'm looking with a guy, but most of the other people looking are couples, husband and wife or boyfriend and girlfriend. These couples are not always all that young. Most are maybe in their early thirties. Yes, that's something I've noticed: in Australia, people don't get married when they are eighteen or twenty or even twenty-five. They wait until they're about thirty. In Somalia, girls often get married when they are sixteen or seventeen. A Somali husband and wife will expect to have five or six kids, even more, so they can't wait until they are thirty to begin a family. In Somalia, having a family is your great purpose in life. In Australia, it's a big deal, sure, but it's not the only big thing. Here, both the husband and wife want to have a career, and a career is a big deal, as big as having a family. The time is going to come when I will be working as a community development officer helping disadvantaged people, and I'll see plenty of girls who are pregnant when they're eighteen. In Australia, it's a disaster if you're a girl and you're pregnant when you're eighteen. It's going to make your life much more difficult. In Somalia, a girl is eighteen, she's married, she's having her second child, it's no problem. This is all just something I've noticed. I was talking about looking at houses …

All the houses in Brunswick, in Northcote, in Carlton, North Melbourne, South Melbourne, Ascot Vale, Flemington, even Coburg – the suburbs close to the city – are too expensive. So Denim and I look at Broadmeadows, further out, then at Roxburgh Park, even further out. Cheaper. I find a place in Roxburgh Park that I might be able to afford. Two bedrooms, sunny, back yard, front yard, nice. A lady from the real estate company waits in the living room while we're looking. She has pamphlets in her hand that show coloured pictures of the house from the inside, and what is known as a floor plan. The lady is about thirty. She's wearing a grey skirt, a grey coat, a white shirt and black shoes.

When I wander over to her and say: 'Okay, I like it,' she gives me a surprised look.

'Really?' she says.

'Sure. I like it.'

She nods her head slowly and says: 'Um.'

I know what she's thinking. I'm young, I'm dark-skinned. She's thinking that I'm just filling in time by looking at houses. She thinks I probably don't have a cent in the bank. She's thinking: *People of this fellow's colour don't buy houses.*

'Are you thinking of … of making an offer for the house? Is that what you want to do?'

'Sure.'

She again nods her head slowly. 'Have you arranged finance?'

'Sure, I've arranged finance.'

And I have. I've been to the ANZ bank, I've shown that I have a five thousand dollar deposit, they've looked at my payslips. The loan officer at the ANZ bank, a friendly guy, said: 'We can come to an arrangement, Mr Aden.'

So: 'Sure,' I tell the confused real estate lady, 'I have finance.'

I tell Mum that I'm buying her a house of her own.

She says: 'Good. Make sure the neighbours are okay.'

A few weeks later, I say: 'I've found the house. It's nice. Front yard, back yard, two bedrooms.'

Mum says: 'Where?'

'In Roxburgh Park.'

'Where in God's name is Roxburgh Park?'

'Past Broadmeadows.'

She knows where Broadmeadows is.

She says: 'So still in the state of Victoria?'

'You can get to the middle of Melbourne in thirty minutes. Okay, forty.'

'Okay.'

Then the house is mine, and I proudly take Mum to Roxburgh Park to show it off to her.

She walks in through the front door, looks around. 'Could have been bigger. I'm not a dwarf,' she says.

And I'm thinking: *Dear God, give me patience, I beg of you.*

All the same, Mum moves in with the nine kids. And yeah, she's pleased. I've never in my life known her to be so pleased about anything that she doesn't have any criticisms. So this is as good as it gets. The Adens of Somalia are now the Adens of Australia.

Well, not all of the Adens. Dad is gone, Jamila is gone. So we believe. And no sooner have the Adens colonised Australia than I think about travelling overseas. In 1997, I'm twenty-two years old and I've seen a bit of the world, but not in the way I want to see the world. If you're a kid in Bucharest freezing to death in the European winter, maybe two coins in your pocket worth ten cents, you're not about to enjoy the sights. I'm restless. I want to see the world with money in my pocket. I'm twenty-two – maybe I'll be married before long, maybe kids in a few more years. But now I have this liberty and I don't want to waste it. In the whole world, the best experience you can ever have is to be a healthy young man of twenty-two with some money in your pocket and the freedom to go north, south, east and west. If you're good-looking, so much the better. I have the hunger for life of a man who has escaped a bullet through the head a dozen times. I want to travel. And I do.

CHAPTER 22

Tourist

I leave Australia on my holiday in late 1998. My ticket will take me around the world. As long as I keep heading in an anticlockwise direction, I can go where I wish. I have my backpack, my guidebooks, my credit cards. I fly from Melbourne to Amsterdam, full of the joy of liberty and hungry for adventure. On the aeroplane, I can hardly keep the smile off my face. People must think I've been taking happy pills.

Amsterdam is very pretty, of course; everybody knows that. I stroll along the walkways beside the canals, gaze at the rows of neatly painted two- and three-storey houses. So many people here ride bicycles, maybe because Amsterdam is perfectly flat. This is the first experience in my life of sightseeing. I notice things that would have meant nothing to me when I was on my desperate journey in 1991. I mean, I would have noticed them back then, but my head was so full of the struggle I was in that I couldn't stop, as I do now, and think: *Hmm, why are the houses of Amsterdam so narrow?* Or: *Hmm, why are so many of the bicycles here white?* Or: *The sky here is such a pale blue. I have never realised how many moods you see in the sky.* That's one of the awful things about being a refugee: your mind is so taken up with the basic things that you have no freedom to enjoy sweetness and beauty. And without sweetness and beauty, is life worth living?

I see plenty of dark-skinned people in Amsterdam, some of them Somalis. But my guidebook says many of these people have come to the Netherlands from countries in Africa and from such places as Indonesia that were once colonies of the Dutch. None of them look like refugees; they all look like they've lived here for years. And I would know. I can look at people passing in the street and tell you straight away which one is a refugee. I can tell you sometimes which ones *used* to be refugees.

Once you've been a refugee, once you've been homeless and hunted, far from the care of anyone who loves you, then you are a refugee for life. You might become a very comfortable refugee – you might have your own house in a lovely suburb, money in your pocket, your mother just down the road – but you will still be a refugee.

Mohammad, the Somali guy I spoke about earlier, once said: 'Australians are like children. They have never seen anything bad.' It's not true that Australians are like children exactly, but Mohammad was right in a way. In this country, apart from the people who came here as refugees, the only people who have ever known what it is to be hunted, made homeless, murdered in a casual way, are the Australian black people, the Aborigines. And I can guarantee you they have never forgotten what it is to be a refugee.

★

From Amsterdam, I travel to Copenhagen in Denmark. Like Amsterdam, Copenhagen is neat and clean. The Danish people are what you would call civilised. The traffic in Copenhagen is exactly the opposite of the traffic in Mogadishu. People here stop at the red lights. They stop at the places where people on foot are crossing the road. It's like they all want to earn certificates for being good guys. In Mogadishu, the traffic is controlled by maniacs. People stop at red lights if they feel like it – otherwise, forget it. If you're a pedestrian in Mogadishu, good luck. Still, I have to say, Mogadishu is more exciting. There's a big part of me that likes good manners on the road, and another part of me that likes the chaos of my old city.

I don't want to write a travel book. What I need to say is that I get a very big buzz out of travelling. I go to Frankfurt after Copenhagen. Another huge Western city, one I've visited before.

I think: *Abdi, you know what? See if you can find Abu. Thank him for taking you to Australia. Why not?*

Why not? Because he might try to strangle me.

Okay, maybe don't see Abu.

Be sane, Nuurow.

But there is another guy in Frankfurt I want to see, a Somali who may know something about my sister. I spoke a few pages back about the international Somali telegraph or web. Word came to me about this guy almost a year earlier. It was just a vague thing – someone said he'd heard from someone else and from someone else again that this guy in Frankfurt might know something, or he might not. I had a telephone number and I'd tried to call him but never got any answer.

If I don't have any luck calling this guy, whose name is Absame, from inside Germany, I'll give up. But this time, when I dial him without the international code, he answers. I'm surprised. I tell him who I am and ask him if I can come to his place and talk about my sister, Jamila. We both know that Absame could tell me all he knows over the telephone, but since I am in Germany, in Frankfurt, it would be rude not to call in.

I take a taxi to Absame's apartment and once there, I'm offered food and drink. I accept, of course, before I raise the subject of Jamila. It must seem strange that I don't burst into Absame's place and say immediately: 'About Jamila, tell me all you know!' That's not the Somali way. We may visit friends, relatives, with a very, very big issue to discuss. But we always observe good manners. We don't want it to appear that the main reason we have come to visit is to get some information. That would be bad manners. And yet both Absame and I know very well that I wouldn't even be here if I wasn't searching for news of my sister.

When we are finally ready to talk about my sister, Absame says: 'Your sister is dead, my brother.'

I look away, at the wall, at the floor.

Absame says: 'I am sorry to be the one who brings you this news. We were a big group, running from the soldiers. Jamila was with us. This was in the year of 1992. But the soldiers caught us, except for me and two others. They killed everyone.'

I couldn't move from where I was sitting. I put my hands over my face. Tears came to my eyes and ran through my fingers. I had accepted years ago that Jamila was dead but, really, I hadn't accepted it at all. The pain is like the blade of a knife plunged into my stomach.

I take my sorrow with me to Italy. How will I tell Mum? She, too, has accepted that Jamila is dead, without believing it. Now I have to say to her: 'Your daughter, so much hope you had for her, but she is gone. God forgive me for telling you this.' It will not destroy my mother. African women are prepared for sorrow.

Rome has some of the swarm of Mogadishu. The traffic is almost as mad. A century ago, more, the Italians came to Somalia and said: 'We're staying.' The Italians wanted an empire, like the

English and the French, but there wasn't much territory left for stealing – the English and the French had grabbed most of it. Actually, the English and the French had already taken big chunks of Somalia, and the Italians had to settle for what was still available, which was not so much. The Italians called their piece of Somalia an 'Italian Protectorate'. Yeah, sure. Protected from the French and the English. I look at the faces of the Italians I see in the street, and I think: 'Maybe your grandfathers went to my homeland to steal as much as they could get their hands on.'

I'll tell you something funny. For the past twenty years (I am speaking now from the year 2015), the big Western countries have been troubled by Somali pirates. The pirates are crazy guys, mad with bravery, no thought about anything but today. They attack big ships using little boats with outboard motors. They board the ships, get control of them, then hold the crews and the cargo (mostly oil) to ransom. They make millions of dollars. It is the main industry of Somalia. The pirates are bad guys, some of them completely insane. But the Italians who came to my country a century and a half ago? And the British, and the French? Same thing. Pirates.

I return to Amsterdam after I've visited maybe seven or eight European countries. In a few more days, I'll fly home. I find a fairly cheap hotel not far from the centre of town then wander about the streets until I find a place to eat. The restaurant is crowded, mostly with people as young as I am, in their early twenties, some a little older. And while I'm eating, I notice a guy on the other side of the restaurant, glancing at me every so often. He's a Somali guy, so it's not that unusual that he should be checking me out. He's not eating; he's waiting with a couple of friends – not Somalis – for a table to become available. I raise my hand in greeting, and he makes a gesture that means: 'Can I join you?' And I make the gesture recognised all over the world – a sort of beckoning movement of the hand – that means 'Sure! Come on over!'

He shakes my hand and sits down. 'Hanad,' he says. 'You don't need to tell me your name. You're Abdi. I've seen you before. You know where?'

'Where?'

'In Bucharest,' says Hanad. 'Sure! You were just a kid. I saw you there in Bucharest. Man, you're the most famous Somali of all time. You got out of Bucharest. I got out too, but it took me much, much longer.'

I lean over the table and hug him as if he's my own flesh and blood.

'You know,' Hanad says, 'I heard you're looking for your sister. Somebody told me. You were here a couple of months ago, right? And asking questions about your sister, if anyone has seen her?'

'I was looking for her,' I say. 'But I spoke to a guy in Frankfurt who told me she's dead. The soldiers took her and killed her.'

Hanad says: 'No, man. That guy got it wrong. Your sister is alive. She lives in Bussum. That's like an hour from here. Sure. In Bussum.'

I sit back in my chair, amazed. I stare at Hanad. Can I believe him? He must have my sister mixed up some other girl. 'I think you're wrong,' I say. 'It can't be my sister.'

'It's your sister, man. It's Jamila. She talks about you. She talks about Abdi, her brother. You don't believe me? Okay, buy me a meal and I'll drive you to her place in Bussum. A deal?'

My sister has been probably dead, then definitely dead and then alive, and only an hour from where I'm sitting. I'm dazed. I don't let myself truly believe it is Jamila that Hanad is talking about. Maybe he's nuts. When I see her with my own eyes, then I will believe it. Not until I see her standing before me, breathing and talking.

Hanad drives me to Bussum in his van. I'm saying to myself all the way, under my breath: 'It's not her. It's not her.' And when we reach the apartment block, I follow Hanad up the steps, still whispering to myself: 'It's not her.' Hanad presses the doorbell. I hear from inside the sounds of kids speaking Dutch. I don't know a word of Dutch, but I would guess that a kid is calling: 'Mum, the doorbell!' Then the door opens, and standing there, fully alive, is my sister, Jamila. I haven't seen her since she was a kid, and she is a woman now, but this Jamila. This is my sister.

Jamila says in Somali: 'Hanad, is that you?'

Hanad says: 'It's me. And this is your brother. This is Abdi.'

Jamila pushes back a little kid who is trying to squeeze past her to get a look at the visitors. 'Abdi?' she says. 'Are you Abdi?'

I say: 'Jamila, it's me. It's Abdi. I've been searching for you.'

Jamila gasps. She puts her hands to her face. 'Your voice! It's you!'

I step inside and embrace her in the Western way, a huge hug, not so common in Somali culture. Such a weird feeling! This woman is my little sister. Impossible!

I meet the whole family; Jamila's husband Mahmuud, her two kids, a girl and a boy. The apartment is full of laughter and shouting in the Somali way. One of the greatest reliefs of finding Jamila alive is that I can phone Mum in Melbourne and say: 'That *tacsiyo* I held for Jamila? A waste. She's alive in the Netherlands, she has a husband and two children, she's a beautiful young woman. Happy day!' And Mum will say: 'Happy, happy day!' Then she will say: 'Is she at university?'

Over the next two days, I hear Jamila's story. She tells it without tears, but there is a tension in her face that I keep a careful watch

on, urging her to stop when the events become too painful. She left Mogadishu about four years ago, and had gone first to Djibouti to stay with friends of our family. She was baffled by what was happening in Somalia and hoped desperately that Mum would appear and make her safe again. She fled to Ethiopia with the family who had charge of her, because they had to, then from Ethiopia they travelled to Italy as refugees. Things were very hard, very hard. Hiding from the Italian police made it more difficult than ever for the family to stay together. Jamila by this time was eighteen. The family were forced to say to Jamila: 'You're on your own now.' In the way that these things happen, Jamila joined a group of Somali refugees who smuggled themselves into Switzerland by train. The group hoped to be accepted as refugees by the Swiss, but no deal. It was in Switzerland, hiding, that Jamila met Mahmuud, who became her husband once he'd found a way to get them into the Netherlands. And she and Mahmuud have been in the Netherlands ever since.

In this brief account I have been forced to leave out a number of the most painful things my sister endured and the terrible things she saw and suffered, because she would be distressed if they appeared in a book such as this one. But let me say this: her courage and will to keep living fill me with admiration. Like me, she should have died a number of times, but didn't. And like me, nightmares sometimes plague her sleep.

★

I return to Melbourne after four months of travel full of gladness. Can you imagine what it feels like, how joyful it is, to know that, at the end of your journey, you have a home to return to, a city to call your own? At Melbourne airport, how different from my first experience of arriving here! The officer at the immigration counter looks at my passport, then looks up at me, the living, breathing Abdi. He smiles. 'Mister Aden,' he says. 'Welcome home.'

CHAPTER 23

Birth

The tale of a refugee ceases to be eventful once he (that's me) finds a welcoming land and settles down. The bad guys disappear; the tense episodes are over. The hero of the story finds a fulfilling job. He meets a wonderful woman and marries her. He attends university, takes out a degree in community relations. He raises a family. He goes out into the community and gives his assistance to young people who are struggling with life.

I hate to admit it, but since I came to Australia, my happiness has made my life less dramatic than it was when I was dodging bullets and explosions in Somalia. But what am I saying? 'I hate to admit it'? Okay, from the point of view of a writer, sure, I hate to admit it. But from the point of view of Abdi Aden, who is married to Angela, and who is the father of three kids, I don't hate to admit it at all.

Robert Hillman, who is helping me with this book, mentioned a book he wrote with a young Iranian woman by the name of Zarah, who was thrown into prison in Tehran more than a decade ago and who survived day after day of torture. Zarah's parents were eventually able to rescue her from the men who were abusing her by paying a large sum of money. Robert met this young woman in Tehran on a visit there to write stories about the Islamic regime for an Australian newspaper. He met her, heard her story, and helped her to come to Australia as an asylum seeker. Not long after she was granted asylum here, she met a good man, married him, settled in Byron Bay, gave birth to two sons, and embraced a life of love, sunshine and surfing. Robert says Zarah is now the happiest person on the entire Australian continent.

The story of Zarah told in Robert and Zarah's book fills two hundred pages, and it is all to do with her struggle in Iran and her time in prison. Nothing has been written about the ten years of happiness that followed. I am sure this is because happiness and fulfilment are not what the best stories are about.

★

When I return from my travels I immediately take up studies at Victoria University at the St Albans campus in the west of Melbourne. I found the community development course here by knocking on doors at all the universities of Melbourne and asking questions. Everyone I spoke to was kind and helpful, but the person who was kindest and most helpful was a woman by the name of Jen Couch at St Albans. She said: 'Community development. A two-year diploma course. You were made for this, Abdi.' Jen explained to me that the course, and the employment that it leads to, empowers people who have never known what it means to gain control of their lives to make choices that allow them to build and grow.

Jen says, 'You were made for this, Abdi,' because she can see that I will be good with people. In a way, my whole life has prepared me for helping people make better choices – even the years running from violence have prepared me. When I was at my most frightened, I feared I would pick up an AK and join the murder industry. But I didn't. I kept my wits. And I listened to my heart, too, of course.

That moment when I decided not to pick up an AK was the moment I qualified for this course at St Albans.

But aiee, aiee, aiee! – it is hard work. I have never before in my life been asked to write an essay, and now almost my whole life is writing essays. But I have help from Jen, and I begin to understand more of what is required to make meaning with English sentences. The best thing is this: I know in my soul that I can do this job, once I have my qualification. I know that Jen's faith is justified, as they say. Will I know what to do if I am asked to help a kid of fifteen who isn't turning up for school, has a record with the cops, an abusive father at home? Yes, I will know. I'll keep calm. I'll find the practical things that can help. I'll speak to the kid without sounding too dramatic. I'll speak to the kid's parents. I'll ask them what would make a difference. They might say: 'In Somalia, kids listen to their parents. This boy won't listen.' And bit by bit, I'll get the kid to listen to his parents, and I'll get the parents to listen to their son. When it seems right, I'll let them all know parts of my own story. How does that sound? I might be able to empower this kid by helping him find the gateways into the community, and by opening those gateways.

I meet Angela, who will become my wife, six months into my course at St Albans. I'm in the city with some Somali friends, all of us enjoying ourselves. We've been to a restaurant, we've tried out a disco, but just for the moment we're walking along Russell Street to the taxi rank, ready to head off home. And while we're waiting for a taxi, I notice two girls – well, not girls but young women – standing beside a car studying a street directory. They're chattering together, every now and again glancing up from the street directory and looking north, south, east and west in a puzzled way. I can tell that they haven't got a clue. And the car they're standing beside has Tasmanian number plates. These girls are lost, for sure.

I wander over and ask them if I can help and, in the way that girls respond to approaches like this from guys, no matter how good-looking, they ignore me. They think I'm trying to pick them up. Five minutes later, still no taxi and the girls are more lost than ever. I tell my friends I'm going to ask them again if I can help. My friends say: 'Forget it. They don't trust you, man.' But I do it anyway.

This time the one I most like the look of says: 'Well, maybe you can help us. We're trying to find Bridge Road.' It's Angela, but I don't know her name, naturally. So they're looking for Bridge Road, which is about five hundred metres away. I told you they were clueless. A taxi has just arrived. I tell the girl who will one day be my wife: 'You know what? Just do a U-turn and follow the taxi into Flinders Street. Me and my friends will be turning left, but you go straight ahead. That's Bridge Road.'

So I happen to help out a girl who has just arrived from Tasmania. She's nice, but I can't expect to ever meet her again. Except that I do. I'm strolling down Toorak Road way up in Toorak Village, once again with some Somali friends, once again out for a good time – a restaurant, a disco (I am the greatest Somali fan of disco in the world – it's the truth) – when I happen to glance through the front window of a bistro, and there's Angela at a table with her girlfriends.

I step inside to say hello. 'Hi, you must be following me!'

Angela and her friends look at me blankly. I say: 'Remember me? In Russell Street? Did you find what you were looking for?'

Recognition dawns on their faces. Angela says: 'Yes, we did. Thank you.' She says it in a way that is intended to end the conversation, so I smile and rejoin my friends.

Twice I've met Angela. At this stage, I'm just 'that guy' and she's just 'that girl'. But then I meet her a third time, and I have to say, we're now talking about fate. Think of it – three chance meetings. How can that not be fate?

On this third time, I'm down in Albert Park with my Somali friends at a restaurant that sits out over the lake. I'm looking for a good time, some good food, maybe some disco a little later. And there at the bar I see Angela and her girlfriend. I'm thinking: *This is insane!*

She's noticed me, and gives me a wave.

I say: 'Okay, I see it now, you're stalking me.'

And Angela says: 'From the first instant I saw you, I knew deep in my heart that you were the only man for me.'

I'm kidding. She doesn't say anything of the sort. But at least we chat, and learn each other's name, and exchange telephone numbers. It's progress. I like her. I really do. Her intelligence, her smile, her whole manner. And after one date, then two, then three, I'm crazy about Angela. Has never happened before. Crazy about her.

It's eight more months before we settle down together in my Ascot Vale apartment, and another six months before we marry. We celebrate twice, in Australian style and with a traditional Somali wedding at the Community Centre Hall in Broadmeadows. I'm in Somali dress, at my mum's insistence. The daylight hours of a Somali wedding ceremony are set aside for feasting, but for men exclusively. Angela and her bridesmaids are in glorious Somali costume for the evening feasting of the women. Even in traditional costume, Angela, with her fair English hair and skin, looks about as Somali as Julie Andrews, but very beautiful.

We eat and drink and dance ourselves into a stupor, as custom demands. But this is what I wish: that my dad was here. The war that I had to flee killed him. Imagine if we had made it to Australia together. That's what clutches at my heart. But then I think:

Nuurow, how many things have to be right before you can accept your good fortune? Your dad is not here, okay. But Mum's here, Angela's here, you're here. So give me a break, Nuurow. You're the luckiest man on the planet.

I'm the luckiest man on the planet? Then what can I say about the birth of my first child, my first son, Isak, named after my father, a year after my wedding? What can I say? This is way beyond good luck. This is Abdi in heaven. I hold Isak in the delivery room, his tiny fists reaching out, his face shining, and I weep tears of joy, perfect joy. Angela is watching me from the bed, smiling in spite of her exhaustion. This is our son. This is our family.

CHAPTER 24

Student

In the second year of my course, students are placed with various community and local government organisations to gain experience. I'm taken on by Maribyrnong City Council, out in the west of Melbourne, where you find concentrations of immigrants from East and Central Africa – Ethiopians, Somalis, Kenyans, Sudanese. It will be my job to work with Somalis, mostly kids here with their mothers but not their fathers, who may still be in camps in East Africa or dead or lost.

Here's my big advantage in helping these kids: I speak Somali; I'm from Somalia; I've been through stuff as bad as these kids have experienced. I have what is known as 'credibility'. These kids, they're lost; they don't know what the hell is going to become of them. Some of them think in the same way they did when they were in the camps. They think they have to be tough to survive, that they need to know how to fight. Hardly any of them grasp that they need to know how to *think*. They don't see any way into this new society of Australia. They believe that they're on the outside and will always be on the outside. So I have to be patient when I work with these kids. I have to show them the gateways. I don't say to them: 'Hey, look at me. I worked it out, look at me.' But even without saying a word about my own circumstances, the kids can see that I am a youth officer with the council; that I am able to speak English;

that I am earning a living, and that I can go the whole day without looking for a fight. I say to these kids: 'In Somalia, there was only one way. Here, many more. A hundred ways.'

They trust me, these kids. When the cops look at them, they see resentment and fear and anger in their eyes. When I look at them, I see a kid pleading for help. He doesn't know how to say to a white policeman: 'Help me, please.' He doesn't even know that he wants help.

The diploma course runs for two years, but there are places for one or two students who do particularly well to enter a third year, a degree year, of the course. And as it happens I am one of the two students asked to stay on for the degree year. So what can I say here? What I really want to say is: 'Man, I deserved it! I worked so hard!' But I can't say that because it would be – and this is an expression I have picked up in Australia – 'blowing my own trumpet'. It is considered very bad manners to 'blow your own trumpet'. As a matter of fact, it's also bad manners in Somali culture to go about telling people how clever you are, or what a big, important man you are. I have good manners. I would *never* blow my own trumpet. But – I deserved it! I really did! Okay, that's all I have to say about getting into the degree year. Except to say that I am very happy about the whole thing. More than very happy. I'm a refugee, I came here with about enough English to ask for a Coke at a milk bar. And now look at me! Fantastic!

★

It's the end of 2002 and I have my degree. My mum is genuinely proud of me, maybe for the first time ever. Well, it's the first time that she actually says she's proud of me. If you want praise from my mum, get ready for a long, long wait. But when she gives it, it's the best thing.

So that's great. Abdi the scholar had a certificate. But not a job, just for the time being. I have to scramble about, looking for a way to make a living. This is a big deal. I have a family to support. For the sake of improving my CV, I accept a short-term job at the Juvenile Detention Centre in Parkville. As the name tells you, the place is full of kids who can't be put into an adult prison. I'm only here a few hours a week, but it's long enough to see how hard a life these kids have had, and have now, and will have in the future. It breaks my heart. All I can do in the short time I'm at the centre is listen to the kids, make a few suggestions, tell them to look me up when they're released. Let me say this: where you're going to put people when they break the law if it's not a prison, I don't know. But prisons are bad for everyone. Just bad.

These few hours at the Juvenile Centre don't earn me much. So I take on a gardening job with a guy I meet who has his own business. After three days of mowing lawns and pruning rose bushes, it occurs to me that I could start a business of my own and make a fortune. Why not? Everyone in Melbourne has a garden, and about one person in ten is prepared to mow the lawn and prune the rosebushes himself. Or herself. I've been keeping up with my delivery job, and I've saved enough to cover the cost of a couple of motor mowers, a leaf blower, garden rakes and so on. So now it's Abdi's Mowing, a subsidiary of Abdi International Enterprises. And man, mowing people's lawns is a gold mine. Within a month or so, I hire a Somali guy to help me keep up with the demand, then I hire another guy. Six months pass and Abdi's Mowing is going so well that I could just about sell shares in the company. Here's my secret: I make sure, absolutely, that the guys I employ, my Somalis, do a really, really good job. I check on them. I say: 'Hey, use the whipper snipper to make the edges straight.' And I say: 'Don't leave any grass behind.' I pay these guys more than anyone else has ever paid them, and they're loyal to me. One of them, Rage, says to me: 'Abdi, good that you're my boss, a good, good thing.' I'm rolling in money after a year, and if I wanted to, I could keep at it and become a millionaire in five years. But you know, mowing lawns, how much of that can you take? Even if other guys are doing the work, how much satisfaction can you expect out of money? Some, but not enough. The lawns are neat, the rose bushes are pruned, but deep down I have wanted to work with people all my life. Even if the lawn is not mowed for ten years, it's no big deal to make it neat again – about a couple of hours. But people, my Somalis, if I can't do anything for them for ten years, there's no hope.

At the end of 2003, I sell Abdi's Mowing and concentrate on getting myself back into community development. I've made an application to the Hume Shire for a position as a youth worker. Hume Shire covers a lot of the west of Melbourne, a bit further out than Maribyrnong Shire, including new suburbs like Roxburgh Park, where a fair number of Somalis have settled. Also Broadmeadows. And it's to Broadmeadows I go when I am accepted by Hume Shire. I'm supposed to reopen a community centre that's been closed for a few years due to a lack of funding. It's a mess, but I get it spruced up and run a list of programs for kids in the area – arts projects, photography and hip-hop classes – anything that's likely to engage these kids. Well, kids and young adults. Some are Somalis, sure, but some are Lebanese, most of them Maronite Christians, and boy, those Lebanese have seen some really ugly stuff! They're tough kids raised in a culture of struggle and crime. But if they trust you, they'd die for you – they're not like the Somali soldiers who've become mass murderers while drugged out of their brains. And they trust me. I don't talk any nonsense to them. I don't pretend that they are angels at heart. What I have to say to them if they want advice is this: you can have one sort of life, or you can have another. But it works better if you find a job and build. I don't mean build a house, although that's good, I mean build a life that can go on for a long time. I say: 'Is this better than the camps? Sure it is. Australia is like a house of treasure.' None of these kids – girls, too; young women – is about to say: 'Abdi my man, I never thought of that before. Thank you. I'm changing as of now.' But maybe another year down the track. Maybe two years. Like I say, they trust me.

And that reminds me of a story that I must put into this book. One evening, I've just left work and I'm out in the carpark. My own car is in for a service so I'm driving Angela's. I get to my car and a couple of guys from the youth centre are trying to break into it.

'Guys!' I call out. 'What the hell? This is my wife's car!'

The guy in charge signals to the other guy to stop. Then he comes over to me, looking guilty. 'Abdi, we didn't know it was yours. Sorry, man. No damage done. We're cool?'

I give a little lecture on how wrong it is to steal *any* car, and the two guys listen with their heads bowed. 'Sure, man. My bad. You should've told us that you were driving your wife's car. How are we supposed to know?'

★

Angela gives birth to our second son, Omar, in 2005. Isak by this time is three. This is the best thing on earth, the best thing ever, little babies coming into your life. I gaze at Omar in Angela's arms, with Isak on my lap, and I think: *Abdi, the world is trying to drive you crazy with happiness.*

In 2007, three years into my employment as a youth worker with Hume, out third son, Kofi, is born, and I get to feel that joy all over again. Angela goes back to her job in loans at Westpac after the birth of each child, and we rely on my mother to babysit and help out in a hundred ways, just like every other young family in Australia.

Working with young men and women in my Hume job is more fulfilling than I could have imagined. Jen Couch says that I have a gift for what I do. If that's true, then I thank God for giving me the gift I would have chosen out of a thousand. Do you know one of the best things? When I talk to these kids, they look me in the eye. What a compliment that is! Because most of them have lost the habit of looking anyone in the eye except for their close friends. If they're talking to the police, or to anyone in authority, mostly they're thinking: *When the hell can I get out of here?*

If you wrench a young man out of his culture (or hers, if it's a young woman, but I'm talking about mostly guys), you have made him horribly insecure. Okay, you're in Australia now, you're never going to see a soldier with an AK again, so that should fix things. But it doesn't. For some people it only fixes one thing. Security comes when you learn the language, when you learn how this society functions, when you see reward for hard work, when you begin to trust the laws that hold the country together. In their insecurity, these guys from the camps respond with resentment and often with aggression. Their pride is at stake. They're scared, they're lost. Back in Somalia, some cop says: 'Hey you, get your arse off the street!' and the young guy thinks: *Wouldn't be such a big shot without that gun.* But he gets off the street. He thinks the cop is an idiot, but he can cope. In Australia, some cop says: 'Hey you, get yourself out of here, creep,' and the young guy feels much greater resentment than he would back in Mogadishu. It's as if the whole of society is rejecting him. His anger grows and it doesn't go away.

When I feel myself standing between that kid and a year in juvenile detention, I know I'm privileged. This is where I can do something special. This is where I give something back to the world. I say to the kid: 'Brother, sit down with me, five minutes, tell me about it.' I know my programs inside out. I know that I can find something for the kid he hasn't even thought of yet. And this is what I end up thinking: *Nuurow, when the soldiers were firing at you and all the bullets missed, you know why? So that you could stand between this kid and disaster. That's the reason.*

Coda

I'm looking at an album of snapshots.

First, my family – Angela, Isak, Omar, Kofi and Abdi. Will you look at my smile? And Angela's smile? We are the parents of these beautiful children. A gift from God to the Aden family. A gift from the Aden family to the world. Do you think I look proud? Well, just *how* proud I couldn't make you believe. Sometimes I gaze at the three kids playing, and I think: *No way. These are my kids? I deserve this happiness?* Then I think: 'Deserve, don't deserve, what the hell? Just accept it, Nuurow.'

Then here I am on the last day of my employment with Hume Shire. Nine years I worked there. By the ninth year, I could go anywhere and people would say: 'Hey, Abdi! Do you remember me, Abdi?'

And here I am with Jen Couch, who gave me the confidence to be someone. You know, everyone needs someone like Jen in his or her life, someone who says: 'Young man, you were made for this. You've got all the right stuff.'

This is me with Jamila. She came to visit us in 2003. And you can see by the way we're looking at each other that we still think it's a miracle that the other is still alive. Yeah, it is a sort of miracle. But here's the thing about miracles. For every person who is granted a miracle, there's a million who pray for one but die in despair. Sure, be thankful for your miracle. But bow your head in sorrow for the other million.

Now, this picture really pleases me. It shows me with a certificate from the Banksia Gardens Community Centre out in Broadmeadows. The certificate says: 'Abdi Aden! What a man! He designed a homework program for the centre that helps refugee kids in school improve their English – all that good gear! Also a soccer program! Yeah, Abdi – come on down!' Not those exact words. I wanted to do something that made it a bit easier for refugee kids to enjoy school, and the best thing of all to help refugee kids in school is to make sure they can actually understand what's being said. You see, if you're a kid in high school, say, and you're struggling along, and you only understand every tenth word in English, what happens is that you literally go back to where you came from. You go into a shell with the language you've spoken since you were a kid, and with the culture you understand, and you say to yourself in a sulky way: 'To hell with Australia! I can't understand a damn thing! I want to be back in Khartoum (or Mogadishu, or Tripoli)!' You get some more English and it's like handcuffs have been removed from your wrists. So that program makes me proud, I promise you. I started it when I was working for Hume Council, back in 2006. I don't work for the council these days, but I'm an Official Ambassador for the Banksia Gardens Community Centre. I always mention the centre in my public-speaking gigs. You know who's also part of the Banksia Gardens thing? Father Bob. Sure. He's a Patron. Love Father Bob. Mullah Bob. And the lady who runs the whole Banksia Gardens Centre, Gina Dougall, wonderful lady. Love her too.

Here I am with Mum. Look at us. I'm proud of her; she's proud of me. Sort of. She's thinking: *Best if he goes to university and gets a PhD. Then after that, another PhD. Then after that ...* And so on. And so on. And so on.

Here's me and Angela together. What can I say? I love her, she loves me. Also, she knows me. She knows about the things I haven't even mentioned about myself in this book. She knows everything. And she still loves me. A blessing.

Here's the family outside the house we bought in the west of Melbourne, the house where we still live. The Australian dream. My arm is around Angela's shoulders. We're grinning our heads off for the camera. Some buddy of mine is taking the snap. He says: 'Hey, Abdi, smile for the camera.' What's he mean? I am smiling! If I smile any harder, they'll have to take me to hospital for face surgery.

And this is me up on stage talking to an audience about my life, about refugees. Most of my work these days is as an inspirational speaker. I talk to audiences of all sorts, including lots of school kids. I'm always asked about refugee policy in this country. 'Abdi, does it make you cry to see refugees packed into detention centres?' And 'Abdi, what do you feel when refugees are treated like criminals?'

I try to explain that refugees have been with us for thousands of years. Even in primitive times, tens of thousands of years ago, tribes were forced to make journeys when drought and natural disasters drove them from places they knew – from their traditional homes. During the many centuries of civilisation, when borders came into being, wars have created great crowds of refugees. Human beings do not give up their lives easily. They pack their belongings and take to the road, hoping for a new life in a new land. Often the people who lived in these new lands didn't make these refugees welcome. Think of the Jewish people, and their long, long struggle for acceptance. The thing is, you can't expect a person who is hunted in his own land, or starved, or unable to make a living to simply say: 'Okay, time for me to die.' We have refugees because human beings want to remain alive. That's not unreasonable.

At this time in the history of our world, a number of countries have chosen, or had forced on them, the industry of war. War is an easy business to run. Young men will always be attracted to AKs. Young men, some of them, many of them, will always feel empowered when they know that they have been given the right to murder. Of course they will. They grow up without jobs, without a future, then suddenly they have more power than they ever imagined. They have a gun. But the industry of war doesn't produce anything except corpses. People estimate that more than half a million Somalis – men, women and children – have died so far in the civil war. I heard that, of my fifty class mates, I am one of just two still alive. So families yearn to escape. They don't want to live in a country where murder goes on all day every day. Or, if not murder then it is poverty that drives people onto the road. And they think of the countries where people live in freedom, where people earn a good wage; countries where children can go to school for twelve years, then maybe to university. They think of Big Europe, of America, of Canada, of Australia. The Dream Lands. For most of these people, their journey will end in a camp, in worse poverty than they fled. Some, including Abdi Aden, against all odds, will reach Big Europe, Australia, Canada, America.

I'm still talking. The audience is still listening. I say: 'There are millions of refugees in the world today, and millions more people still living in their own ravaged lands who wish to take to the road, and will, one day. Australia cannot take in hundreds of thousands of refugees each year – millions over a decade. I understand that. But nor can we say to the refugees on the road, on the seas: 'You have no right even to *try* to reach Australia.' These people do have a right to try. They have a right to their dreams. And I think we can find more imaginative things to say to them than: 'Don't even try. We will punish you if you do. We will keep you in camps that will cripple your brain. We will make you sorry you ever dreamt of Australia.'

I want to say to the government: stopping the boats is no great feat. Think harder. This problem will be with us for decades to come. It will get bigger and bigger. Please, some imagination. And I would say: Maybe it's better to be more generous than you have to be rather than less generous than you could be.

And I tell the audiences about when I appeared on series two of *Go Back to Where You Came From*. This TV show on SBS takes a small group of Australian citizens – some very critical of asylum seekers – and flies them to places in the world where refugees come from. They learn first-hand about the conditions that drive people to seek a new life in another country. The show is also about the asylum seekers themselves, people such as me.

People who have seen me on the show ask me: 'Abdi, when people tell you to go back home, what do you say?'

And this is my answer. I say: 'No, thanks. Madmen with AKs will kill me.' And then I say: 'Don't you want me here? Really? With these good looks?'

Photographs

Page 1: With my father, Isak Aden, and little sister, Jamila, in around 1979. This family photograph was taken in a photographer's studio in Afgooye, Somalia.

* Page 2: Boys playing soccer on Lido Beach, Mogadishu, in 2013: © Michelle Shephard/*Toronto Star*/Getty Images

Page 12: Hooyo – Mum – in Mogadishu in the late 1980s

Page 22: Abe – Dad (right) – with work friends in Paris in the 1980s

* Page 40: Armed gunmen ride through the streets of Mogadishu in 1992: © Scott Peterson/Liaison/Getty Images

* Page 58: Soldier protecting a Red Cross convoy, Somalia, in 1992: © Alexis Duclos/Gamma-Rapho/Getty Images

* Page 82: Mandera Refugee Camp, Kenya, in 1992: © Scott Peterson/Liaison/Getty Images

* Page 108: A Somali passes the ruins of a building in Mogadishu in 1993: © Manoocher Deghati/AFP/Getty Images

* Page 146: A block of flats in Bucharest, Romania, in snow: © Daniel Mihailescu/AFP/Getty Images

Page 210: Aged around seventeen and living in Melbourne

Acknowledgements

For many years my wife and other family members have encouraged me to tell my story. However, this always appeared to be a long-distant dream. Sharing my journey has been therapeutic and given closure to a harrowing experience that never seemed a reality until now.

Thank you to HarperCollins for your belief in my story. Your wonderful support and dedication has kept this journey alive. Thanks especially to Catherine Milne for believing in me from the start.

To Robert Hillman, my brother and very special friend, your understanding has taken us down a path that will remain with us for life. Without your creative, extremely talented mind, this would not have been possible.

Abdi Aden